PRAISE FOR THE REFORMATION HERITAGE
BIBLE COMMENTARY SERIES

The *Reformation Heritage Bible Commentary* is a unique series that promises to be a valuable resource for laity and preachers. The verse-by-verse commentary focuses on major topics, providing clear interpretation and devotional insight in keeping with how the Reformers approached Scripture, and emphasizing themes that were central in their teaching. Illustrative quotes from key Reformers and their heirs, including Lutheran, Calvinist, Anglican, and Wesleyan sources, provide insights in their own words, without trying to survey the range of views represented in this heritage. This focused approach gives a clear reading of the text which engages one's mind and heart.

—The Rev. Dr. Rodney A. Whitacre
Professor of Biblical Studies
Trinity School for Ministry
Ambridge, Pennsylvania

Busy pastors and teachers of the Scriptures need commentaries that are biblical, theological, and practical. Fortunately, the Reformation Heritage Bible Commentary series fulfills those requirements. The scholarship is reverent, demonstrating that the truths of the Reformation are relevant today just as they were in the 16th century. The volumes are accessible to a wide variety of readers, for it is written in a wonderfully clear way. I commend this work gladly.

—Thomas R. Schreiner, PhD
James Buchanan Harrison Professor of New Testament
The Southern Baptist Theological Seminary
Louisville, Kentucky

The Reformation Heritage series is a "Heritage of Reformation theology" now put at the fingertips of every serious Bible student, young or old.

This commentary helps anyone to dive deeply into the Scriptures, verse by verse, even word by word. I was blessed with its academic rigor in straightforward language, the sidebar articles explaining overarching Biblical themes, and the voices of the Reformers demonstrating again that this Good News of Jesus is a message for all times. If one yearns to know the unique message of the Scripture and its meaning for life, now and forever, then join me in having the Reformation Heritage Series in your library today.

—Rev. Gregory P. Seltz
Speaker, *The Lutheran Hour*

The *Reformation Heritage Bible Commentary* promises to be an asset to the library of serious Bible students, whether layman or clergy. This series exemplifies the reformers' commitment to sola scriptura, that the revelation of God's saving purposes is in Scripture alone, which is primarily about Christ alone. The blend of overviews and insights from our Protestant forefathers with exegesis and application from contemporary Reformed theologians makes for an interesting read. Contemporary readers will also appreciate the devotional notes in these commentaries. Because the study of God's word is not just an academic endeavor, it engages the mind, heart and will of those who trust Christ for their salvation. While many modern commentaries seem to focus on the application of the Scriptures, the intent here is Gospel centered interpretation, resulting in devotional application. This is a work of serious scholastic intent combined with theological scrutiny and integrity. I am grateful for such a work and confident that it will be profitable for years to come in aiding the church's effort to know Christ more fully as He is revealed in holy Scripture.

—Kenneth R. Jones
Pastor of Glendale Baptist Church, Miami, FL
Co-host of nationally syndicated talk show—*White Horse Inn*
Contributed to: "Experiencing the Truth," "Glory Road," and
"Keep Your Head Up"; all published by Crossway.
Contributed to *Table Talk* and *Modern Reformation* magazines
Frequent conference speaker

The Reformation of the church brought with it biblical insights that revitalized churches and radically changed the course of theological studies as giants like Luther, Melanchthon, Calvin, Chemnitz, and Wesley commented extensively on Holy Scripture. The new *Reformation Heritage Bible Commentary* is a one-stop resource where the observations of these and other distinguished Reformation leaders are brought together around specific books of the New Testament.

—The Rev. Dr. R. Reed Lessing
Professor of Exegetical Theology and Director of the Graduate School
Concordia Seminary, St. Louis, MO
Member of the Society of Biblical Literature,
the Catholic Biblical Association, and
the Institute of Biblical Research

GALATIANS
EPHESIANS
PHILIPPIANS

ALSO FROM CONCORDIA

BIBLICAL STUDIES

The Reformation Heritage Bible Commentary Series
  Colossians/Thessalonians, Edward A. Engelbrecht and Paul Deterding
  Revelation, Mark Brighton
  Mark, Daniel Paavola (forthcoming November 2013)

The Living Word. An online Bible learning program, featuring studies on individual books of the Bible. www.OnlineBibleLearning.org

The Lutheran Study Bible, Edward A. Engelbrecht, General Editor

The Apocrypha: The Lutheran Edition with Notes, Edward A. Engelbrecht, General Editor

LifeLight Indepth Bible Study Series
  More than 50 studies available on biblical books and topics

Concordia's Complete Bible Handbook for Students, Jane L. Fryar, Edward A. Engelbrecht, et al.

Concordia Commentary Series: A Theological Exposition of Sacred Scripture
  Leviticus, John W. Kleinig
  Joshua, Adolph L. Harstad
  Ruth, John R. Wilch
  Ezra and Nehemiah, Andrew E. Steinmann
  Proverbs, Andrew E. Steinmann
  Ecclesiastes, James Bollhagen
  The Song of Songs, Christopher W. Mitchell
  Isaiah 40–55, R. Reed Lessing

  Ezekiel 1–20, Horace D. Hummel
  Ezekiel 21–48, Horace D. Hummel
  Daniel, Andrew E. Steinmann
  Amos, R. Reed Lessing
  Jonah, R. Reed Lessing
  Matthew 1:1–11:1, Jeffrey A. Gibbs
  Matthew 11:2–20:34, Jeffrey A. Gibbs
  Luke 1:1–9:50, Arthur A. Just Jr.
  Luke 9:51–24:53, Arthur A. Just Jr.
  Romans 1–8, Michael Middendorf (forthcoming May 2013)
  1 Corinthians, Gregory J. Lockwood
  Colossians, Paul E. Deterding
  Philemon, John G. Nordling
  2 Peter and Jude, Curtis P. Giese
  1–3 John, Bruce G. Schuchard
  Revelation, Louis A. Brighton

HISTORICAL STUDIES

From Abraham to Paul: A Biblical Chronology, Andrew E. Steinmann

The Church from Age to Age: A History from Galilee to Global Christianity, Edward A. Engelbrecht, General Editor

History of Theology, 4th Rev. Ed., Bengt Hägglund

Reformation Heritage
BIBLE COMMENTARY

✦ GALATIANS
✦ EPHESIANS
✦ PHILIPPIANS

JERALD C. JOERSZ

CONCORDIA PUBLISHING HOUSE • SAINT LOUIS

Copyright © 2013 Concordia Publishing House
3558 S. Jefferson Ave., St. Louis, MO 63118-3968
1-800-325-3040 · www.cph.org

This publication contains The Holy Bible, English Standard Version®, copyright © 2001 by Crossway, a publishing ministry of Good News Publishers. The ESV® text appearing in this publication is reproduced and published in cooperation between Good News Publishers and Concordia Publishing House and by permission of Good News Publishers. Unauthorized reproduction of this publication is prohibited.

English Standard Version®, ESV®, and the ESV® logo are trademarks of Good News Publishers located in Wheaton, Illinois. Used by permission.

The Holy Bible, English Standard Version (ESV) is adapted from the Revised Standard Version of the Bible, copyright Division of Christian Education of the National Council of the Churches of Christ in the U.S.A. All rights reserved.

Scripture quotations marked KJV are from the King James or Authorized Version of the Bible.

Portions of this book adapted or taken from the maps, original articles, or notes of *The Lutheran Study Bible*, copyright © 2009 by Concordia Publishing House. All rights reserved.

Quotations marked LW are from Luther's Works, American Edition: volumes 1–30 © 1955–76 Concordia Publishing House; volumes 31–54 © 1957–86 Augsburg Fortress; volumes 56–75 © 2009– . Concordia Publishing House. All rights reserved.

Hymn texts and other material with the abbreviation *LSB* are from *Lutheran Service Book*, copyright © 2006 Concordia Publishing House. All rights reserved.

The quotations from the Lutheran Confessions are from *Concordia: The Lutheran Confessions*, second edition; edited by Paul McCain, et al., copyright © 2006 Concordia Publishing House. All rights reserved.

Manufactured in the United States of America

Library of Congress Cataloging-in-Publication Data

Library of Congress Cataloging-in-Publication Data

Joersz, Jerald C.
    Galatians, Ephesians, Philippians / Jerald C. Joersz.
        p.   cm. — (Reformation heritage Bible commentary)
    ISBN 978-0-7586-2769-8
    1. Bible. N.T. Galatians--Commentaries. 2. Bible. N.T. Ephesians—Commentaries. 3. Bible N.T. Philippians—Commentaries. I. Joersz, Jerald C.- II. Title. III. Title: Galatians, Ephesians, Philippians.
    BS2715.53.E54 2013
    227'.077--dc23   2011044778

1 2 3 4 5 6 7 8 9 10   22 21 20 19 18 17 16 15 14 13

CONTENTS

ABOUT THIS SERIES

The great reformers' influence upon the Bible's interpretation and application could not help but revitalize our churches. This is as true today as it was 500 years ago. This renewal happens in part because the reformers drew upon the insights of the Renaissance, which linked the medieval church back to her earlier roots in the ancient world. There the biblical texts sprang up. The reformers were among the earliest students to pursue classical studies, not only due to personal interest but especially due to the benefits such study brought to the study of the Bible. By reading the New Testament Scriptures in their ancient languages and context, the reformers dispelled many misunderstandings.

Second, the fires of controversy, which followed Luther's proclamation of justification by grace through faith on account of Christ alone, served to refine the study of Sacred Scriptures. So many ideas that medieval people took for granted or that were accepted based on human authority alone were tested and retested, leading to more careful study of God's Word.

Third, the reformers themselves taught with special insight due to their constant reading, study, translating, and preaching of the Sacred Scriptures. Their approach to the Scriptures and the insights they gained have continued to inform biblical studies even to the present day. For all of these reasons, Concordia Publishing House wished to produce a readable commentary series that would serve the current generation by sharing with them (1) insights from the reformers and (2) commentary that stemmed from their heritage.

In preparing this commentary, we drew upon the insights of the following reformers and heirs to their evangelical approach to teaching the Scriptures:

John Hus (c. 1372–1415)	John Knox (c. 1513–72)
Martin Luther (1483–1546)	Martin Chemnitz (1522–86)
Thomas Cranmer (1489–1556)	Johann Gerhard (1582–1637)
Philip Melanchthon (1497–1560)	Johann Albrecht Bengel (1687–
John Calvin (1509–64)	1752)
	John Wesley (1703–91)

Not every commentary in this series will include quotations from each of these reformers or heirs of the Reformation since these authors did not all comment on Books of the Scriptures with equal frequency. Other reformers may be included, as well as citations of Reformation era confessional documents such as the Augsburg Confession and Westminster Confession. Readers should not conclude that citation of an author implies complete endorsement of everything that author wrote (heaven knows, these were fallible men, as they themselves acknowledged). The works of other significant Reformation era commentators are less available in English. We have intentionally stayed away from more radical reformers such as Andreas Bodenstein von Karlstadt, Ulrich Zwingli, Thomas Münzer, etc.

The commentary is not simply a compilation of sixteenth century views but a thorough verse-by-verse commentary built from the reformers' approach of *Scripture interprets Scripture* and supplemented from their writings. Along with quotations from the reformers and their heirs, readers will also find quotations from some early and medieval Church Fathers. This is because the reformers did not wish to overthrow the earlier generations of teachers but to profit from them where they were faithful in teaching the Word.

Some readers will note that the writers listed above represent different branches in the Protestant family of churches, and they may wonder how compatible these writers will be alongside one another. It is certainly the case that the reformers held different views, especially concerning the Sacraments, biblical authority, and other matters. Some authors for the series may at times describe differences between the various reformers.

However, while it is true that these differences affect the fellowship and work of the churches of the Reformation, it is also true that the reformers shared significant agreement. For example, the great historian Philip Schaff noted, "Melanchthon mediated between Luther and Calvin" (*History of the Christian Church* vol. VII, second revised ed. [New York: Charles Scribner's Sons, 1894], 260). Early Reformation works like Melanchthon's *Commonplaces* and the Augsburg Confession served as models for the various traditions of Protestant confession and doctrine. What is more, as the writers focused on a particular biblical text for interpretation, they often reached very similar conclusions regarding that text. The text of Scripture tended to lead them toward a more unified expression of the faith. This is something I have described as "the text effect,"[1] which illustrates for us a way in which the Bible brings us together despite differences and always remains the most important guide for Christian teaching

---

[1] *Friends of the Law* (St. Louis: Concordia, 2011), 136.

and practice. In view of the 500th anniversary of the Reformation in 2017, I believe it is fitting for us to draw anew upon the time honored insights of these great servants of God.

The Bible Translations

Among the translations for our commentary we have chosen, on the one hand, what many regard as the finest English translation ever produced: the King James Version. The KJV is a product of the Reformation era, and although it is now more than 400 years old, remains a most valuable tool for study. Along with the KJV we are pleased to present the English Standard Version, which has rapidly become one of the most widely used modern English translations. The success of the ESV is due in part to the translators' efforts to follow sound, classical principals of translation very like those used by the KJV translators. The result is a very readable English translation that also allows readers to grasp the biblical expressions and terms that appear repeatedly in the Bible. Due to this approach, we find the ESV an especially helpful translation for Bible study. Our notes are keyed to the ESV, but we have placed the KJV in parallel with the ESV for easy comparison. Since the ESV text is based on the broad consensus of biblical scholars who have consulted the early Greek manuscripts, it differs at points from the KJV text, which was produced when fewer manuscripts were available for study. Where significant differences between the translations appear, the notes include comment.

Our Prayer for You

The following prayer embodies the sense of study and devotion we wish to convey to all who take up these commentaries:

Blessed Lord, You have caused all Holy Scriptures to be written for our learning. Grant that we may so hear them, read, mark, learn, and inwardly digest them that, by patience and comfort from Your holy Word, we may embrace and ever hold fast the blessed hope of everlasting life; through Jesus Christ, our Lord. Amen.

Rev. Edward A. Engelbrecht, STM
Senior Editor for Bible Resources

Today, as in Paul's day, the precious Gospel that frees us from sin, death, and the power of the devil is constantly under assault by those who would compromise, contradict, or dilute it. This robs it of its sweetness and can even draw our eyes away from our Lord Jesus Christ. This is a matter of utmost seriousness, for there is no other Gospel (Gal 1:6–7).

In these three Epistles, St. Paul reminds us, again and again, that our life and hope are entirely in God's gracious and capable hands. Even before the foundation of the world, He predestined us, in love, for adoption (Eph 1:4). Our Lord Jesus willingly humbled Himself to death on a cross for us (Php 2:8). Our resurrected and ascended Savior graciously intercedes for us now and will come again in glory.

This is the Gospel Paul boldly proclaims and the Church confesses. Though written to three different Christian communities and read by countless others, each of these Letters directs us to Christ and the salvation and freedom He has won for us. They call us to walk in joyful faith and to boldly confess our Lord Jesus and His Gospel.

In Ephesians 5, St. Paul considers the mystery of Christ and His bride, the Church. As he does so, he shows us God's desire for husband and wife who enjoy his gift of marriage. Grateful for all His gifts, we dedicate this volume to the author's wife Ann Joersz who departed to be with Christ on May 7, 2010 after their 44 years of marriage. "Oh blest communion, fellowship divine! We feebly struggle, they in glory shine; Yet all are one in Thee, for all are Thine. Alleluia! Alleluia!" (*LSB* 677:4; *H82* 287:4; *TPH* 426:3; *TUMH* 711:4)

Steven P. Mueller, Ph.D.
General Editor

ABBREVIATIONS

AD	*anno Domini* (in the year of [our] Lord)	Gk	Greek
		Hbr	Hebrew
Aram	Aramaic	NT	New Testament
BC	before Christ	OT	Old Testament
c.	circa	p.	page
cf.	confer	pp.	pages
ch.	chapter	St.	Saint
chs.	chapters	v.	verse
Ger	German	vv.	verses

Canonical Scripture

Gn	Genesis	Lm	Lamentations
Ex	Exodus	Ezk	Ezekiel
Lv	Leviticus	Dn	Daniel
Nu	Numbers	Hos	Hosea
Dt	Deuteronomy	Jl	Joel
Jsh	Joshua	Am	Amos
Jgs	Judges	Ob	Obadiah
Ru	Ruth	Jnh	Jonah
1Sm	1 Samuel	Mi	Micah
2Sm	2 Samuel	Na	Nahum
1Ki	1 Kings	Hab	Habakkuk
2Ki	2 Kings	Zep	Zephaniah
1Ch	1 Chronicles	Hg	Haggai
2Ch	2 Chronicles	Zec	Zechariah
Ezr	Ezra	Mal	Malachi
Ne	Nehemiah		
Est	Esther	Mt	Matthew
Jb	Job	Mk	Mark
Ps	Psalms	Lk	Luke
Pr	Proverbs	Jn	John
Ec	Ecclesiastes	Ac	Acts
Sg	Song of Solomon	Rm	Romans
Is	Isaiah	1Co	1 Corinthians
Jer	Jeremiah	2Co	2 Corinthians

Gal	Galatians	Heb	Hebrews
Eph	Ephesians	Jas	James
Php	Philippians	1Pt	1 Peter
Col	Colossians	2Pt	2 Peter
1Th	1 Thessalonians	1Jn	1 John
2Th	2 Thessalonians	2Jn	2 John
1Tm	1 Timothy	3Jn	3 John
2Tm	2 Timothy	Jude	Jude
Ti	Titus	Rv	Revelation
Phm	Philemon		

The Apocrypha

Jth	Judith	2Macc	2 Maccabees
Wis	The Wisdom of Solomon	Old Grk Est	Old Greek Esther
Tob	Tobit	Sus	Susanna
Ecclus	Ecclesiasticus (Sirach)	Bel	Bel and the Dragon
Bar	Baruch	Pr Az	The Prayer of Azariah
Lt Jer	The Letter of Jeremiah	Sg Three	The Song of the Three Holy Children
1Macc	1 Maccabees	Pr Man	Prayer of Manasseh

Other Books

1Esd	1 Esdras	Ps 151	Psalm 151
2Esd	2 Esdras	1En	1 Enoch
3Macc	3 Maccabees (Ptolemaika)	2En	2 Enoch
4Macc	4 Maccabees	Jub	Jubilees

Abbreviations for Commonly Cited Books and Works

AC   Augsburg Confession. From *Concordia*.

ANF   Roberts, Alexander, and James Donaldson, eds. *The Ante-Nicene Fathers: The Writings of the Fathers Down to AD 325*, 10 vols. Buffalo: The Christian Literature Publishing Company, 1885–96. Reprint, Grand Rapids, MI: Eerdmans, 2001.

Ant   Josephus, Flavius. *Antiquities of the Jews*. In *The Works of Josephus*. Translated by William Whiston. Peabody, MA: Hendrickson Publishers, 1987.

Ap   Apology of the Augsburg Confession. From *Concordia*.

Bengel   Bengel, John Albert. *Gnomen of the New Testament*. 5 vols. Edinburgh: T. & T. Clark, 1877.

Calvin   Calvin, John. *Commentaries on the Epistles of Paul to the Galatians and Ephesians and to the Philippians, Colossians, and Thessalonians*. John Pringle, trans. Edinburgh: Thomas Clark, 1841; Calvin Translation Society, 1851.

Chemnitz   Chemnitz, Martin. *Chemnitz's Works*. 8 vols. St. Louis: Concordia, 1971–89.

Church   Huss, John. *The Church*. David S. Schaff, trans. New York: Charles Scribner's Sons, 1915.

Concordia   McCain, Paul Timothy, ed. *Concordia: The Lutheran Confessions*. 2nd ed. St. Louis: Concordia, 2006.

Cranmer   *The Remains of Thomas Cranmer, D.D.* Henry Jenkyns, ed. 4 vols. Oxford: Oxford University Press, 1833.

Ep   Epitome of the Formula of Concord. From *Concordia*.

ESV   English Standard Version.

FC   Formula of Concord. From *Concordia*.

Gerhard   Gerhard, Johann. *Theological Commonplaces*. Richard J. Dinda, trans. Benjamin T. G. Mayes, ed. St. Louis: Concordia, 2009–.

H82   *The Hymnal 1982, according to the Use of The Episcopal Church*. New York: The Church Hymnal Corporation, 1985.

KJV   King James Version of Scripture.

Knox   Knox, John. *Writings of the Rev. John Knox*. London: The Religious Tract Society, 1900.

LC   Large Catechism. From *Concordia*.

LSB   Commission on Worship of The Lutheran Church—Missouri Synod. *Lutheran Service Book*. St. Louis: Concordia, 2006.

LW   Luther, Martin. *Luther's Works*. American Edition. General editors Jaroslav Pelikan and Helmut T. Lehmann. 56 vols. St. Louis: Concordia, and Philadelphia: Muhlenberg and Fortress, 1955–1986. Vols. 56–75: Edited by Christopher Boyd Brown. St. Louis: Concordia, 2009–.

LXX   Septuagint. Koine Greek Old Testament.

NIV   New International Version.

NPNF1   Schaff, Philip, ed. *A Select Library of Nicene and Post-Nicene Fathers of the Christian Church*, Series 1. 14 vols. New York: The Christian Literature Series, 1886–89. Reprint, Grand Rapids, MI: Eerdmans, 1956.

NPNF2	Schaff, Philip, and Henry Wace, eds. *A Select Library of Nicene and Post-Nicene Fathers of the Christian Church*, Series 2. 14 vols. New York: The Christian Literature Series, 1890–99. Reprint, Grand Rapids, MI: Eerdmans, 1952, 1961.
RSV	Revised Standard Version.
SA	Smalcald Articles. From *Concordia*.
SD	Solid Declaration of the Formula of Concord. From *Concordia*.
TPH	*The Presbyterian Hymnal*. Louisville, KY: Westminster/John Knox Press, 1990.
Tr	Treatise on the Power and Primacy of the Pope. From *Concordia*.
TUMH	*The United Methodist Hymnal*. Nashville, TN: The United Methodist Publishing House, 1989.
Wesley	Wesley, John. *Explanatory Notes upon the New Testament*. 12th ed. New York: Carlton & Porter, 1754.

Timeline for the New Testament

Anatolia, Greece, and Rome	Egypt and Africa	Dates	Syria, Canaan, and Israel	Mesopotamia and Persia
		4 BC	Angel appears to Zechariah (c. Nov 15; Lk 1:8–22)	
		3 BC	The Annunciation (inter Apr 17–May 16; Lk 1:26–38); John the Baptist born (Aug; Lk 1:57–66)	
	Holy family in Egypt	2 BC	Jesus born (mid Jan to early Feb; Mt 1:25; Lk 2:1–7); Magi visit; flight to Egypt (mid to late in the year; Mt 2)	
		1 BC	Death of Herod the Great (after Jan 10; Mt 2:19); return to Nazareth (Mt 2:19–23)	
		AD 6	Judas the Galilean leads revolt against Rome; Judea, Samaria, and Idumaea combined to form the Roman province of Judea	
		c. 10	Rabbi Hillel dies	
		11	Jesus in temple before the elders (c. Apr 8–22; Lk 2:42)	
Tiberius, Roman emperor		14–37		
Revolt in Gaul; grain shortages cause unrest in Rome		21		
		29	Baptism of Jesus (Fall; Lk 3:1–2)	
		30	Jesus at Passover (c. Apr 8; Jn 2:20)	
		32	Jesus at Passover (c. Apr 15; Jn 6:4); Jesus arrives at Feast of Booths (c. Oct 14; Jn 7:14); Feast of Booths (Oct 17 or 18; Jn 7:37)	

Anatolia, Greece, and Rome	Egypt and Africa	Dates	Syria, Canaan, and Israel	Mesopotamia and Persia
Roman senators unable to pay debts; subsidized by Emperor Tiberius		33	Triumphal entry (Sun, Mar 29); Last Supper (Thurs eve, Apr 2); crucifixion (Fri, Apr 3); resurrection (Sun, Apr 5); ascension (May 14; Lk 24:51; Ac 1:9); Pentecost (May 24)	Jews of Parthia, Media, Elam and Mesopotamia travel to Jerusalem for Pentecost
	Ethiopian eunuch baptized, returns home (Ac 8:26–39)	c. 35		
		35–42		Revolt of Seleucia on the Tigris against Parthian rule
		36	Paul's conversion (Ac 9:1–31)	
Caligula (Gaius), Roman emperor		37–41	Josephus, Jewish historian, born	
	Philo of Alexandria leads Jewish delegation to Rome	c. 39	Caligula attempts to place statue of himself in Jerusalem temple	
		41	Martyrdom of James (late Mar; Ac 12:2); Peter in prison (Apr; Ac 12:3–4); Passover (May 4; Ac 12:4); Peter leaves Jerusalem (May; Gal 2:11)	
		41–44	Herod Agrippa I rules Judea	
Claudius, Roman emperor		41–54		
Peter on mission in Asia Minor (spr/sum; 1Pt 1:1–2); [in Corinth (fall); at Rome (mid Nov)]		42	Peter in Antioch (May 41–Apr 42; Gal 2:11)	
		44	Herod Agrippa at festival in Caesarea (Mar 5; Ac 12:19); death of Herod Agrippa (Mar 10; Ac 12:21–23)	

Anatolia, Greece, and Rome	Egypt and Africa	Dates	Syria, Canaan, and Israel	Mesopotamia and Persia
		47–48	Paul's 1st missionary journey (Ac 13:1–14:28)	
Paul goes to Macedonia; Barnabas and John Mark go to Cyprus (mid May; Ac 15:36–16:10)		49	Conference in Jerusalem (Ac 15:1–35); Peter goes to Antioch (Feb; Gal 2:11); Paul confronts Peter (Apr; Gal 2:11)	
		49–56	[Peter in Antioch (seven years)]	
Paul's 2nd missionary journey (Ac 15:39–18:22)	Philo of Alexandria leads second Jewish delegation to Rome	49–51		
Paul's 3rd missionary journey (Ac 18:23–21:17)		52–55		
Nero, Roman emperor		54–68		
		55–57	Paul imprisoned in Caesarea (Ac 23:23–26:32)	
Paul's journey to Rome (Ac 27:1–28:16)		57–58		
Paul in custody in Rome (Ac 28:17–31)		58–60		
		62	Martyrdom of James, the Lord's brother	
Paul assigns Titus at Crete (Ti 1:5)		64–65		
Paul in Ephesus, where he leaves Timothy (spr–sum; 1Tm 1:3)		65		

Anatolia, Greece, and Rome	Egypt and Africa	Dates	Syria, Canaan, and Israel	Mesopotamia and Persia
	Tiberius Julius Alexander, of Jewish descent, appointed Roman prefect of Egypt	66		
		66–70	Jewish revolt against Romans	
Peter and Paul martyred		68		
Emperor Vespasian		69–79		
		70	Titus destroys Jerusalem temple; Rabbon Yohanan ben Zakkai at Yavneh Academy	Jerusalem Jews settle in Babylonia, which becomes the new center of Judaism
		c. 73	Fall of Masada	
Emperor Titus		79–81		
Emperor Domitian		81–96		
		c. 90–115	Rabbon Gamaliel II at Yavneh Academy	
Jews revolt in Cyprus	Jews revolt in Egypt and Cyrene	115–17		Trajan captures Mesopotamia; Jews revolt
	Founding of Antinoöpolis by Emperor Hadrian	130		
		132–35	Bar Kokhba revolt; death of Rabbi Akiva, Yavneh Academy leader who hailed Bar Kokhba as the messiah	

Paul's Missionary Journeys

PAUL'S MISSIONARY JOURNEYS (ACTS 13–21)

First journey (AD 47–48): The Holy Spirit sent Saul, Barnabas, and John Mark from Antioch in Syria via Seleucia to Salamis, then overland to Paphos (Ac 13:1–12). The three continued to Perga, where John Mark left them for Jerusalem (13:13). Saul, also called Paul (13:9), and Barnabas continued to Antioch in Pisidia (13:14–50), Iconium (13:51–14:6a), Lystra, and Derbe (14:6b–20), from whence they retraced their steps back to Pisidian Antioch, then went to Attalia and Syrian Antioch (14:21–28).

Second journey (AD 49–51): Paul and Barnabas separated (15:36–39) while in Syrian Antioch. Paul and Silas went through Syria and Cilicia (15:40–41). They came to Derbe and Lystra, where Timothy joined them (16:1–5). The Spirit led them throughout Galatia and Phrygia to Troas, where they continued, via the island of Samothrace (not shown) to Macedonia;

then they traveled to Neapolis and Philippi (16:6–40). They continued via Amphipolis and Apollonia to Thessalonica, Berea, Athens, and Corinth (17:1–18:17). Paul stayed 18 months there (18:11). He journeyed via Cenchreae and Ephesus to Caesarea Maritima, Jerusalem and Syrian Antioch (18:18–22).

Third journey (AD 52–55): Paul took the inland route from Syrian Antioch and eventually arrived in Ephesus, where he stayed for two years and three months (18:23–19:41). He visited Macedonia and Achaia, and then sailed from Philippi to Troas (19:21; 20:1–12) on his way to Jerusalem. From Troas, he sailed via Assos, Mitylene, Miletus (where he met the Ephesian elders), Rhodes, and Patara to Tyre (20:13–21:6). He sailed to Ptolemais and Caesarea Maritima, and went on foot from there to Jerusalem (21:7–17).

Early Gentile Churches

EARLY GENTILE CHURCHES

Congregations in Galatia, Ephesus, and Philippi were among the earliest Christian churches outside of Israel and Syria. More churches in the region were described in the Book of Revelation later in the first century. These locations (marked with squares) included the following: *Ephesus* was an important stop on Paul's second and third missionary journeys (Ac 18:19–21; 19). It successfully vied with *Smyrna* and Pergamum to be the chief city of Asia Minor.

Like Smyrna and the other cities mentioned by John, Ephesus embraced the emperor cult. It also held the temple of Artemis. Pergamum boasted of a great library and many pagan temples. *Thyatira* was known for its cloth dyers (Ac 16:14) and for general worldliness. *Sardis* lived to recall its past glory. *Philadelphia* was known for its pagan temples. *Laodicea*, located at an important trade-route junction, was a wool producer and a center of medicine (cf. Col 4:13–16).

GALATIANS ✦

INTRODUCTION TO
GALATIANS

Overview

Author

Paul the apostle

Date

c. AD 51–53

Places

Galatia; Jerusalem; Arabia; Damascus; Syria; Cilicia; Antioch

People

Galatians; Paul; Cephas (Peter); James, the Lord's brother; John; Barnabas; Titus; Gentiles; Jews; false brothers

Purpose

To demonstrate that faith in Christ accomplishes both justification and sanctification

Law Themes

The threat of subtle false teaching; hypocrisy; works cannot justify; the Law's curse; works of the flesh; the Law of Christ

Gospel Themes

One saving Gospel; God's gracious call; justified through faith in Christ; the gift of the Spirit; adoption as God's sons; freedom in Christ

Memory Verses

Only one Gospel (1:6–9); justification through faith, not works (2:16); life in Christ (2:19–20); the Law and the Gospel promise (3:23–29); freedom (5:1, 13–14); fruit of the Spirit (5:16–24); three crosses (6:14)

Reading Galatians

A guardian calls the seven-year-old boy in from play to make an introduction. Pointing to a young man, he explains that tomorrow at dawn this fellow will lead the boy to and from school, making certain the boy has the tools of learning: wooden tablets and a stylus. Though the young man is a slave, the boy must mind him and learn from him until the boy is ready to be self-sufficient.

In the Letter to the Galatians, the apostle Paul refers to such first-century life situations in order to explain our relationship to the Law (moral, civil, and ceremonial commands) and the Gospel (God's promise to us in Christ). A typical schoolboy's guardian (Gk *paidagogos*; 3:24) had temporary authority. Similarly, the Law given by Moses served as a temporary guardian, according to the will of our legal guardian (4:2), the Lord Himself. As Paul explains, the Lord had greater plans to fulfill the Law and His life-changing promise. He adopted us (4:5), making us co-heirs with His true Son, our Savior Jesus. In this way, Paul explains and illustrates the binding and life-changing effects of the Law and the Gospel, the two essential teachings of the Christian faith.

Luther on Galatians

The Galatians had been brought by St. Paul to the true Christian faith, from the law to the gospel. After his departure, however, false apostles came along. They were disciples of the true apostles, but they so turned the Galatians around that they believed they had to be saved by works of the law and were committing sin if they did not keep the law—as even several dignitaries in Jerusalem maintained, Acts 15.

To refute them, St. Paul magnifies his office; he will not take a back seat to any other apostle. He boasts that his doctrine and office are from God alone, in order that he might silence the boast of the false apostles who helped themselves to the works and reputation of the true apostles. He says it is not true, even if an angel were to preach differently, or he himself, to say nothing of disciples of apostles, or of apostles themselves. This he does in chapters 1 and 2, and concludes that everyone must be justified without merit, without works, without law, through Christ alone.

In chapters 3 and 4 he proves all this with passages of Scripture, examples, and analogies. He shows that the law brings sin and a curse rather than righteousness. Righteousness is promised by God, fulfilled by Christ without the law, given to us—out of grace alone.

In chapters 5 and 6 he teaches the works of love that ought to follow faith. (LW 35:384)

For more of Luther's insights on this Book, see *Galatians, Chapters 1–4; 5–6* (LW 26, 27).

Calvin on Galatians

The false apostles, who had imposed on the Galatians, endeavoured to obtain their favour by pretending that they had received a commission from those apostles. Their chief influence arose from insinuating the belief that they represented the apostles, and delivered their message. To Paul, on the other hand, they refused the name and authority of an apostle. They objected that he had not been chosen by our Lord as one of the twelve,—that he had never been acknowledged by the college of the apostles,—that he did not receive his doctrine from Christ, or even from the apostles themselves. All this tended not only to lower Paul's authority, but to class him with the ordinary members of the church, and therefore to place him far below the persons who made these insinuations.

If this had been merely a personal matter, it would have given no uneasiness to Paul to be reckoned an ordinary disciple. But when he saw that his doctrine was beginning to lose its weight and authority, he was not entitled to be silent. It became his duty to make a bold resistance. When Satan does not venture openly to attack doctrine, his next stratagem is to diminish its influence by indirect attacks. Let us remember, then, that in the person of Paul the truth of the gospel was assailed. If he had allowed himself to be stripped of the honour of apostleship, it followed that he had hitherto claim what he had no title to enjoy; and this false boasting would have made him liable to suspicion in other matters. The estimation in which his doctrine was held depended on the question whether it came, as some had begun to think, from an ordinary disciple, or from an apostle of Christ. (Calvin, *Galatians* xxii–xxiii)

Gerhard on Galatians

The apostles had learned that the Galatians had allowed themselves to be misled by false apostles who were corrupting the pure teaching of the Gospel that the Galatians had received from Paul regarding justification by faith (or gratuitous justification through faith alone in Christ) by mixing in the righteousness of works. The false apostles were teaching that man is not justified by faith alone in Christ but that to attain righteousness before God and hence eternal life there is an additional need for the observance of the Law and, in fact, not only of the moral but also of the ceremonial law. With great strength, the apostolic spirit in this Epistle sets itself against their corrupting influences. (Gerhard E 1.260)

Bengel on Galatians

This is the sum: Moses and Jesus; the law and the promise; doing and believing; works and faith; wages and the gift; the curse and the blessing,—are represented as diametrically opposed to each other. . . . Man is not justified by the works of the law, and therefore [is justified] in no other way save by faith. (Bengel 14–15)

5

Wesley on Galatians

This epistle is not written, as most of St. Paul's are, to the Christians of a particular city, but to those of a whole country in Asia Minor, the metropolis of which was Ancyra. These readily embraced the Gospel; but, after St. Paul had left them, certain men came among them, who (like those mentioned, Acts xv) taught that it was necessary to be circumcised, and to keep the Mosaic law. They affirmed, that all the other apostles taught thus: that St. Paul was inferior to them; and that even he sometimes practised and recommended the law, though at other times he opposed it. The first part, therefore, of this epistle is spent in vindicating himself and his doctrine, proving, 1. That he had it immediately from Christ himself, and that he was not inferior to the other apostles: 2. That it was the very same which the other apostles preached and, 3. That his practice was consistent with his doctrine. The second contains proofs, drawn from the Old Testament, that the law and all its ceremonies were abolished by Christ. The third contains practical inferences; closed with his usual benediction. (Wesley 650)

Challenges for Readers

Ignoring Sanctification. In the first part of Galatians, Paul focuses strongly on the chief topic of the Christian faith: that Christ justifies us by grace through faith. The dominance of this teaching can lead some readers to ignore Paul's other important message in the Letter: through faith Christ leads us in a new way of life.

The "New" Look on Paul. Some recent interpreters of the Dead Sea Scrolls and other early Jewish literature have argued that Paul did not correctly understand or represent the teachings of Judaism in his day, because early Jewish literature clearly emphasizes themes of election, grace, and faith. Note that, in contrast to Judaism, Paul taught that God saves us by grace through faith alone, without our merit or obedience to the Law.

Genderless Christianity. Feminist interpreters and those influenced by feminism have radically altered the historic interpretation and application of Gal 3:28. They argue that gender and social order should have no influence on roles of service in Christianity. This interpretation has been forcefully used to encourage women's ordination in liberal Protestant church bodies and has even been used to support the ordination of homosexuals.

Galatia. Some scholars contend that the term "Galatia" refers to the northern region of the province, but it most probably refers to the southern area, where Paul and Barnabas established churches on the first missionary journey. Regardless, Galatians was likely intended as a circular Letter to be read in several churches.

Blessings for Readers

The proper distinction of Law and Gospel, described in Galatians, leads one away from the misunderstandings of God's Word mentioned above. Paul certainly affirmed a limited role for the Law in the life of a believer. He explained the life-changing blessings of the Gospel, which make us God's children and give us freedom to do good, not evil. Yet Galatians shows that, though we never outgrow the Law because we are sinners (cf. 5:16–26), it is God's promise that assures our place in His family (4:5–7), with all the privileges He bestows by Word and Spirit.

As you study Galatians, pray that the Holy Spirit would teach you rightly to discern and apply God's Law and Gospel. He who generously gives His good Spirit through the promise will surely grant you a discerning heart.

Outline

Paul uses his rhetorical training in a most sophisticated way, as seen in this Letter's structure and its argumentation. In 1:6–12, Paul confronts the chief problem: false teachers have come to Galatia and preached a different gospel, one that requires the reintroduction of Judaic practices (most prominently, circumcision) in order for the Gentile Christians in Galatia to truly be part of the "Israel of God" (6:16). Paul's solution is presented briefly in 2:15–21: faith in Christ accomplishes both justification (2:15–16) and sanctification ("our endeavor to be justified"; 2:17–21). The rest of the Book gives Paul's supporting argumentation for his solution (e.g., 2:15–16 is explained by 3:1–5:1; 2:17–21 is explained by 5:2–6:10).

    I.   Greetings (1:1–5)
   II.   The Problem (1:6–12)
       A.   Is There Another Gospel? (1:6–10)
       B.   The Gospel Preached by Paul Is the Only Gospel (1:11–12)
  III.   Background to the Problem, Moving toward a Solution (1:13–2:14)

IV. The Solution (2:15–21)
    A. How One Gets Justified (2:15–16)
    B. How One Lives as a Justified Person (2:17–20)
    C. The Gospel Preached by Paul Is the Only Gospel (2:21)
V. The Supporting Arguments for the Solution of 2:15–21 (3:1–6:10)
    A. First Argument about Receiving Justification (3:1–18): Foolish Galatians and Faithful Abraham
        1. Rebuke (3:1–5)
        2. Appeal to Scripture (3:6–14)
        3. Illustration of a human covenant (3:15–18)
    B. Second Argument about Receiving Justification (3:19–4:7): How One Becomes an Heir
        1. Why the Law? (3:19–22)
        2. The end of the Law's function as guardian, the coming of the inheritance by faith (3:23–29)
        3. Illustration of a human heir (4:1–7)
    C. Third Argument about Receiving Justification (4:8–20): Appeal to a Shared Past
        1. What the Galatians were before faith (4:8–11)
        2. Paul's anguish over a wayward child (4:12–20)
    D. Fourth Argument about Receiving Justification (4:21–5:1): Allegory of Sarah and Hagar—Be Free!
    E. First Argument about Living as a Justified Person (5:2–15): The Uselessness of Circumcision
        1. Paul's direct command (5:2–6)
        2. The Law divides the community (5:7–15)
    F. Second Argument about Living as a Justified Person (5:16–26): The Fruits of the Flesh and the One Fruit of the Spirit
        1. The community living by the flesh is divided (5:16–21)
        2. The community living by the Spirit is united (5:22–26)
    G. Third Argument about Living as a Justified Person (6:1–10): A Specific Application for the Community United by the Spirit
        1. Bearing and restoring one another (6:1–5)
        2. Serving one another (6:6–10)
VI. Summarizing Conclusion (6:11–18)

PART 1

GREETINGS (1:1–5)

ESV	KJV
1 ¹Paul, an apostle—not from men nor through man, but through Jesus Christ and God the Father, who raised him from the dead—²and all the brothers who are with me, To the churches of Galatia: ³Grace to you and peace from God our Father and the Lord Jesus Christ, ⁴who gave himself for our sins to deliver us from the present evil age, according to the will of our God and Father, ⁵to whom be the glory forever and ever. Amen.	1 ¹Paul, an apostle, (not of men, neither by man, but by Jesus Christ, and God the Father, who raised him from the dead;) ²And all the brethren which are with me, unto the churches of Galatia: ³Grace be to you and peace from God the Father, and from our Lord Jesus Christ, ⁴Who gave himself for our sins, that he might deliver us from this present evil world, according to the will of God and our Father: ⁵To whom be glory for ever and ever. Amen.

1:1 *apostle.* Paul begins this Letter with the powerful word "apostle" (Gk *apostolos*), which means literally "the sent one." In a wider or more general sense it can refer to a "messenger" or "envoy" (Php 2:25; 2Co 8:23). But Paul calls himself an "apostle" (15 times in the NT) because he wants his readers specifically to know that he has been directly appointed and commissioned by the risen Christ. Luther wrote, "[Paul] does not come as a private person but as the emissary of a king" (LW 26:16). *not from men nor through man.* Paul's apostleship was not of human origin ("men"), nor did it come through human agency ("man"; cf. Am 7:14–15). Already in this first verse he alludes to a charge leveled at him by his critics to which he will later respond. They probably claimed that he had been sent by Christian leaders in Antioch (Ac 13:2–3), not by the risen Lord Himself (Ac 9:15–16). *but through Jesus Christ and God the Father.* This phrase further emphasizes that God, not humans, has authorized him to be His apostle. In Gk the first two persons of the Trinity are controlled grammatically by one preposition, indicating that God the Father called Paul through His very own Son, whom He raised from the dead (cf. Rm 1:1–4, for all three persons of the Godhead). In his Letters to the Romans and Ephesians, Paul similarly stresses at the outset that his call came straight from God. He was "set apart for the gospel of God" (Rm 1:1) and became an "apostle of Christ Jesus by the will of God" (Eph 1:1; see commentary notes; cf. Ac 26:15–18).

1:2 *brothers.* "Brother" is one of Paul's favorite terms for fellow Christians in general (e.g., Rm 8:29; Eph 6:23; see note on Eph 1:12). In this verse he probably has in mind his coworkers in Christ's mission (cf. Php 4:21). *churches.* These were congregations in the towns that Paul and Barnabas visited on the first missionary journey (Ac 13:4–14:28). *Galatia.* Some scholars think that "Galatia" designates the northern region of the Roman province (see map p. xxii). Others argue that it is the southern area where Paul and Barnabas established churches on the first missionary journey. The latter location seems most probable. In any case, Galatians may have been intended as a circular Letter to be read in several churches. What an impact his Letters must have made when they were first read aloud in their gatherings!

1:3 *Grace to you and peace.* Paul's characteristic greeting was especially on target in the Galatia situation, where the message of grace was seriously compromised and peace undermined. *Grace.* We have here a one-word summary of entire Gospel: God's free and undeserved favor toward sinful humanity revealed in Jesus Christ (6:18; see notes on Eph 2:8–9). A central theme of Paul's Letters, it expresses not only God's loving disposition toward human beings, but also His activity of redeeming the world through Christ. *peace.* Through Christ God has made us truly whole: one with Him (Rm 5:1; Col 1:20) and consequently one with each other (Eph 2:14–17; 4:3). God's peace brings us inner peace (Rm 15:13; Php 4:6–7), a precious blessing indeed.

1:4 *present evil age.* Christ "gave Himself for our sins" in order to (the Gk term denotes purpose) rescue us from the bondage that characterizes this age. The present age is evil because it is the realm where sin, death, and the power of Satan reign (Eph 2:1–3). Christ's death broke the stranglehold of these tyrannical powers. He delivered us from "the domain of darkness and transferred us to the kingdom of His beloved Son" (Col 1:13; cf. Heb 2:14) The Gk word for "deliver" that Paul uses here in Gal 1:3 is a strong one (*exaire-omai*). It means to set free from peril or confining circumstances (Ac 7:34; 12:11; 23:27). "To be saved is nothing other than to be delivered from sin, death, and the devil [Colossians 1:13–14]. It means to enter into Christ's kingdom [John 3:5], and to live with Him forever" (LC IV 25). Because believers already participate in the age to come (Gal 2:19–20; 5:5), they live in the world but are not of it (Jn 17:14–15). Thus they are not to conform themselves to this age's sinful values and lifestyles, but to be transformed by the renewal of a mind committed to discerning and doing God's will (Rm 12:2). *the will.* Our deliverance from the powers of this evil age did not just come along by chance. Already in eternity God the Father conceived and set in motion a plan to rescue us from our sins through the blood of Christ (Eph 1:5–7).

1:5 Paul customarily concludes the numerous doxologies in his Letters with the heartfelt affirmation "Amen" (Rm 1:25; 9:5; 11:36; 15:33; 16:27; 6:18; Eph 3:21; Php 4:20; 1Tm 1:17; 6:16; 2Tm 4:18). But this Letter's opening differs from Paul's other Letters in one important respect. He includes a doxology in the salutation (greeting). Because God's deliverance from this evil age is foremost on his mind as he writes to this troubled church, he bursts forth with unrestrained praise to God. Indeed, all of God's promises find their "yes!" in Christ, and for this reason we "utter our Amen to God for His glory" (2Co 1:20). The Letter opens with a doxology but conspicuous by its absence is an opening thanksgiving prayer—the only Pauline Letter without it. This conveys a sense of urgency and forecasts an impending rebuke. *Amen.* This affirming "let it be so" became a liturgical response spoken by the congregation at the end of the liturgy in earlier Christian worship (cf. 1Co 14:16).

Devotion and Prayer in 1:1–5 Paul's opening greetings usually introduce in some way the chief themes of his Letters, setting the tone and atmosphere for what he intends later to say. His strong negative statement, "not from men nor through man, but through Jesus Christ and God the Father," imparts a sense of urgency and prepares the reader for Paul's extended defense of his apostleship to follow. He immediately reminds the Galatians that the risen Lord who called him directly is the same Lord who gave Himself for our sins to deliver us from this present evil age. He has set us free—free from bondage to the Law, a central theme of the Letter (5:1; cf. 4:9). God alone deserves all glory and praise. As will soon become apparent, all human efforts to achieve righteousness on the basis of obedience to the Law rob God of His due glory. Such efforts take away from us true peace, for God gives rest to our hearts only through the forgiveness of sins. For the sake of love Paul was willing to be patient with human weaknesses and failings, but he was uncompromising in his defense of the truth of the Gospel (2:5; Col 1:5). • Heavenly Father, by the power of Your Son's resurrection and His forgiveness, set our hearts free of all things that trouble our consciences and give us Your eternal peace. Amen.

PART 2

THE PROBLEM (1:6–12)

Is There Another Gospel? (1:6–10)

ESV	KJV
[6]I am astonished that you are so quickly deserting him who called you in the grace of Christ and are turning to a different gospel—[7]not that there is another one, but there are some who trouble you and want to distort the gospel of Christ. [8]But even if we or an angel from heaven should preach to you a gospel contrary to the one we preached to you, let him be accursed. [9]As we have said before, so now I say again: If anyone is preaching to you a gospel contrary to the one you received, let him be accursed. [10]For am I now seeking the approval of man, or of God? Or am I trying to please man? If I were still trying to please man, I would not be a servant of Christ.	[6]I marvel that ye are so soon removed from him that called you into the grace of Christ unto another gospel: [7]Which is not another; but there be some that trouble you, and would pervert the gospel of Christ. [8]But though we, or an angel from heaven, preach any other gospel unto you than that which we have preached unto you, let him be accursed. [9]As we said before, so say I now again, if any man preach any other gospel unto you than that ye have received, let him be accursed. [10]For do I now persuade men, or God? or do I seek to please men? for if I yet pleased men, I should not be the servant of Christ.

1:6 *deserting*. The ESV translation more precisely retains the force of the Gk, more so than the KJV (note the KJV's passive rendering "are . . . removed"). The Galatians were actively turning away from the Gospel through which God had called them (cf. 2Th 2:14). They were actually no longer "in the same place" as they were, whether they realized it or not. Paul now calls them fully to account for their departure from the very heart of the Gospel—the "gospel of the grace of God" (Ac 20:24). Deserting the Gospel of Jesus Christ was the same thing as abandoning God Himself. *called.* Like a laser beam, this single expression pinpoints God's initiative in our salvation (cf. 5:13; Eph 4:1; Rm 8:30; 1Co 1:9). *different gospel.* Paul insists in v. 7 that his opponents' "gospel" is really no gospel at all, for there can be no "other gospel." The "gospel" promoted by some in Galatia is "news," all right, but it is not *the* good news of God's *grace* foretold by the prophets and fulfilled in Christ (cf. Rm 10:15; Is 52:7; 61:1)! Their message came on the scene as a revised version of God's Gospel (cf. 1Th 2:2). They claimed they were telling "the rest of the story," insinuating that Paul's proclamation was deficient and that they were proclaiming the full or complete gospel.

1:7 *not . . . another.* The opponents' "gospel" did not just harmlessly modify the Word of truth; it perverted it (Eph 1:13). Christ's Gospel stands all by itself, without parallel and exclusive of all other messages—however cogent and attractive they may seem. Just as there is one Savior, so there is only one Gospel (Gal 2:5, 14). The Gospel is the vehicle through which God creates the Church and keeps its members united with Christ and with each other (1Pt 1:23–25; Jn 17:20–21; 1Jn 1:1–4). Error leads away from Jesus Christ, not toward Him. Hence, to tamper with the Gospel inevitably endangers faith and tears the fabric of Christian unity. *some who trouble you.* The Apostolic Council addressed the contentious issue as to whether Gentiles had to be circumcised to be saved (Ac 15). Following the Council, the Christian leaders who gathered there shared their conclusions with the churches in a letter. They mentioned that Jewish Christians had been troubling the Church "with words," and had "unsettled" (same Gk word as v. 7, *tarasso*) minds (15:24). Paul uses an even stronger word for them in Gal 5:12 that means to upset people and throw them into confusion. *distort.* The Gk term means to change the state or condition of something, such as changing the sun into darkness (Ac 2:20) or laughter to grief (Jas 4:9). Add to or subtract from the Gospel, mix rules and regulations up with it, and you have just polluted and contaminated it! It becomes something fundamentally different. This is what the Galatian intruders did! They consciously intended to change the Gospel by adding the Law as a supplement. The bottom line: their "gospel" failed the acid test of "grace alone."

1:8 *accursed.* The word (Gk *anathema*) can refer to something or someone delivered over to destruction (e.g., Dt 7:26 where the

LXX also uses *anathema*) and thus cursed (1Co 12:3; 16:22; Rm 9:3). Whoever preaches a false gospel—no matter how gifted or impressive the preacher may be—stands under the apostolic anathema. Such strong language may sound offensive to modern ears, but maintaining the Gospel's purity is a serious matter of eternal consequence. Luther wrote, "God's Word shall establish articles of faith, and no one else, not even an angel can do so [Galatians 1:8]" (SA II II 15). This principle includes those who want to be called Christians and boast of their adherence to the teaching of Christ (FC SD Intro 7).

1:9 *said before.* Paul repeats a warning that he and his coworkers had issued on an earlier visit or through earlier contacts (cf. 5:21). He is not merely repeating what he had said in the previous verse. He extends the scope of the warning, adding the phrase "if anyone." You can imagine Paul being so agitated that he could hardly get this Letter off to the churches quickly enough. Melanchthon wrote, "Ungodly teachers are to be deserted because they no longer act in Christ's place, but are antichrists" (Ap VII and VIII 48). *received.* The Gk word belongs to technical vocabulary among rabbis of Paul's day for passing on authoritative teaching or traditions. Paul was God's instrument for imparting revelation given to him directly by Christ and "received" by the Galatia churches. See the note on Php 4:9. *accursed.* See the note on v. 8.

1:10 *approval.* Paul's critics evidently were charging him with merely seeking human favor. But he always insisted that, in obedience to God, the interests of others must come first, and his second (1Co 4:2–5). *please man?* (Gk "men"; see note, v. 1) To Paul's way of thinking, being faithful to God was far more important than being popular. Calvin wrote,

> This is a remarkable sentiment. Those whom ambition leads to hunt after the applause of men, cannot serve Christ. He declares for himself, that he had freely renounced the estimation of his fellow-men; and contrasts his present position with that which he occupied at an early period of life. He had been regarded with the highest esteem, had received from every quarter loud applause; and, therefore, if he had chosen to please men, he would not have found it necessary to change his condition. But we may draw from it the general doctrine which I have stated, that those who resolve to serve Christ faithfully [specifically, pastors], must have boldness to despise the favour of men. (Calvin, *Galatians* 16–17)

15

Devotion and Prayer in 1:6–10 Paul was so deeply agitated by developments in the Galatia churches that he uncharacteristically begins this Letter not with an expression of thanksgiving but with a stern warning. He is astonished that these Christians had so quickly ignored his previous cautions and had now departed from the one true Gospel he had consistently preached. They had been convinced by the persuasive and deceitful words of some to accept "another gospel"—which was "no gospel" at all. Their false teachings struck at the very heart of the pure Gospel of God's grace alone and thus endangered saving faith in Jesus Christ. Evil influences (v. 4) are continually seeking to "qualify" the grace of God in Christ by adding to or subtracting from the scriptural Gospel. How blessed we are to have pastors who proclaim to us God's unqualified love toward us in the Lord Jesus who forgives our sins and sets our hearts at rest!
• May Your precious Word, O Lord, be taught in all truth and purity so that we may receive Your divine blessing. Amen.

The Gospel Preached by Paul Is the Only Gospel (1:11–12)

ESV	KJV
[11]For I would have you know, brothers, that the gospel that was preached by me is not man's gospel. [12]For I did not receive it from any man, nor was I taught it, but I received it through a revelation of Jesus Christ.	[11]But I certify you, brethren, that the gospel which was preached of me is not after man. [12]For I neither received it of man, neither was I taught it, but by the revelation of Jesus Christ.

1:11 *brothers.* Paul's opening rebuke might seem very hard-nosed to us today. But let's not jump to the conclusion that he harbored within him personal animosity toward his fellow-Christians in Galatia. The Galatians had gone astray, but he still regards them as brothers and sisters in Christ, members of God's family (3:15; 4:5, 12, 28; 5:11, 13; 6:1, 18). In fact, it is precisely because they are "brothers" that he is so intensely concerned about them and their spiritual welfare. *was preached.* The Gk text shows a play on words for the sake of emphasis, reading literally, "the gospel 'gospelled' ["preached"] by me." Paul deliberately uses the passive "was preached" to show how conscious he was of his calling to be God's instrument for proclaiming the Gospel. Let it be known, the Gospel did not come from him!

1:12 *I.* The pronoun (Gk *ego*) stands at the beginning of the sentence for emphasis. *a revelation of Jesus Christ.* Paul writes that God "was pleased to reveal His Son to me" (v. 16). The risen Jesus disclosed that He was the Christ, the Son of God and the Savior of the world. Again, Paul's Gospel came not by human mediation, but directly from Christ who is also its content (cf. Rm 16:25; 2Co 4:4–6).

PART 3

BACKGROUND TO THE PROBLEM, MOVING TOWARD A SOLUTION (1:13–2:14)

ESV	KJV
[13]For you have heard of my former life in Judaism, how I persecuted the church of God violently and tried to destroy it. [14]And I was advancing in Judaism beyond many of my own age among my people, so extremely zealous was I for the traditions of my fathers. [15]But when he who had set me apart before I was born, and who called me by his grace, [16]was pleased to reveal his Son to me, in order that I might preach him among the Gentiles, I did not immediately consult with anyone; [17]nor did I go up to Jerusalem to those who were apostles before me, but I went away into Arabia, and returned again to Damascus. [18]Then after three years I went up to Jerusalem to visit Cephas and remained with him fifteen days. [19]But I saw none of the other apostles except James the Lord's brother. [20](In what I am writing to you, before God, I do not lie!) [21]Then I went into the regions of Syria and Cilicia. [22]And I was still unknown in person to the churches of Judea that are in Christ.	[13]For ye have heard of my conversation in time past in the Jews' religion, how that beyond measure I persecuted the church of God, and wasted it: [14]And profited in the Jews' religion above many my equals in mine own nation, being more exceedingly zealous of the traditions of my fathers. [15]But when it pleased God, who separated me from my mother's womb, and called me by his grace, [16]To reveal his Son in me, that I might preach him among the heathen; immediately I conferred not with flesh and blood: [17]Neither went I up to Jerusalem to them which were apostles before me; but I went into Arabia, and returned again unto Damascus. [18]Then after three years I went up to Jerusalem to see Peter, and abode with him fifteen days. [19]But other of the apostles saw I none, save James the Lord's brother. [20]Now the things which I write unto you, behold, before God, I lie not. [21]Afterwards I came into the regions of Syria and Cilicia; [22]And was unknown by face unto the churches of Judaea which were in Christ:

[23]They only were hearing it said, "He who used to persecute us is now preaching the faith he once tried to destroy." [24]And they glorified God because of me.

2 [1]Then after fourteen years I went up again to Jerusalem with Barnabas, taking Titus along with me. [2]I went up because of a revelation and set before them (though privately before those who seemed influential) the gospel that I proclaim among the Gentiles, in order to make sure I was not running or had not run in vain. [3]But even Titus, who was with me, was not forced to be circumcised, though he was a Greek. [4]Yet because of false brothers secretly brought in— who slipped in to spy out our freedom that we have in Christ Jesus, so that they might bring us into slavery—[5]to them we did not yield in submission even for a moment, so that the truth of the gospel might be preserved for you. [6]And from those who seemed to be influential (what they were makes no difference to me; God shows no partiality)—those, I say, who seemed influential added nothing to me. [7]On the contrary, when they saw that I had been entrusted with the gospel to the uncircumcised, just as Peter had been entrusted with the gospel to the circumcised [8](for he who worked through Peter for his apostolic ministry to the circumcised worked also through me for mine to the Gentiles),

[23]But they had heard only, That he which persecuted us in times past now preacheth the faith which once he destroyed.

[24]And they glorified God in me.

2 [1]Then fourteen years after I went up again to Jerusalem with Barnabas, and took Titus with me also.

[2]And I went up by revelation, and communicated unto them that gospel which I preach among the Gentiles, but privately to them which were of reputation, lest by any means I should run, or had run, in vain.

[3]But neither Titus, who was with me, being a Greek, was compelled to be circumcised:

[4]And that because of false brethren unawares brought in, who came in privily to spy out our liberty which we have in Christ Jesus, that they might bring us into bondage:

[5]To whom we gave place by subjection, no, not for an hour; that the truth of the gospel might continue with you.

[6]But of these who seemed to be somewhat, (whatsoever they were, it maketh no matter to me: God accepteth no man's person:) for they who seemed to be somewhat in conference added nothing to me:

[7]But contrariwise, when they saw that the gospel of the uncircumcision was committed unto me, as the gospel of the circumcision was unto Peter;

[8](For he that wrought effectually in Peter to the apostleship of the circumcision, the same was mighty in me toward the Gentiles:)

9and when James and Cephas and John, who seemed to be pillars, perceived the grace that was given to me, they gave the right hand of fellowship to Barnabas and me, that we should go to the Gentiles and they to the circumcised. 10Only, they asked us to remember the poor, the very thing I was eager to do.

11But when Cephas came to Antioch, I opposed him to his face, because he stood condemned. 12For before certain men came from James, he was eating with the Gentiles; but when they came he drew back and separated himself, fearing the circumcision party. 13And the rest of the Jews acted hypocritically along with him, so that even Barnabas was led astray by their hypocrisy. 14But when I saw that their conduct was not in step with the truth of the gospel, I said to Cephas before them all, "If you, though a Jew, live like a Gentile and not like a Jew, how can you force the Gentiles to live like Jews?"

9And when James, Cephas, and John, who seemed to be pillars, perceived the grace that was given unto me, they gave to me and Barnabas the right hands of fellowship; that we should go unto the heathen, and they unto the circumcision. 10Only they would that we should remember the poor; the same which I also was forward to do.

11But when Peter was come to Antioch, I withstood him to the face, because he was to be blamed. 12For before that certain came from James, he did eat with the Gentiles: but when they were come, he withdrew and separated himself, fearing them which were of the circumcision. 13And the other Jews dissembled likewise with him; insomuch that Barnabas also was carried away with their dissimulation. 14But when I saw that they walked not uprightly according to the truth of the gospel, I said unto Peter before them all, If thou, being a Jew, livest after the manner of Gentiles, and not as do the Jews, why compellest thou the Gentiles to live as do the Jews?

1:13 Paul will tell his personal story as evidence for what he says in vv. 11–12 (see the temporal and sequential "then" in 1:18, 21; 2:1). His violent pre-Christian past was etched in his memory. Rehearsing it displayed the magnitude of God's mercy shown to him (1Tm 1:13; 1Co 15:9–10). *heard.* Reports had been circulated about him and his fanatical efforts to annihilate the Christian Church (cf. vv. 22–23). As the accounts of his conversion in Acts also suggest, he likely included the story of his soiled past as part of his defense and proclamation of the Gospel on various other occasions. *Judaism.* The term (only in vv. 13–14 in the NT) designates the faith and way of life that distinguished Jews from Gentiles (including especially circumcision, dietary laws, Sabbath observance, and the system of feasts and sacrifices). Note Ac 13:43 where the ESV speaks of "converts to Judaism." (literally, "proselytes"). *persecuted.* See the note on Php 3:6. Twice in this chapter Paul says that he persecuted God's Church because he was obsessively driven by his desire to destroy it (Gk *portheo*; here and v. 24). *church of God.* The NT word "church" (*ekklesia*) is used in the LXX to translate the Hbr word for congregation or assembly. In the NT it refers to the church in geographical locations (such as Corinth) as well as to the universal Church of all believers in Christ (1Co 1:2). Since the Church is the body of Christ (Eph 5:23; Col 1:18), to persecute the Church is to persecute Christ (Ac 9:4–6). Persecution of the Church equals hostility aimed at God Himself! In contrast to his former life in Judaism, Paul now belongs to those who believe in Christ, the new "Israel of God" (see note, 6:16). *violently.* Paul persecuted the Church "to an extraordinary degree," intensively and extensively. He once thought it a noble cause to shut up saints in prisons. He voted for their execution and punished them in the synagogues. He tried to make them blaspheme, raged in "fury against them," and even hunted them down in foreign cities (Ac 26:10–11).

1:14 *advancing in Judaism.* See the note on v. 13. In his defense defending the Gospel and his apostleship Paul made a special point of his being brought up at the feet of Gamaliel "according to the strict manner of the law of our fathers, being zealous for God" (Ac 22:3). He lived as a Pharisee, "the strictest party" of the Jewish religion (Ac 26:5). But more, he outstripped his contemporaries in the teachings and practices of the Jewish religion, shown especially by his ardent zeal for persecuting God's Church. See the note on Php 3:5. *traditions.* According to the Pharisees, the rabbis' ancestral interpretations and rulings drawn from the Law were on the same level as the Law (Torah) itself. These were passed on in the oral law and later accumulated in writing in the form of teachings, commandments, stories, etc. (Hbr *halakah*, cf. Mk 7:5).

1:15 *set me apart . . . called.* Paul did not decide to "change religions." As God set apart and called the prophets of old (Jer 1:5; Is 49:1–6), so also He chose Paul to bring the Gospel to the Gentiles to carry out His divine purpose. A former persecutor of the Church, he knew from experience that God called him by grace (1Co 15:9). Calvin wrote,

The word of the Lord which came to Jeremiah, though expressed a little differently from this passage, has entirely the same meaning. "Before I formed thee in the belly, I knew thee; and before thou camest forth out of the womb I sanctified thee, and I ordained thee a prophet unto the nations." Before they even existed, Jeremiah had been set apart to the office of a prophet, and Paul to that of an apostle. (Calvin, *Galatians* 20)

1:16 *consult.* Paul was converted and received his commission independently of the other apostles (cf. v. 17). In fact, his encounter with the risen Lord was such a powerful, life-changing experience that there was no need for him to take the issue up with anyone. *anyone.* The Gk text reads literally, "with flesh and blood." Paul received no instruction from anyone in Jerusalem immediately after his conversion. He mentions this to prove that his Gospel did not depend on any human source but came to him only by way of divine revelation. His opponents assumed that he had no authorization to preach Christ and Him crucified (1Co 1:23) to nations other than Israel without also insisting that converts keep certain requirements in the Law (i.e., "among the Gentiles"). See the notes on vv. 11, 12.

1:17 Paul gives us no specific information regarding his activity in Arabia or Damascus, though his purpose in mentioning them is clear. He reports his departure to these locations as further evidence that he received his apostolic authority apart from any contact with the church's leadership in Jerusalem. *Arabia.* This is probably a reference to the Nabataean Kingdom located in the area around Damascus in Syria, founded in the second century BC. See map, p. xxi. Aretas IV ruled at Petra (9 BC–c. AD 40) as king when Paul was converted (2Co 11:32). Some commentators believe that Paul went to Arabia to begin mission work among the Gentiles. *Damascus.* See map, p. xxi. Damascus was one of the cities of the Decapolis under the supervision of Syria's imperial legate (its official emissary). It came under Roman control in 66 BC. At Paul's time, it was a Nabataean city and had a large Jewish population.

1:18 *Cephas.* Peter's surname Cephas (Aram *kepha*; Gk *petros*, "stone"), which Jesus gave to him (Jn 1:42), recalls Peter's rock-solid confession that Jesus is "the Christ, the Son of the living God" (Mt 16:18). Peter did not receive this confession from "flesh and blood" but from the Father in heaven (Mt 16:17). It does not seem far-fetched to imagine that this was among the topics discussed between

Paul and Peter during their 15-day visit. Paul customarily used the name Cephas for Peter, though not always (cf. 2:7–8). *remained with him.* Paul avoids the impression that he went to Jerusalem to receive instruction from Peter, though certainly they would have shared information about Jesus. The carefully chosen word "visit" (*historeo*) intimates that Paul mainly desired to get to know Peter. Notably, both saw the risen Lord with their own eyes (1Co 9:1; 15:5; Lk 24:34).

1:19 *James the Lord's brother.* James was probably the oldest, and certainly the best known, of Jesus' four brothers (Mk 6:3). There is no biblical evidence showing that he was Jesus' cousin or a brother from a previous marriage of Joseph, as some have speculated. Though not one of the Twelve, James became a prominent apostle in the Jerusalem Church (Ac 12:17; 15:13; 21:18–19; 1Co 15:7). He was likely the author of the Epistle of James (Jas 1:1). Two other men bore this name in the NT (James the son of Alphaeus and James the son of Zebedee). Again, Paul emphasizes the minimal amount of contact that he had with Jerusalem leadership at this stage of his career. He did "visit" with Peter, but he did not even "see" any of the other apostles except James.

1:20 By oath, Paul affirms his integrity, since the truth of the Gospel he proclaims is at issue. Some may have found the sudden about-face in Paul's life hard to believe. Others may have accused him of not telling the whole truth about the source of his preaching.

1:21 *Syria and Cilicia.* These regions were combined into one Roman province with its capital at Antioch. See map, p. xxi. Paul mentions his post-conversion work here to show again his distance from Jerusalem. According to Luke's report in Acts, he spent some time in both Cilicia (at Tarsus) and Syria proper (Antioch, the capital). See Ac 9:30, 11:25–26, and 13:1. "Then" shows again that Paul wants to give a careful sequential account, leaving out nothing that might arouse suspicion.

1:22 *the churches of Judea.* Luke reports in Acts that following Stephen's death, "a great persecution against the church" broke out, forcing believers out of Jerusalem and scattering them throughout Judea and Samaria (Ac 8:1). Some Christians whom Paul apprehended in Damascus for imprisonment may have been refugees (cf. Ac 22:5). *Judea.* This Roman province included all of Galilee, Samaria, and Judea proper. *in Christ.* This phrase was Paul's signature way of identifying persons individually and corporately as "Christian" (occurring

73 times in his Letters). What better shorthand could there be for the blessings we have through our union with Him and our fellow Christians? "In Christ" we have freedom (2:4), are justified (2:17), have the blessing of Abraham, and receive the promised Spirit through faith (3:14). We are all sons of God (3:26) and are one with Him (3:28; cf. 1Co 1:9).

1:23 *hearing it said.* The churches did not know Paul personally (v. 22), but they kept hearing about his past reputation as "the persecutor." *the faith.* In Paul, faith (Gk *pistis*) can mean either the faith in Christ by which we are saved (2:26), or as here, the content that is believed (i.e., teaching; cf. 1Tm 1:19; 4:1).

Devotion and Prayer in 1:11–24. "Reading between the lines" we can readily see that one leg of the Galatia agitators' strategy was to directly attack Paul's apostleship. His authority, they said, was derivative or secondary. It was "from men" and "through man" (v. 1). Their real bone of contention, of course, was that Paul allowed Gentiles to become Christians without circumcision. Selecting key facts from his personal history, Paul vigorously defends his apostleship. It came directly from God through His Son who appeared to Him on the road to Damascus and commissioned Him to be an apostle. The one and only Gospel, which he proclaimed, came to him by revelation independent of human sources. This Gospel totally transformed Paul from being "in Judaism" (vv. 13–14) to being "in Christ." Today, enemies of God's Church continue to question the divine origin of the Christian message, causing doubts and confusion among many believers in Christ. As God called Paul "by His grace," so He now seeks to change hearts through the Good News of His Son. We join Christians everywhere in glorifying God for all faithful witnesses to His grace in Christ. • Keep us faithful to Your Word, O Lord, when doubts threaten. Amen.

2:1 *after fourteen years.* This could mean 14 years after Paul's conversion (1:15–16), after his first visit to Jerusalem (1:18), or after the time spent in Syria and Cilicia (1:21). The exact chronology of Paul's life and career has been difficult to determine. In any case, the overall argument remains clear: during this long period, Paul had no direct contact with Jerusalem. *Barnabas . . . Titus.* A friend and co-worker of Paul, Barnabas was a Levite from the island of Cyprus. Luke pays him a wonderful tribute: "he was a good man, full of the Holy Spirit and of faith" (Ac 11:24). His name meant "son of encouragement" (Ac 4:36). He was responsible for bringing Paul from Cyprus to Antioch (Ac 11:25), from which they both were sent off on the first missionary journey (Ac 16:1–3). Titus was a Greek convert (uncircumcised) of Paul (Ti 1:3) and his assistant in dealing with the church at Corinth (2Co 2:13; 7:6–7, 13–15; 8:6, 16–24; 12:8). Calling Barnabas and Titus "very suitable witnesses" (i.e., test cases), Luther wrote,

> By presenting himself with both of them he intended to make it clear that he was at liberty to be a Gentile with Titus and a Jew with Barnabas . . . [to prove] the freedom of the Gospel in each case. (LW 27:200)

2:2 *revelation.* Paul went up to Jerusalem for no other reason than that God told him to go there (just as after his conversion, Ac 22:17–21). He did not go because there was an official need for him to have his message validated or authorized by church leaders there. He had already been preaching the Gospel independently of them for many years. *influential.* In this context, the Gk word (*dokeo*) means to "be influential" or "have a reputation." In v. 9 Paul identifies them primarily as James, Cephas, and John. He extended to them the courtesy of a private consultation, which showed his high regard for them and signaled the bond of fellowship. For the sake of the Church's unity and God's mission to Jews and Gentiles, Paul desired to get a vote of confidence from the Jerusalem leadership. *not run in vain.* The apostle was not fearful of failure in pursuing a successful career. But he was genuinely concerned that those who had believed the Gospel would hold fast "to the word of life" until "the day of Christ" (Php 2:16; see note).

2:3 *not . . . circumcised . . . Greek.* That Titus was not compelled to be circumcised shows that Paul's views prevailed in the Jerusalem Church. That the Church did not press the point likely weakened the circumcision party's future efforts to make it's case. Significantly, despite opposition from a circumcision group, Peter (like Paul) went by divine revelation to uncircumcised Gentiles and associated with them (a sign of fellowship (Ac 11:2–18).

2:4 *false brothers.* Some Jewish Christians (commonly labeled Judaizers) within the Jerusalem Church demanded the circumcision of Gentile converts (Ac 15:1, 5). Their claim to be fellow believers was belied by their conduct. Their behavior showed them to be Christians in name only (cf. 1Co 5:11). They adhered to a "gospel" that

Paul regarded as false (1:6–9). It is difficult to determine for certain whether Paul is referring to the just mentioned event in Jerusalem, to later developments in Galatia, or to what happened perhaps in Antioch. *secretly brought in.* The Gk word (*pareisaktos*; only here in the NT) carries the idea of someone who comes into a group by stealth (note "slipped in"), under false pretenses and with false motivations. The expression may suggest collusion between the infiltrators who wormed their way into the churches from the outside, and "insiders" who facilitated their spying operation. In any case, the context here indicates that they took the initiative. *freedom.* This is a central topic in the Letter to the Galatians. It shows up four times as a noun (Gal 2:4; 5:1, 13), six times as an adjective (3:28; 4:22, 23, 26, 30, 31), and once in verbal form (5:1). According to Paul's principal argument, to introduce works of the Law as the basis for our acceptance before God brings back into bondage a person set free by the Gospel of grace in Christ. We can see from this verse that it was not only the false gospel taught by the Galatian interlopers that infuriated Paul, but also their underhanded methods. Paul similarly indicted the "false apostles" who infiltrated the Church at Corinth "disguising themselves as apostles of Christ." They "disguise themselves as servants of righteousness. Their end will correspond to their deeds" (2Co 11:13–15).

2:5 Paul did not yield an inch to the Judaizers. He held his ground to preserve the purity of the Gospel, the message of God's free grace. He also wanted to make certain that its truth was maintained for the Galatians' sake (and for the sake of all future readers of the Letter). The Gospel's truth stands in sharp opposition to so-called "truth" of Paul's opponents. Luther wrote,

> The truth of the Gospel is this, that our righteousness comes by faith alone, without the works of the Law. The falsification or corruption of the Gospel is this, that we are justified by faith but not without the works of the Law. (LW 26:88)

Other Lutheran reformers noted,

> In such a case we have nothing to concede. We should plainly confess and endure what God sends because of that confession, and whatever He allows the enemies of His Word to inflict on us. (FC Ep X 6)

2:6 *what they were makes no difference.* Paul respected the Jerusalem leaders but refrained from overstating their importance. The Galatian agitators were evidently appealing to the status and prestige of the Jerusalem apostles in order to denigrate Paul's own teaching and work. They were so superior to Paul, they said, that his ministry lacked validity. *no partiality.* The LXX uses this word to translate a Hbr expression ("lift the face") that means "show partiality or favoritism" (cf. 2Ch 19:7; Mal 1:8; Lk 20:21). Likewise, Paul's words can be translated literally "God does not receive the face." This terminology is combined into single terms used often in the NT to emphasize that God shows no partiality (Ac 10:34; Rm 2:11; Eph 6:9; Col 3:25; Jas 2:1; 1Pt 1:17). Before God, all are on equal footing. *added nothing.* The "pillars" in Jerusalem added nothing to Paul (i.e., his message or divine commissioning).

2:7 *entrusted.* The risen Lord had given Paul the responsibility of faithfully administrating the Gospel, which included both its proclamation and preservation. He remained ever conscious of this sacred stewardship (1Co 9:17; 1Th 2:4; 1Tm 1:11; Ti 1:3). As today, God's servants in the holy ministry need to be keenly aware of the social and cultural contexts in which their audiences live as they communicate effectively the one Gospel (1Co 4:1–2). Melanchthon wrote,

> St. Paul clearly affirms that he was neither ordained nor confirmed by Peter. Nor does he acknowledge Peter to be one from whom confirmation should be sought. (Tr 10)

2:8 *his apostolic ministry.* The Gk term *apostole* ("apostolate") is a technical term for the office and work of an apostle of Christ (Ac 1:25; Rm 1:5; 1Co 9:2). In Paul's self-consciousness as Christ's servant, "apostleship" and "grace" are wedded together (v. 9): "we [he and his fellow apostles] have received grace and apostleship" (Rm 1:5; 12:3; 1Co 3:10; 15:9–10, 15; Eph 3:8; Php 1:7).

2:9 *pillars.* We still use "pillars" of those recognized for their spiritual leadership in our congregation's history (cf. v. 6). Leaders like this were extremely important in the Church's early days, for they supported and gave stability to the Church (cf. 1Tm 3:15). There may even be an allusion to the "pillars" in God's new sanctuary, the Church (Rv 3:12; cf. Eph 2:21–22; 1Co 3:16; 2Co 6:16). *right hand of fellowship.* A handshake would give assurance that a formal agreement would be held in honor. *fellowship.* The handshake also outwardly expressed the apostles' partnership in the Gospel. See the commentary notes on Php 1:5, 7.

2:10 *remember the poor.* The Jerusalem pillars recognized the divine legitimacy of Paul's calling and work. The word "only" implies that they attached no conditions or additional requirements to their agreement. But they did have one request: that Paul and Barnabas administer financial relief for the saints in Jerusalem, who were caught in persecution and famine. In keeping with the OT's heavy emphasis on helping the poor (e.g., Dt 24:10–22; Ps 10:2, 9; 12:5; 14:6 etc.), Paul had early on made such help a policy in his missionary work (Ac 11:29–30). In the years following, he led a specific campaign to collect funds to relieve the poverty of the Jerusalem Church. This became a major task to which Paul vigorously devoted himself (Rm 15:25–28; 1Co 16:1–4; 2Co 8–9). "The Collection," as it came to be called, served the higher purpose of demonstrating the Church's unity. Largely, these funds were gifts of Gentile churches to Jewish Christians. Among the many terms he attaches to the offering ("service," "gift," "generous gift," "collection," "liberal gift," and "service that you perform"), the Gk term *koinonia* (which here means a "sign of fellowship"; ESV "contribution") seems most apt (Rm 15:26).

Devotion and Prayer in 2:1–10 By divine revelation, Paul goes to Jerusalem with Barnabas and Titus to visit Church leaders. Despite some opposition in their midst, they approved of his message and mission to the Gentiles when they saw God's grace manifested in Paul's ministry. They laid down no stipulations regarding Paul's apostleship, nor did not they even demand that the Gentile Titus be circumcised. The visit concluded with a warm handshake signifying a solid partnership in the Gospel. Paul highly respected the Church's leaders in Jerusalem, but refused to exaggerate their importance as some did as a way of denigrating Paul's work. In the face of strong opposition from legalists out to discredit his Gospel of God's free grace, Paul stood his ground and prevailed. We thank God for this courageous apostle who preserved the truth of the Gospel. Christians today also face continual threats to their freedom in Christ. Even the temptations of their own sinful flesh threaten to rob them of liberty that is theirs through Christ's forgiveness. We rejoice that the Gospel comes from God and thus cannot be deprived of its power to set us free. • Lord, grant us strength in our partnership in the Gospel. Amen.

2:11 *Antioch*. A Hellenistic city and trading center in NW Syria, Antioch ranked with Rome and Alexandria as one of the three greatest cities in the Greco-Roman world. A significant Jewish population resided there. Barnabas and Paul helped to establish the first Gentile Church there (Ac 11:19–26). *to his face*. Paul publicly and personally took issue with Peter. *condemned*. Peter stood self-condemned but also convicted before God. When a Jesuit wrote to Knox that only heretics disagreed among themselves, as happened among the reformers, Knox replied:

> Did not Paul disagree from Peter? (Gal. ii.) Yea, he did so disagree from him, that he resisted him plainly to his face, because he walked not according to the right way of the truth of the gospel. These were two principal pillars; the one appointed to the Jews, and the other to the Gentiles. (Knox 285)

2:12 *eating with*. Peter had learned from God at Joppa in a vision that he should not regard any person as unclean: "God shows no partiality" and "to the Gentiles also God has granted repentance that leads to life" (Ac 10:34; 11:18). When you had table fellowship with Gentiles in those days, you were assuming freedom from the Law (also Jewish food laws) and full acceptance of them (Ac 10:35, 48). *fearing*. Peter's duplicitous behavior probably came from heavy religious and emotional pressure, not from a change in his convictions. *circumcision party*. See the note on v. 4.

2:13 *rest of the Jews*. These were Jewish Christians in Antioch—"Jews by birth," as Paul relates in v. 15. *even Barnabas*. "Even" (Gk *kai*) his trusted friend and colleague of many years lacked the courage of his convictions and succumbed to behavior inherently dishonest. Imagine what a terrific shock it must have been to Paul that Barnabas, too, did what was expedient instead of what was right! Shortly after this event, Paul and Barnabas parted company after a sharp disagreement over Barnabas' proposal to take John Mark along on a return visit to Galatia. It is possible that hard feelings still lingered between them following Paul's rebuke in Antioch (but apparently not permanently, as 1Co 9:6; Col 4:10 demonstrate). The Lutheran Confessions cite Paul's example in a discussion of matters neither commanded nor forbidden by God (adiaphora):

> Paul yields and gives way to the weak concerning food and ‹the observance of› times or days (Romans 14:6). But to the false apostles, who wanted to impose these on the conscience as

necessary things, he will not yield even in matters that are adiaphora. . . . When Peter and Barnabas yielded somewhat in such an emergency, Paul openly rebukes them according to the truth of the Gospel as people who were not acting right in this matter (Galatians 2:11–14). (FC SD X 13)

2:14 *conduct was not in step.* Measured by the Gospel of freedom in Christ, the deliberate withdrawal from fellowship with Gentiles not only lacked integrity but betrayed God's truth. Further, Paul rebuked behavior inconsistent with the Gospel because of its scandalous effect on others. He makes the matter public again in this Letter to correct error in Galatia. Though public rebuke of public sin is neither required nor always advisable, it is permissible in some contexts (cf. LC I 284). *the truth of the gospel.* See the note on v. 5. *you force the Gentiles to live like Jews?* Such strong-arming would have been seen as an open violation of the Jerusalem agreement (see note on vv. 3, 9). But intense group pressure was surely exerted on the Gentile Christians to adopt, "for the sake of peace," Jewish customs and practices. "To live like Jews" translates a Gk word occurring only here it the NT (*ioudaizo*). The term designates someone living according to Mosaic laws or traditions, thus "in a Judean or Jewish fashion."

Devotion and Prayer in 2:11–14 Peter and Barnabas's conduct at Antioch illustrates how difficult it is to remain faithful to clear biblical principles in the face of strong group pressure. Sometimes Christians cave in to such pressure and act in ways inconsistent with a core truth of the biblical Gospel. Such was the case with Peter, a distinguished leader in the Church. For the sake of the Gospel's truth, Paul publicly rebuked Peter for his hypocritical conduct. He withdrew table fellowship with Gentiles under pressure from some Jewish Christians. His actions loudly communicated that the Gentiles must live like Jews, keeping their laws and customs. The Scriptures repeatedly condemn the sin of hypocrisy, pretending to be a Christian (Mt 23:28; Lk 12:1; 1Pt 2:1; cf. Lk 20:20). But the Gospel assures us that God freely forgives all our sins, also the sins of false witness: "the blood of Jesus his Son cleanses us from *all* sin" (1Jn 1:7; cf. 1Jn 1:9; 1Co 1:9). • Lord Jesus, forgive all thoughts, words, and actions that have shown a lack of Christian integrity on my part. May my entire life be a clear testimony to the freedom that You have won for me through Your death and resurrection. Amen.

PART 4

The Solution (2:15–21)

How One Gets Justified (2:15–16)

ESV	KJV
¹⁵We ourselves are Jews by birth and not Gentile sinners; ¹⁶yet we know that a person is not justified by works of the law but through faith in Jesus Christ, so we also have believed in Christ Jesus, in order to be justified by faith in Christ and not by works of the law, because by works of the law no one will be justified.	¹⁵We who are Jews by nature, and not sinners of the Gentiles, ¹⁶Knowing that a man is not justified by the works of the law, but by the faith of Jesus Christ, even we have believed in Jesus Christ, that we might be justified by the faith of Christ, and not by the works of the law: for by the works of the law shall no flesh be justified.

2:15 *We ourselves.* Paul speaks from a Jewish perspective. *Gentile sinners.* The phrase gives us a glimpse into how the pious Law-observing Jews felt toward nations without the Law. They noticed every sin and failure in others while explaining their own troubles in the kindest way. Calvin wrote,

> The word *sinner*, signifies here . . . a "profane person," or one who is lost and alienated from God. Such were the Gentiles, who had no intercourse with God; while the Jews were, by adoption, the children of God, and therefore set apart to holiness . . . . They who believe in Christ, confess that they are sinners, and renounce justification by works. (Calvin, *Galatians* 45)

2:16 *not justified by works of the law.* The word "justify" in the Scriptures denotes a verdict, a legal act whereby God declares a person righteous, that is, innocent, not guilty, forgiven (cf. v. 17; 3:8, 11, 24; 5:4). A sinner's justification (Rm 5:6–8) does not depend on obedience to what the Law requires. *through faith in Jesus Christ.*

This does not mean "the faithfulness of Jesus Christ" (cf. note 2 of the ESV), but "faith in Jesus Christ." The words immediately following show that He is not the subject of believing, but the object of our faith: "so we also have believed in Christ Jesus." *not by works of the law.* Luther rightly (in idiomatic German) included the word "alone" (Ger *allein*) in a parallel passage at Rm 3:28. Melanchthon wrote,

> The term *alone* [*sola*] offends some people. . . . If the exclusive term *alone* displeases, let them remove from Paul also the exclusives *freely, not by works, it is the gift,* and so on. (Ap IV 73)

Cranmer wrote,

> His great mercy [God] showed unto us in delivering us from our former captivity, without requiring of any ransom to be paid, or amends to be made upon our parts, which thing by us had been impossible to be done. (Cranmer 2:139)

How One Lives as a Justified Person (2:17–20)

ESV	KJV
[17] But if, in our endeavor to be justified in Christ, we too were found to be sinners, is Christ then a servant of sin? Certainly not! [18] For if I rebuild what I tore down, I prove myself to be a transgressor. [19] For through the law I died to the law, so that I might live to God. [20] I have been crucified with Christ. It is no longer I who live, but Christ who lives in me. And the life I now live in the flesh I live by faith in the Son of God, who loved me and gave himself for me.	[17] But if, while we seek to be justified by Christ, we ourselves also are found sinners, is therefore Christ the minister of sin? God forbid. [18] For if I build again the things which I destroyed, I make myself a transgressor. [19] For I through the law am dead to the law, that I might live unto God. [20] I am crucified with Christ: nevertheless I live; yet not I, but Christ liveth in me: and the life which I now live in the flesh I live by the faith of the Son of God, who loved me, and gave himself for me.

2:17 *is Christ then a servant of sin?* Paul's opponents likely argued that if Jews who keep the Law are reckoned as "sinners" in need of God's justifying grace, then Christ is made an agent of sin. Paul's doctrine of justification by faith alone, in their view, also encouraged people to break the Law and to become lax in carrying out their moral responsibilities. Paul categorically rejects these arguments as invalid. A "new obedience" follows faith. Melanchthon wrote,

> Our churches teach that this faith is bound to bring forth good fruit [Galatians 5:22–23]. It is necessary to do good works commanded by God [Ephesians 2:10], because of God's will. We should not rely on those works to merit justification before God. (AC VI 1)

2:18 *if I rebuild . . . transgressor.* If a builder tears down a wall, builds a new one, and then tears the new one down, his actions imply that the new wall was a mistake. The Gospel Paul preached broke down the wall of separation (the Law's requirements) between Jew and Gentile (cf. Eph 2:14–18). For Paul (and by implication, Peter) to reinstate the Law as a way of salvation in the place of Christ would be to make himself a "transgressor" all over again. Christ would then be of no advantage to anyone (5:2), and would have "died for no purpose" (v. 21).

2:19 *I died.* Paul's relationship to the Law as a means of becoming righteous before God and acceptable to Him has come to an end for him personally. The Law can save no one because no one can live up to its requirements. The Law does serve the important purpose of showing us how sinful we are (Rm 7:13). Melanchthon wrote, "The Law only accuses and terrifies consciences" (Ap XII 34). All who are in Christ (v. 17) are no longer under the Law's jurisdiction: "But now we are released from the law, having died to that which held us captive. . . ." (Rm 7:6). The Law has no claim on believers. Because Christ has redeemed them from the Law's curse, they are free from its curse (3:13).

2:20 *It is no longer I who live, but Christ who lives in me.* Luther explains, "By [faith] you are so cemented to Christ that He and you are as one person" (LW 26:168). *in the flesh.* Here "flesh" refers to our earthly life. Knox wrote,

> But the true faithful, when all hope of natural means fail, flee to God himself, and to the truth of his promise. . . . Not that . . . the faithful have at all hours such a sense of the life everlasting, that they fear not the death and the troubles of this life . . . not so; for the faith of God's children is weak. (Knox 375)

The Gospel Preached by Paul Is the Only Gospel (2:21)

ESV	KJV
[21]I do not nullify the grace of God, for if righteousness were through the law, then Christ died for no purpose.	[21]I do not frustrate the grace of God: for if righteousness come by the law, then Christ is dead in vain.

2:21 If obedience to the Law is in any sense regarded as part of God's justification of the sinner, then Christ's death becomes unnecessary. Salvation by Christ's atoning death (v. 20) and salvation by human effort are mutually exclusive. "Grace alone" and "Christ alone" distinguish Christianity from all other religions of the world. Those who compromise the Gospel undermine the foundations of the Christian religion.

Devotion and Prayer in 2:15–21 Paul now spells out the serious theological implications of Peter's vacillating behavior. By his actions Peter was telling the Gentiles that they were not acceptable to God unless they submitted to the Law. To the Jews, Peter was saying he had sinned by eating with the Gentiles. In response, Paul presents the Letter's core argument: God justifies sinners by grace through faith for the sake of Christ who loved us and gave Himself for us. All human works are excluded. Those who appeal to the Law in addition to Christ as a means of salvation reject the grace of God as invalid and render Christ's saving work on the cross meaningless. Prevalent today is the common notion that good works, at the least, "won't hurt" one's chances to go to heaven—and will likely help. Actually quite the opposite is true. Efforts to achieve salvation through works of the Law are spiritually harmful, and even dangerous, for they negate God's grace and strip Christ of His reason for coming. Once we know Christ and His great love, there is no going back, nor would we ever want to! He has loved us and given Himself for us to free us from the Law's condemnation and captivity. He now lives within us so that we may live for Him • O God, our earthly life in Christ now has a high purpose, to live for You (2:19). Grant me full confidence in Christ Jesus, who alone can save me. Amen.

PART 5

THE SUPPORTING ARGUMENTS FOR THE SOLUTION OF 2:15–21 (3:1–6:10)

First Argument about Receiving Justification (3:1–18): Foolish Galatians and Faithful Abraham

Rebuke (3:1–5)

ESV	KJV
3 ¹O foolish Galatians! Who has bewitched you? It was before your eyes that Jesus Christ was publicly portrayed as crucified. ²Let me ask you only this: Did you receive the Spirit by works of the law or by hearing with faith? ³Are you so foolish? Having begun by the Spirit, are you now being perfected by the flesh? ⁴Did you suffer so many things in vain—if indeed it was in vain? ⁵Does he who supplies the Spirit to you and works miracles among you do so by works of the law, or by hearing with faith—	3 ¹O foolish Galatians, who hath bewitched you, that ye should not obey the truth, before whose eyes Jesus Christ hath been evidently set forth, crucified among you? ²This only would I learn of you, Received ye the Spirit by the works of the law, or by the hearing of faith? ³Are ye so foolish? having begun in the Spirit, are ye now made perfect by the flesh? ⁴Have ye suffered so many things in vain? if it be yet in vain. ⁵He therefore that ministereth to you the Spirit, and worketh miracles among you, doeth he it by the works of the law, or by the hearing of faith?

3:1 *bewitched*. The Gk term occurs only here in the NT. It means to exert an evil influence on someone through the eye, such as casting a spell. Paul wonders whether the Galatians in effect have been hypnotized. *publicly portrayed as crucified*. Paul preached Christ's death so vividly that his audiences could almost see Jesus die with their own eyes (cf. 1Co 2:1–2). It is hard to understand how they could now have such a spiritual blind spot! Calvin wrote,

> To show how energetic his preaching was, Paul first compares it to a picture, which exhibited to them, in a lively manner, the image of Christ. But not satisfied with this comparison, he adds, *Christ hath been crucified among you*, intimating that the actual sight of Christ's death could not have affected them more powerfully than his preaching. (Calvin, *Galatians* 59)

3:2 *receive the Spirit.* Paul assumes that the Galatians have already received the Holy Spirit and His gifts through faith in Jesus Christ proclaimed in the Gospel (5:22; cf. Rm 10:17; 1Th 2:13). Where faith is, there is the Holy Spirit and where the Spirit is, there is faith (3:5, 14; 4:6; 5:5). With a rhetorical question, Paul wants the Galatians to admit the obvious: the Holy Spirit came to them when they believed the Gospel; He did not come through works of the Law. *by hearing.* "The Holy Spirit renews the heart. He is given and received, not through the Law, but though the preaching of the Gospel (Galatians 3:14)" (FC SD VI 11). We are "brought to" the Church through the Holy Spirit and incorporated into it when we hear God's Word, "which is the beginning of entering it" (LC II 52).

3:3 *by the flesh.* Paul's use of "flesh" (*sarx*) in Galatians (18 times) illustrates the range of NT nuances this term can have: literally, flesh that covers the bones or a living being with flesh (1:16; 2:16; 6:13); the functioning body (4:13, 14); the body with its physical limitations (2:20); the body dominated by sin—weak, self-centered, and self-indulgent (5:13, 19, 24); earthly descent (4:23); outward side of life, as in "human standards" (6:12). In 3:3 Paul focuses on the sinful dimension of human beings (third use in list above). That the Judaizers require circumcision for a "full gospel" (cf. Rm 2:23–29) comes from the fallen human nature, not from God's Spirit.

3:4 *Did you suffer.* The NT makes no specific mention of the Galatians undergoing suffering. "Suffer" in this context may have the more general sense of "experience," but in most instances the experience entails hardship (death, persecution, physical suffering).

3:5 *miracles.* When the Gospel came to the Galatians God manifested His miraculous power through His Spirit among them. Miracles often accompanied the apostolic proclamation (Rm 15:19; 1Th 1:5; 2Co 12:12).

Appeal to Scripture (3:6–14)

ESV	KJV
⁶just as Abraham "believed God, and it was counted to him as righteousness"? ⁷Know then that it is those of faith who are the sons of Abraham. ⁸And the Scripture, foreseeing that God would justify the Gentiles by faith, preached the gospel beforehand to Abraham, saying, "In you shall all the nations be blessed." ⁹So then, those who are of faith are blessed along with Abraham, the man of faith. ¹⁰For all who rely on works of the law are under a curse; for it is written, "Cursed be everyone who does not abide by all things written in the Book of the Law, and do them." ¹¹Now it is evident that no one is justified before God by the law, for "The righteous shall live by faith." ¹²But the law is not of faith, rather "The one who does them shall live by them." ¹³Christ redeemed us from the curse of the law by becoming a curse for us—for it is written, "Cursed is everyone who is hanged on a tree"—¹⁴so that in Christ Jesus the blessing of Abraham might come to the Gentiles, so that we might receive the promised Spirit through faith.	⁶Even as Abraham believed God, and it was accounted to him for righteousness. ⁷Know ye therefore that they which are of faith, the same are the children of Abraham. ⁸And the scripture, foreseeing that God would justify the heathen through faith, preached before the gospel unto Abraham, saying, In thee shall all nations be blessed. ⁹So then they which be of faith are blessed with faithful Abraham. ¹⁰For as many as are of the works of the law are under the curse: for it is written, Cursed is every one that continueth not in all things which are written in the book of the law to do them. ¹¹But that no man is justified by the law in the sight of God, it is evident: for, The just shall live by faith. ¹²And the law is not of faith: but, The man that doeth them shall live in them. ¹³Christ hath redeemed us from the curse of the law, being made a curse for us: for it is written, Cursed is every one that hangeth on a tree: ¹⁴That the blessing of Abraham might come on the Gentiles through Jesus Christ; that we might receive the promise of the Spirit through faith.

3:6 Having rebuked the Galatians' foolishness, Paul now turns to an example from Scripture in order to make his case for justification through faith. *just as.* The usual formula for Scriptural proof was "As it is written" (e.g. Rm 1:17; 2:24; 3:10). Not only the Galatians' experience of receiving the Spirit, but especially also Scripture itself sup-

39

ports what Paul is saying. God declared Abraham righteous by faith, but not because of his obedience. This issue comes under discussion at some length in Rm 4:1–25, where Paul gives a detailed interpretation of OT passages in Gn 15, Ps 32, and Gn 17. He argues that "Abraham believed God, and it was counted to him as righteousness" (Rm 4:3; cf. Gn 15:6). Abraham did not earn righteousness before God as his due wages (Rm 4:4–6). He was not counted righteous because he was circumcised, for he was declared righteous by God *before* his circumcision. This reveals God's purpose to "make him the father of all who believe [including Gentiles] without being circumcised, so that righteousness would be counted to them as well" (Rm 4:11).

Introduction to 3:7–5:26 Now begins a sustained argument from Scripture to disprove two incorrect rabbinic understandings of Abraham's role, namely that: (1) Abraham was counted righteous because of his faithfulness under testing (regarded as meritorious); and (2) Abraham's faith (Gn 15:6) included obedience to the Law of circumcision (Gn 17:4–14) which was necessary for a right standing before God. Melanchthon wrote,

> This is absolutely a Jewish opinion, to hold that we are justified by a ceremony, without a good tendency of the heart, that is, without faith. . . . Paul contradicts this, and denies (Romans 4:9) that Abraham was justified by circumcision. He asserts that circumcision was an illustration presented for exercising faith. (Ap XIII 18–19)

3:7 *sons of Abraham.* The Judaizers may have been telling the Galatian Christians that they should become sons of Abraham by circumcision. Paul counters by saying, on the basis of the text just quoted (Gn 15:6), that all men and women who believe are already spiritual heirs of Abraham by faith in the promise fulfilled in Christ.

3:8 *Scripture, foreseeing.* Paul personifies the Holy Scriptures, equating them with God speaking (cf. 3:22; 4:30; Rm 9:17). Thus, what Scripture says, God says. Bengel wrote,

> The term *foreseeing* implies divine *foreknowledge*, more ancient than the law. The great excellence of sacred Scripture is, that all the points likely to be controverted are foreseen and decided in it. . . . It is God who has given testimony to these things; God foreknew that He would act in this manner with the Gentiles; God therefore already at that time acted in a similar manner with

Abraham; God also caused it to be consigned to writing, and that too when at the time that it was written, it was still future. (Bengel 20)

preached the gospel beforehand. The Scripture (God speaking) pre-announced the good news to Abraham. The unique verb Paul uses (Gk *proeuangelizomai,* "proclaim good news in advance") affirms the fundamental unity of the Bible. We find the fulfillment of the OT promise of justification by faith in the NT (Rm 1:1–3). In the Gospel, God fully disclosed the secret hidden for long ages (Rm 16:25–26; Eph 3:2–6). *blessed.* Paul now quotes from Gn 12:3; 18:18 to establish his central point: that the promise to Abraham embraced also the Gentiles, who, like Abraham, are justified by faith and have peace with God (Rm 5:1). (Note the passive "be blessed," following the LXX and indicating that this is God's action and not a result of anything we do.)

3:9 *of faith.* The Gk phrase *ek pisteos* appears nine times in Gal (based on Hab 2:4; cf. Gal 3:11; Rm 1:17; Heb 10:38). In this verse, "those who are *of faith*" means "those who believe." Abraham belonged among "the people of faith." When Paul focuses on faith as the means through which we personally receive God's justifying grace, the ESV correctly translates the phrase "by [or through] faith" (2:16; 3:8, 11, 22, 24). Paul's carefully chosen words in v. 3 set in bold contrast the Gospel promise on the one hand, and the Law and good works on the other. Try as they may, the "circumcision party" (2:12) would no longer be able legitimately to hold up Abraham as an example of obedience to the Law as they argued that circumcision is a necessary requirement in addition to the Gospel Paul preached.

Devotion and Prayer in 3:1–9 Paul expresses astonishment that the Galatians have been mesmerized by the foolish notion that salvation is completed by works of the Law. To prove that a person is not justified by works of the Law but through faith in Jesus Christ (v. 15), Paul appeals to the Galatians' experience (vv. 1–5) and to Scripture's witness concerning Abraham (vv. 6–9). The Galatians were converted when they heard the Gospel of Christ. They could hardly escape its full impact, for it was proclaimed vividly to them—like a well done multimedia presentation today. They received the Holy Spirit "by hearing with faith," not by works of the Law. Paul turns the Judaizers' argument on its head by showing, on the basis of key texts from Genesis, that Abraham was justified by his faith in God's promises, not because of his obedience to the Law. All who share Abraham's faith in God's promise share also in the blessing of salvation given to Abraham. Our sinful flesh likes to take confidence in good works as a means to assure God's favor. Such self-serving confidence amounts to a rejection of salvation by grace alone through faith in Christ alone. Thank God that we can look to Jesus, our crucified Savior, through whom our sins are completely forgiven. • How blessed we are, Lord, to be the heirs of Your promises! Thank You for granting me faith through Your Word. Amen.

3:10 *all who . . . everyone.* Paul returns to the principle (see v. 11) that he has already laid down in 2:16: *"no one"* will be justified before God *"by works of the law"* (a phrase occurring three times in that verse alone!; see note on 2:16). He has in mind all those who rely on the Law or on their obedience to the Law for their acceptance and life with God—whether they are Jewish or Gentile Christians. Significantly, the Gk translated "no one" in 2:16 reads literally *"all flesh* shall not be justified. . . ."* That covers all humanity with no exceptions. *a curse . . . Cursed.* All who rely on the works of the Law ("under the Law," v. 23; 4:4, 5, 21) to become righteous before God are under divine condemnation—which is the exact opposite of being "justified before Him." Luther summarizes Paul in this way: "In 'keeping' the Law he [the doer of the Law] does not keep it" (LW 26:268; see FC SD VI 4). Paul's Jewish readers would have found this comment about cursing absolutely shocking. Many modern readers would likely consider such a thought as going way overboard, if not excessively harsh and even outlandish. A God who would curse someone does not fit in with popular ideas of God as a benevolent or benignly tolerant deity who welcomes human efforts to earn his favor. *all things written in the Book of the Law.* Paul, an authoritative interpreter of the OT, makes use of the LXX when quoting Dt 27:26 and drawing on Dt 28:58. These texts in the LXX emphasize obedience to "all things" written in the whole Law (Dt 30:10; cf. 28:1, 15).

3:11–12 Faith and Law are teachings that are fundamentally different from one another. Faith says only God can justify us and give us life (Hab 2:4). The Law promises life only to those who keep its every command (Lv 18:5). A person can only rely on one. Only by faith are we saved.

3:13 *redeemed.* Paul uses this term (*exagorazo*) here and in 4:5 in the figurative sense of "deliver" or "liberate." *Cursed is everyone* *who is hanged on a tree*. Having previously quoted Dt 27:26 placing under a curse all those who do not keep everything written in God's Law, Paul now quotes Dt 21:23 and applies it to the crucified Christ (cf. Ac 10:39; 13:29; 1Pt 2:24). In its original context, Dt 21:23 spoke about the hanging of a criminal's corpse on a tree or pole after execution. *Cursed*. The curse pronounced on all humans for their failure to keep the Law perfectly is transferred to Christ, who kept the Law perfectly. Paul's identification of Christ and the curse becomes a graphic way of saying that He bore the curse *for us* (Gk *hyper hemon*) and thus delivered us (cf. Rm 5:8; Eph 5:2; 1Th 5:10; Ti 2:14). Luther wrote, "Whatever sins I, you, and all of us have committed or may commit in the future, they are as much Christ's own as if He Himself had committed them" (LW 26:278; cf. 2Co 5:21).

3:14 *receive the promised Spirit*. By faith in Jesus Christ, whose atoning work delivered us from the curse of the Law, all believers (both Jews and Gentiles) receive the gift of the Spirit. They become children of Abraham, "heirs according to the promise" (3:29; cf. Eph 3:6; Heb 6:17; 11:9). See the note on v. 2. Luther wrote concerning the promise of the Spirit received through faith: "Now the Spirit is freedom from the Law, from sin, death, the curse, hell, and the wrath and judgment of God" (LW 26:293).

Devotion and Prayer in 3:10–14 These verses go to the heart of biblical Christianity, the doctrine of justification. They deal with the central question of religion: how people come into a right relationship with God. In the doctrine of justification, Luther has reminded us, all the other doctrines of our faith are included, and "if it is sound, all the others are sound as well" (LW 26:283). Paul first declares that the Law cannot make us right with God, because God's curse falls on all who do not keep it in its entirely. One sin, no matter how trivial it may seem to us, makes us a transgressor of the whole Law and accountable to God (Jas 2:10). Paul then announces the good news that Christ has redeemed us from the Law's curse by becoming a curse for us. Christ's death on the cross releases us from the guilt of every sin we have committed or will commit. By believing in Christ, the promise of life becomes ours. • O Holy Spirit, strengthen us in the new life of faith begun in our Baptism. Amen.

Illustration of a human covenant (3:15–18)

ESV	KJV
¹⁵To give a human example, brothers: even with a man-made covenant, no one annuls it or adds to it once it has been ratified. ¹⁶Now the promises were made to Abraham and to his offspring. It does not say, "And to offsprings," referring to many, but referring to one, "And to your offspring," who is Christ. ¹⁷This is what I mean: the law, which came 430 years afterward, does not annul a covenant previously ratified by God, so as to make the promise void. ¹⁸For if the inheritance comes by the law, it no longer comes by promise; but God gave it to Abraham by a promise.	¹⁵Brethren, I speak after the manner of men; Though it be but a man's covenant, yet if it be confirmed, no man disannulleth, or addeth thereto. ¹⁶Now to Abraham and his seed were the promises made. He saith not, And to seeds, as of many; but as of one, And to thy seed, which is Christ. ¹⁷And this I say, that the covenant, that was confirmed before of God in Christ, the law, which was four hundred and thirty years after, cannot disannul, that it should make the promise of none effect. ¹⁸For if the inheritance be of the law, it is no more of promise: but God gave it to Abraham by promise.

3:15 *no one annuls . . . ratified.* Paul cites a human example perhaps from Greek law. In Greek law, wills were irrevocable. New conditions could not be imposed, nor could an heir be removed. Once wills were ratified and sealed they could not be altered by a supplementary testament. Some Jewish wills were of this kind. Roman law was less restrictive, allowing the testator to alter his will at any time until his death, when it was validated and could never be changed.

3:16 *offspring.* This word (Gk *sperma*, "seed") denotes physical descent or ethnicity. God made promises to Abraham (Gn 12:1–3, 7; 13:14–17; 17:8; 22:16–18; 24:7) about his "offspring" ("seed"; Hbr *zeraʿ*). The singular "seed" in the OT texts can have a double nuance: a single descendant or many descendants (that is, a collective sense; cf. Gal 3:29). In typical rabbinic fashion, Paul uses this grammatical point to prove a pivotal theological point. Christ is the ultimate heir of the inheritance promised to Abraham. Through the one Seed (Christ), believers become the seed (descendants) of Abraham. We have here another example of the earthshaking impact Paul's conversion has on him. After Christ got a hold of him (Ac 9:1–16), Paul understood God's "promise" to Abraham in a totally new way.

3:17 *430 years.* Ex 12:40 tells us that Israel spent 430 years in Egypt (cf. Gn 15:13; Ac 7:6, where the number of years is rounded to 400). NT scholars have offered various suggestions regarding the events covered by this number. Paul's main point, however, should not be lost. A lengthy period of time elapsed between the covenant made with Abraham and the giving of the Law. *make the promise void.* God's gracious promise is not invalidated by the Law given much later (see previous comparison, v. 15).

3:18 *inheritance.* The promise (*epangelia*; the noun is used 8 times in Gal 3, the verb once in v. 19) God gave to Abraham belongs to all who are justified through faith in Christ, whether Jews or Gentiles. Note especially the word "gave" (Gk *charizomai,* "give graciously"). Our inheritance (justification) is either based on God gracious promise (as Paul says), or it is given to those who keep the Law (as the Judaizers claimed). Luther wrote, "The forgiveness of sins, righteousness, salvation, and eternal life, . . . means that we are the sons and heirs of God and fellow heirs with Christ (Rom. 8:17)" (LW 26:304).

Second Argument about Receiving Justification (3:19–4:7): How One Becomes an Heir

Why the Law? (3:19–22)

ESV	KJV
[19]Why then the law? It was added because of transgressions, until the offspring should come to whom the promise had been made, and it was put in place through angels by an intermediary. [20]Now an intermediary implies more than one, but God is one. [21]Is the law then contrary to the promises of God? Certainly not! For if a law had been given that could give life, then righteousness would indeed be by the law. [22]But the Scripture imprisoned everything under sin, so that the promise by faith in Jesus Christ might be given to those who believe.	[19]Wherefore then serveth the law? It was added because of transgressions, till the seed should come to whom the promise was made; and it was ordained by angels in the hand of a mediator. [20]Now a mediator is not a mediator of one, but God is one. [21]Is the law then against the promises of God? God forbid: for if there had been a law given which could have given life, verily righteousness should have been by the law. [22]But the scripture hath concluded all under sin, that the promise by faith of Jesus Christ might be given to them that believe.

3:19 *added because of transgressions.* The Law came with a purpose different from the promise. It brings the true nature of sin out into the open. Sin is a violation of God's revealed will (cf. Rm 3:20; 4:15; 7:7). *offspring.* See the note on v. 16. *through angels by an intermediary.* Though unidentified, the intermediary (Gk *mesites*), is probably Moses, who was assisted by angels (cf. Dt 33:2; Ps 68:17). God spoke directly to Abraham, but He administered the Law through intermediaries. This shows the Law's inferiority to the Promise/Gospel. Wesley wrote, "The moral law was added to the promise to discover and restrain transgressions, to convince men of their guilt, and need of the promise, and give some check to sin" (Wesley 479). Regarding the role of angels here, Calvin wrote, "This is declared by Stephen also, who says, that they had 'received the law by the disposition of angels.' " Calvin adds that we should not be surprised "that angels, by whom God bestows on us some of the smallest of his blessings, should have been entrusted also with this office of attending as witnesses at the promulgation of the law" (Calvin, *Galatians* 81–82).

3:20 Paul highlights a central tenet of Jewish teaching that is reflected in the *shema* (the common name given to the three prayers offered daily by pious Jewish of the first century taken from Dt 6:4–9; 11:13–21; Nu 15:37–41): God is one. When God gave the Promise to Abraham, He acted directly on His own according to His sovereign grace. However, when He gave the Law, He did so indirectly through the mediation of angels and Moses. The apostle sees God's direct bestowal of the Promise as an indication of the Promise's superiority over the Law. Bengel wrote, "There is not one God before and another after the giving of the law, but one and the same God" (Bengel 28). The one God's "name" (note that "name" is singular) is "Father, Son, and Holy Spirit (reflecting that there are three persons in the one God; Mt 28:19).

3:21 The rhetorical question anticipates the Jewish response to the previous point. Paul gives an emphatic "No!" to the false conclusion (cf. Rm 3:21) that Law and Promise stand in opposition to each other. The Law and the Promise have different functions. But this does not mean that Paul is *against* the Law, for it is holy, righteous, and good (Rm 7:12, 16; 1Tm 1:8). The Law shows our need for a Savior; but it cannot give us the righteousness that leads to life. The Promise declares that God has given us life through the justifying work of His Son Jesus Christ.

3:22–23 *Scripture imprisoned everything under sin . . . held captive.* The Gk term meaning "imprison" or "confine" (*synkleio*) in this context conveys the idea of transferring or delivering someone into the hands or control of another (it is used three times in NT, figuratively here and at Rm 11:32; and literally in Lk 5:6 where it describes enclosing fish in a net). Scripture, which contains God's Law, "incarcerates" the whole world with no hope for release (cf. Rm 3:9; 11:32). It reveals sin's dreadful power over all human existence. Luther wrote,

> In clear terms this passage consigns and subjects to sin and the curse not only those who sin against the law openly or fail to keep it outwardly but also those who are subject to the Law and bend every effort to keep the Law; such were the Jews. . . . (LW 26:332)

under the law. All human beings are under the power of the Law, which condemns sin and places them under God's curse (v. 10; see note). *until.* The Law kills (2Co 3:6). Luther observes that it does so, however, in such a way that God may be able to make alive. It shows the enormity of sin in order that it may drive us to Christ. This dynamic of the Word happens daily in our personal lives and thus fulfills God's ultimate intent, namely, to bring us to Christ who delivers us from the Law's subjugation.

The end of the Law's function as guardian, the coming of the inheritance by faith (3:23–29)

ESV	KJV
[23]Now before faith came, we were held captive under the law, imprisoned until the coming faith would be revealed. [24]So then, the law was our guardian until Christ came, in order that we might be justified by faith. [25]But now that faith has come, we are no longer under a guardian, [26]for in Christ Jesus you are all sons of God, through faith. [27]For as many of you as were baptized into Christ have put on Christ.	[23]But before faith came, we were kept under the law, shut up unto the faith which should afterwards be revealed. [24]Wherefore the law was our schoolmaster to bring us unto Christ, that we might be justified by faith. [25]But after that faith is come, we are no longer under a schoolmaster. [26]For ye are all the children of God by faith in Christ Jesus. [27]For as many of you as have been baptized into Christ have put on Christ.

28There is neither Jew nor Greek, there is neither slave nor free, there is no male and female, for you are all one in Christ Jesus. 29And if you are Christ's, then you are Abraham's offspring, heirs according to promise.

28There is neither Jew nor Greek, there is neither bond nor free, there is neither male nor female: for ye are all one in Christ Jesus. 29And if ye be Christ's, then are ye Abraham's seed, and heirs according to the promise.

3:24 *guardian.* The Gk *paidagogos* means literally "boy" or "child leader." Greco-Roman households often secured a slave whose duty was to supervise and guard (though not to teach) children from about ages 6–16. Guardians had to walk children to and from school, show them good manners, and discipline them when necessary (like a tutor or even "baby-sitter"). Their temporary role served as the point of comparison. One commentator describes the Law's provisional role as "a stepping stone" to faith, not as something on the same level with faith (as the Judaizers might have supposed). It did not bring people to salvation, but revealed their need for it. The Lutheran Confessions teach that civil laws have a disciplinary or supervisory role in governing external behavior in the world. Melanchthon wrote, "God wants wild sinners to be restrained by civil discipline. To maintain discipline, He has given laws, letters, doctrine, rulers, and penalties" (Ap IV 22). But people are not to think that obedience to such laws earns them the righteousness before God that only comes by faith in Christ Jesus.

3:25 The Law served an interim role for Israelites from Moses to Christ, but when faith came, this arrangement ceased. For Paul "faith" here serves as a kind of "code word" for the new era of salvation through faith in Christ. By faith we are freed from the Law's curse, become righteous before God (v. 11), receive the Spirit (vv. 13–14), and are God's children united with Christ (vv. 27–28).

3:26 *sons of God.* See the notes on v. 25 and on 4:6. Note the subtle shift in this verse from the personal "we" to "you" in the phrase "*you are all.* . . . " All believers in Christ, including the Gentiles in the Galatian churches, without distinction, bear the honorific title "sons of God" once reserved for Israel (Ex 4:22–23; Dt 14:1; Is 43:6; Hos 1:10). They are no longer under a "guardian" (v. 24) and his watchful eye.

3:27 *put on Christ.* Through Baptism, God incorporates believers into union with Christ (cf. Mt 28:19; Rm 6:3–4). Thus His righteousness becomes theirs. Luther wrote, "Christ Himself is our garment . . . the garment of our righteousness and salvation" (LW 26:353; see LC IV 83–84). Today's familiar saying "clothing makes the man" is generally understood to mean that what a person wears expresses who that person is. In the truest sense, to "put on" Christ means to be fully and totally in Him (note the phrase *"into Christ"*; cf. Rm 6:3; 14:14). In Christ believers receive a new identity, purpose, and meaning. See the note on 2:20.

3:28 Neither ethnic or social identities nor gender has a bearing on one's salvation before God. All who are baptized into Christ are one in His body, even while distinctions present in creation remain. Regarding man and woman, for example, Paul's point is not that their identity can be exchanged, nor could Greeks become Jews or Jews become Greeks. The individual characteristics of believers are not abolished by the new creation established by God in Christ Jesus (6:15; 2Co 5:17). But all receive the Gospel the same way: freely for Christ's sake.

3:29 Paul now brings his argument in vv. 15–29 to a close by summarizing two principal points he has made in this section. By believing in Christ Jesus (2:16) and being baptized into Him (3:27) Christians are identified with Christ and with other Christians and become "sons of God" by faith (3:26). Christians also become Abraham's "offspring" (the collective plural) by believing in Christ, who is Abraham's Seed ("offspring" in the singular; see note, v. 16) and thus heirs of the promise given to Abraham. By faith in Christ we find our true identity. We belong to God and are one with fellow Christians, in time and in eternity.

Devotion and Prayer in 3:15–29 Paul discusses the relation between the promise given to Abraham and the Law given later through Moses. He reminds those who insist on keeping the Law, in addition to faith in Christ, that they have made keeping the Law necessary for salvation. The promise given to Abraham, that through his Seed (Christ) all people will be blessed, precedes and has priority over the Law, and cannot be annulled or modified by the Law. Through Christ, God fulfills the promise He gave to Abraham. All united to Christ by Baptism become heirs of the promise by faith and therefore are righteous before God. In the history of our salvation the Law had a temporary, preparatory function until the time of the Promise's fulfillment in Christ arrived—the time of faith. The Law still serves the good purpose of revealing sin and our need for a Savior. But Christ does what the Law cannot do. He gives forgiveness and life. To those who feel alone and whose life seems meaningless, Paul's words (which may sound somewhat abstract and complicated) offer great comfort. By faith in Christ we belong to our gracious God and are united with all our fellow Christians. We now have a new personal history with all those who are heirs of God's promise given to Abraham! • Lord, help us to see that in our congregation all are to be welcomed, whatever their background or place in life. Help us also to reach out to all with the message of Jesus' love. Amen.

Illustration of a human heir (4:1–7)

ESV	KJV
4 ¹I mean that the heir, as long as he is a child, is no different from a slave, though he is the owner of everything, ²but he is under guardians and managers until the date set by his father. ³In the same way we also, when we were children, were enslaved to the elementary principles of the world. ⁴But when the fullness of time had come, God sent forth his Son, born of woman, born under the law, ⁵to redeem those who were under the law, so that we might receive adoption as sons. ⁶And because you are sons, God has sent the Spirit of his Son into our hearts, crying, "Abba! Father!" ⁷So you are no longer a slave, but a son, and if a son, then an heir through God.	4 ¹Now I say, That the heir, as long as he is a child, differeth nothing from a servant, though he be lord of all; ²But is under tutors and governors until the time appointed of the father. ³Even so we, when we were children, were in bondage under the elements of the world: ⁴But when the fulness of the time was come, God sent forth his Son, made of a woman, made under the law, ⁵To redeem them that were under the law, that we might receive the adoption of sons. ⁶And because ye are sons, God hath sent forth the Spirit of his Son into your hearts, crying, Abba, Father. ⁷Wherefore thou art no more a servant, but a son; and if a son, then an heir of God through Christ.

4:1–2 *guardians and managers.* Paul elaborates on his previous comparison. Guardians (Gk *epitropos*) and managers (Gk *oikonomos*) were legally appointed individuals to whom a child's welfare, support, and household affairs, were entrusted. That was their most important duty. In addition, they were charged with the administration of the child's inheritance. Under the Roman legal system, the status of a child still under the care of a guardian was roughly that of a slave (both were unable to experience the inheritance). The precise legal details of the procedure are not known to us, but Paul's main point is clear enough. The inheritance belongs to the child, but under law he cannot have control over it until the date set by the father arrives. It is his by promise, but he is not yet free to enjoy it. We may note in Paul's discussion in chs. 3–4 the numerous times he uses the preposition "under" as he contrasts subjugating restraint with liberty (under a curse, 3:10; under the Law, 3:23; 4:21 [cf. 5:18]; under sin, 3:22; under guardians, 3:25, 4:4; under the basic principles of the world, 4:3).

4:3 *were children*. The pairing of "children" and "enslaved" calls attention to our previous history as a state of confinement. *elementary principles*. Cf. v. 9. In the NT the Gk term (*stoicheia*) has a range of meanings (Gal 4:3, 9; Col 2:8, 20; Heb 5:12; 2Pt 3:10, 12). It is hard to determine whether Paul is specifically referring to elemental evil influences (note that they are "of the world") that enslaved Gentiles during their pagan way of life, or forces that used the Law and its regulations to place people under hopeless bondage (cf. Col 2:8, 20). Perhaps both are meant. All such forms of enslavement are not hopeless and without the possibility of escape, as the devil deceptively would have us believe. On the contrary, the apostle is set to tell us that Christ has come to set people free.

4:4 *fullness of time*. Time had reached its state of fullness. One might imagine a container steadily being filled with the passage of time until it is full. The events of human history had reached the divinely appointed time for God to take action. The phrase corresponds to "date set by his father" in v. 2, when the child will be set free and come into the inheritance promised to him. Thus, at the right time in human history, God acted to fulfill His eternal purpose (see Eph 1:10 and the commentary notes). *born of woman*. The pre-existent Son of God (1Co 8:6; Php 2:6–11; Col 1:15–16) became fully human. The Lutheran Confessions affirm,

> In the fullness of time He received also the human nature into the unity of His person. He did not do this in such a way that there are

now two persons or two Christs. Christ Jesus is now in one person at the same time true, eternal God. (FC SD VIII 6)

Notably, Paul nowhere mentions Mary by name. Throughout his Letters, Paul's theology and devotion centers on Jesus Christ and only on Him. *under the law.* Jesus was born a Jew. In obedience to His Father's will ("God sent") the Son of God placed Himself under an inherited obligation to keep the Law of Moses (cf. Rm 8:3; also FC SD III 58). Though He was without sin (2Co 5:21), for Him to be "under" the Law meant He must be treated as a sinner "under" a curse for us (3:10–11). Consistent with Paul's imagery, Jesus entered our prison (3:23) in order to free us from its confinement. See also note, 3:10.

4:5 *those . . . under the law.* Paul first mentions Jewish Christians. *we.* He then switches pronouns to include both Jewish and Gentile believers (cf. 3:14; see note on 3:10). *adoption as sons.* Paul's readers would be familiar with adoption practice in Roman law and custom. Once legally adopted into a family, a person received all the rights and privileges of a natural born son. See the notes on Eph 1:5.

4:6 *you are sons.* All Christians live as sons and daughters of God through faith in Jesus Christ (3:26). Because they are His, God [has] sent (Gk, past tense) the Spirit of His Son into their hearts (3:2, 14). When they come to faith, believers simultaneously have both Christ and His Spirit. *Abba!* This Aramaic word preserved in Greek comes from the language of small children, similar to the words "Dada" or "Papa" today. On the lips of Jesus, "dear Father" reveals His intimate relationship with His Father (Mk 14:36). By the Spirit's prompting, this same spontaneous cry from believers testifies that they have a new relationship with God given through His Son (Rm 8:9, 15–17). Since they are God's children, they are authorized and privileged to address God in the words of their Lord Himself, "our Father." Surprisingly, God was never addressed as "Abba" in Jewish prayers! We can only wonder what the Judaizers thought about this childlike intimacy with God!

4:7 *you.* Paul personalizes his argument by using the singular "you" in Greek. Each person can regard himself or herself as an heir of all the spiritual blessings God gives to His adopted children. Calvin wrote, "We have Christ present with us, and in that manner enjoy his blessings" (Calvin, *Galatians* 102).

Devotion and Prayer in 4:1–7 A person's status under the Law contrasts like night and day with the position of someone who is

in Christ. Those who are "under the Law" are like slaves who were part of inherited property, not heirs of it! Those who are God's children in Christ are like sons destined to inherit what belongs to their father. At His appointed time, God sent His Son to free us from the Law that we might become God's sons and daughters through faith in Him. We are truly God's children and receive the Spirit of His Son. The Spirit assures us that we are God's children and full heirs of the promise given to Abraham and fulfilled in Jesus Christ. Jesus addressed His Father in the word used by children of their loving father, "Abba"—a word our Heavenly Father is surely thrilled to hear from our lips. Jesus has earned for us the right also to call upon God as our dear Father. When we pray "our Father who art in heaven" we can be assured that the Holy Spirit dwells in our hearts by faith.
• Dear Father, I confidently bring my needs before You. Hear me for the sake of Jesus alone. Amen.

Third Argument about Receiving Justification (4:8–20): Appeal to a Shared Past

What the Galatians were before faith (4:8–11)

ESV	KJV
⁸Formerly, when you did not know God, you were enslaved to those that by nature are not gods. ⁹But now that you have come to know God, or rather to be known by God, how can you turn back again to the weak and worthless elementary principles of the world, whose slaves you want to be once more? ¹⁰You observe days and months and seasons and years! ¹¹I am afraid I may have labored over you in vain.	⁸Howbeit then, when ye knew not God, ye did service unto them which by nature are no gods. ⁹But now, after that ye have known God, or rather are known of God, how turn ye again to the weak and beggarly elements, whereunto ye desire again to be in bondage? ¹⁰Ye observe days, and months, and times, and years. ¹¹I am afraid of you, lest I have bestowed upon you labour in vain.

4:8 *you.* The Gentile converts' pagan past now comes into view. *not gods.* Already in this verse Paul's readers could hardly have missed the point he was preparing to make. Having just said that believers are God's sons and heirs of the Promise, the sad specter of the Galatians reverting to another slavery looms on the horizon. Prior to their acceptance of the Gospel, they were enslaved to entities that were not by nature gods at all (1Co 8:5). They formerly did not know and serve "the living and true God" (1Th 1:9). Behind this dire situation were elemental forces at work. Paul repeatedly emphasizes this in his Letters. The present evil age is dominated by demonic principalities and powers hostile to Christ and His Church (cf. e.g., Rm 8:35, 38; 1Co 2:6, 8; Eph 1:21; 2:2; 6:12; Col 2:10, 15).

4:9 *know God . . . known by God.* Before creation God chose us in Christ. He knew us beforehand and predestined us in grace "for adoption through Jesus Christ" (Eph 1:4–5; Rm 8:29). To be known by God is to be chosen in love by Him (Dt 7:6–9; 1Jn 4:10). Paradoxically, coming to know God is a purely passive experience (1Co 8:3; 13:12). *weak and worthless elementary principles.* The Galatians were exchanging one form of slavery for another, coming under the powers of this evil age (Gk *stoicheia*; see note on v. 3; cf. 2:4). The Judaizers no doubt seductively implied that they would become spiritually richer by obeying Jewish laws—actually an impoverishment compared to Christ's riches (Eph 1:7, 18; 2:4, 7; 3:8, 16).

4:10 *observe.* The Gk denotes scrupulous observance. The Galatians were actually adopting or following the Jewish liturgical calendar being required of them (cf. Ex 13:10; 31:16–17; Nu 10:10; Lv 25:1–7; 1Ch 23:31). Luther wrote,

> Now the Galatians had been forced by the false apostles to observe these same rites as something necessary for righteousness. This is why he says that they have lost grace and Christian liberty, and have turned back to the slavery of the weak and beggarly elements. (LW 26:411)

Their religion had evolved into a rigorous legalism.

4:11 *in vain.* Paul ends with a heavy sigh, so to speak. He could hardly bear the thought that after all his hard labor, the Galatians were in danger of losing the Gospel and the freedom it brings. He entertained the fearsome thought that he had wasted his time in Galatia and that everything, as we say today, had gone down the drain. In the tough arena of his missionary work, this was not an uncommon anxiety in Paul's heart (cf. Gal 2:2; 1Th 3:5).

Paul's anguish over a wayward child (4:12–20)

ESV	KJV
¹²Brothers, I entreat you, become as I am, for I also have become as you are. You did me no wrong. ¹³You know it was because of a bodily ailment that I preached the gospel to you at first, ¹⁴and though my condition was a trial to you, you did not scorn or despise me, but received me as an angel of God, as Christ Jesus. ¹⁵What then has become of the blessing you felt? For I testify to you that, if possible, you would have gouged out your eyes and given them to me. ¹⁶Have I then become your enemy by telling you the truth? ¹⁷They make much of you, but for no good purpose. They want to shut you out, that you may make much of them. ¹⁸It is always good to be made much of for a good purpose, and not only when I am present with you, ¹⁹my little children, for whom I am again in the anguish of childbirth until Christ is formed in you! ²⁰I wish I could be present with you now and change my tone, for I am perplexed about you.	¹²Brethren, I beseech you, be as I am; for I am as ye are: ye have not injured me at all. ¹³Ye know how through infirmity of the flesh I preached the gospel unto you at the first. ¹⁴And my temptation which was in my flesh ye despised not, nor rejected; but received me as an angel of God, even as Christ Jesus. ¹⁵Where is then the blessedness ye spake of? for I bear you record, that, if it had been possible, ye would have plucked out your own eyes, and have given them to me. ¹⁶Am I therefore become your enemy, because I tell you the truth? ¹⁷They zealously affect you, but not well; yea, they would exclude you, that ye might affect them. ¹⁸But it is good to be zealously affected always in a good thing, and not only when I am present with you. ¹⁹My little children, of whom I travail in birth again until Christ be formed in you, ²⁰I desire to be present with you now, and to change my voice; for I stand in doubt of you.

4:12 *as I am*. In this verse and the verses following Paul opens a window into his pastoral heart (note the pastoral appeal, "I entreat you"). He harbors no personal resentment toward the Galatians, treating them with mutual respect and trust. He desires deeply that they emulate him as a man whom Christ set free from the Law's bondage (cf. 1Co 4:16; 11:1; 1Th 1:6; 2:14, and notes on Php 3:17). He assures them as his brothers in Christ that they had not mistreated him while he was with them.

4:13 *bodily ailment.* Paul suffered from some kind of physically debilitating illness, but its exact identity eludes us. We can assume that the Galatians knew exactly what he was talking about. It is possible that he refers to this same ailment in 2Co 12:7–10 as his "thorn . . . in the flesh"—because of which he learned the sufficiency of God's grace in weakness. Numerous suggestions have been offered (e.g., malaria, epilepsy, or an eye infection). Perhaps the sickness provided an occasion for Paul's original visit, when he took the opportunity to rest and recuperate during a stay in Galatia.

4:14 *a trial to you.* Evidently Paul's appearance or condition was repulsive, making people look on him with disdain and disgust. The Gk term for "despise" means literally, "spit out," a way of showing contempt. The challenge was whether the Galatians would also look askance at Paul's message because of his physical state. *as an angel of God, as Christ Jesus.* The church in Galatia welcomed Paul with honor worthy of an angel (cf. 2Sm 14:17). Despite his external appearance they recognized his apostolic authority as the risen Christ's messenger and representative (cf. Lk 10:16; Jn 13:20). Messengers were to be received as actual representatives of their senders. See the notes on "apostle" at Gal 1:1 and Eph 1:1.

4:15 *blessing you felt?* The Galatians had considered themselves extremely fortunate because of Paul's presence among them and the blessings that he brought. *gouged out your eyes.* For someone to sacrifice an eye for someone else in Paul's day was a way of expressing a willingness to sacrifice for another. People showed friendship by sacrificing themselves for others. In today's idiom we might say, "You would have given your right arm for me." The verse pictures the bond that existed between the Galatians and Paul.

4:16 *truth?* Paul's opponents surely painted him in a negative light, convincing the Galatians he was being hostile to them. He does not hesitate a moment to speak forthrightly the truth of the Gospel (2:5, 14) and to expose their deceptive, pandering tactics.

4:17 *They.* These were false teachers. They were agitating the Church and trying to "force the Gentiles to live like Jews" (Gk *ioudaízo*, hence the name "Judaizers"; 2:14). They sought to bar fellowship with Gentiles unless and until they underwent circumcision. *shut you out.* These agitators hoped that by wooing the Galatians into their sphere of influence and isolating them from Paul, the Galatians would, in turn, become their followers. *make much of them.*

The same Gk term (*zeloo*) in this context means to court someone's favor to get that person to come over to one's side. This unsavory strategy was to get the Galatians, through flattery, to "make much of" (same Gk word, *zeloo*) them. Paul's indictment of the errorists' way of operating in Rome applies here as well: "For such persons do not serve our Lord Christ, but their own appetites, and by smooth talk and flattery they deceive the hearts of the naive" (Rm 16:18).

4:18 While Paul was with them and able to defend himself (v. 16) the Galatians were enthusiastic about being Christians, and this was good. They had shown genuine love for him. He hopes to persuade them now through his Letter that their misdirected zeal for keeping the Law serves no good purpose. Had the teachers who endeared themselves to the Galatians been faithful ministers of the one Gospel, Paul would have rejoiced (as in 1Co 3:5–10; Php 1:15–18). It has become apparent that their intentions were less than honorable.

4:19 *little children.* Paul often called the members of the churches he founded his beloved "children" (e.g., 1Co 4:14–15,17; 2Co 12:14; 1Th 2:11–12). Parental affection and intimacy characterizes his relationship with them. *anguish of childbirth . . . Christ is formed in you!* "I am . . . in the anguish of childbirth" translates a Gk word meaning "to have birth-pains" (*odino*; cf. v. 27). In the ancient world labor pains were regarded as the severest pains a human being could experience. Even with skilled midwives, many mothers died in childbirth. Paul compares himself to a mother in such agony. The word "again" implies that this was the second time he suffered anxiety over them, the first time when he first preached the Gospel to them. The analogy cannot be pressed too far, for he does not labor like a mother to bring forth children in his own likeness, but in Christ's image. This is God's work. He creates "the new self" after His likeness "in true righteousness and holiness (Eph 4:24; see the commentary note; cf. Col 3:10). Paul abhorred the adulation of human preachers at the expense of Christ and His Gospel, through which we become God's children (cf. 1Co 1:12–13; 1Pt 1:23; 2:2).

4:20 *my tone.* A one-on-one conversation would help Paul express his deep love and concern.

Devotion and Prayer in 4:8–20 Few sections of Paul's Letters are laden with such a mixture of emotions as this one. He is filled with exasperation (vv. 9–10), anxiety (v. 11), tenderness, empathy, affection (vv. 12–18), anguish (v. 19), sternness, and perplexity (v. 20).

The Galatians had once known slavery to pagan beliefs and practices, and had experienced the freedom Christ brings. But now they had taken a tragic step backward, exchanging their freedom in Christ for another form of slavery—submission to the Law and its requirements. They had become attracted to Jewish legalists who ingratiated themselves to them. The situation seemed nearly out of control. Although he cannot personally speak with the Galatians face to face, Paul genuinely desires and hopes that through this correspondence he can restore their friendship and especially the freedom in Christ they once so gladly embraced. Tragically, enemies of the Gospel continue to camouflage their dishonorable intentions as they lure people away from Christ. Especially those not firmly grounded in and committed to the truth of the Gospel can become easily enamored by smooth and persuasive teachers with plausible-sounding arguments (cf. Heb 2:1; 5:11–14). Thank God for loving pastors like Paul who faithfully proclaim the Gospel. Through His messengers who proclaim the Gospel, Christ Himself is inviting all to return to Him for forgiveness and renewal of faith. • Heavenly Father, I pray for all ministers of the Word and the blessings they bring. Through them, open our eyes to the truth. Amen.

Fourth Argument about Receiving Justification (4:21–5:1):
Allegory of Sarah and Hagar—Be Free!

ESV	KJV
21Tell me, you who desire to be under the law, do you not listen to the law? 22For it is written that Abraham had two sons, one by a slave woman and one by a free woman. 23But the son of the slave was born according to the flesh, while the son of the free woman was born through promise. 24Now this may be interpreted allegorically: these women are two covenants. One is from Mount Sinai, bearing children for slavery; she is Hagar. 25Now Hagar is Mount Sinai in Arabia; she corresponds to the present Jerusalem, for she is in slavery with her children.	21Tell me, ye that desire to be under the law, do ye not hear the law? 22For it is written, that Abraham had two sons, the one by a bondmaid, the other by a freewoman. 23But he who was of the bondwoman was born after the flesh; but he of the freewoman was by promise. 24Which things are an allegory: for these are the two covenants; the one from the mount Sinai, which gendereth to bondage, which is Agar. 25For this Agar is mount Sinai in Arabia, and answereth to Jerusalem which now is, and is in bondage with her children.

²⁶But the Jerusalem above is free, and she is our mother. ²⁷For it is written,

"Rejoice, O barren one who does not bear;
break forth and cry aloud, you who are not in labor!
For the children of the desolate one will be more
than those of the one who has a husband."

²⁸Now you, brothers, like Isaac, are children of promise. ²⁹But just as at that time he who was born according to the flesh persecuted him who was born according to the Spirit, so also it is now. ³⁰But what does the Scripture say? "Cast out the slave woman and her son, for the son of the slave woman shall not inherit with the son of the free woman." ³¹So, brothers, we are not children of the slave but of the free woman.

5 ¹For freedom Christ has set us free; stand firm therefore, and do not submit again to a yoke of slavery.

²⁶But Jerusalem which is above is free, which is the mother of us all.

²⁷For it is written, Rejoice, thou barren that bearest not; break forth and cry, thou that travailest not: for the desolate hath many more children than she which hath an husband.

²⁸Now we, brethren, as Isaac was, are the children of promise.

²⁹But as then he that was born after the flesh persecuted him that was born after the Spirit, even so it is now.

³⁰Nevertheless what saith the scripture? Cast out the bondwoman and her son: for the son of the bondwoman shall not be heir with the son of the freewoman.

³¹So then, brethren, we are not children of the bondwoman, but of the free.

5 ¹Stand fast therefore in the liberty wherewith Christ hath made us free, and be not entangled again with the yoke of bondage.

4:21 *under the law . . . listen to the law?* In the previous section Paul appeals to the Galatians from a personal perspective. Now he prepares to buttress his argument on the basis of Scripture. His opponents knew the Law, but did they really understand it? It is important for modern readers to note that the term "law" (Gk *nomos*) in the NT can have differing senses. "Law" in this verse has two slightly different points of reference. "Law" in the phrase "under the law" focuses on law as a general principle and designates a state of enslavement (3:23; see the note on 3:10) under Moses' Commandments, requiring liberation (4:5; cf. 5:18). The second use of "law" in a more restricted sense means the Books of Moses (the Pentateuch) or possibly Scripture in general, since what follows is based on the narrative history in Gn 16–21.

4:22–23 The false teachers and Paul related the same biblical story but Paul gave a sharply different interpretation of the texts these teachers probably thought clinched their case. Briefly, the story Paul recalls for his readers is this: Unable to bear children, Abraham's wife, Sarah, gave Abraham a son, Ishmael, through her Egyptian slave Hagar (Gn 16:1–16; 17:18). Years later and past their childbearing years, Abraham (age 100) and Sarah (90) received God's promise that Sarah would bear a son, whom they named Isaac. The Judaizers likely interpreted this narrative to mean that the uncircumcised Gentiles corresponded to Ishmael and were illegitimate sons. They were not true descendants of Abraham. Paul's response was devastating and cut the props out from under the Judaizers' whole case. Wrong, Paul says. The uncircumcised Gentile believers corresponded to Isaac, the son of the promise (cf. 3:14, 29). Paul then contrasts the births of Abraham's two sons according to the status of their mothers. Ishmael's mother was Hagar, the slave woman (the LXX uses the Gk word *paidiske*, "female slave" [Gn 16:1], the same term Paul uses in both vv. 22 and 23). Sarah, having despaired of bearing Abraham a child, gave him her Egyptian maid who bore Ishmael (Gn 16:15). Isaac's mother was Sarah, the free woman (21:2–3). The apostle further contrasts the way the sons were born. There was nothing exceptional about Ishmael's birth. He was born in an ordinary manner according to the course of nature (literally, "according to flesh"). Isaac's birth, however, was *extra*ordinary, since Abraham and Sarah were beyond their childbearing years (Gn 17:15–19; 18:11–13). Although also born naturally, Isaac became Abraham and Sarah's son through God's gracious and creative Word of promise (Gn 17:19; 18:10; cf. Rm 4:17–21; Heb 11:11).

4:24 *allegorically.* The English adverb here translates a verb that occurs only here in the Greek Bible. The term refers to the use of a comparison or likeness that stands for something different (see "corresponds to" in v. 25). In his interpretation of the Holy Scriptures, Paul saw in OT historical events a foreshadowing of greater realities fulfilled in Christ and in the new people of God, the Church.

4:25 *Mount Sinai in Arabia.* By identifying Hagar with Mt. Sinai, Paul is saying that she and her descendants stand for the Law.

4:26 *Jerusalem above.* A city's name often becomes a designation for its inhabitants (a figure of speech called "metonymy," in which a word substitutes for what it suggests). The heavenly or spiritual "Jerusalem" represents those who belong to it, namely, members of the one holy Christian Church who have been set free by Christ from the Law and its condemnation—the people who belong to the new covenant in Christ. In contrast, the "present Jerusalem" (v. 25) represents the Jews and their legalistic system. Luther wrote,

Now the heavenly Jerusalem above is the church, that is, believers scattered throughout the world, who have the same Gospel, the same faith in Christ, the same Holy Spirit, and the same sacraments. (LW 26:439)

See Php 3:20 and the commentary notes (cf. Heb 12:22–24). See also Ap VII and VIII 10. *our mother.* In his explanation of the Third Article of the Apostles' Creed, Luther wrote,

The Spirit has His own congregation in the world, which is the mother that conceives and bears every Christian through God's Word [Galatians 4:26]. (LC II 42)

4:27 As further Scriptural support for the argument he is constructing, Paul quotes Is 54:1 verbatim from the LXX. Isaiah comforts Israel exiled in Babylon (a "barren" condition) with the hope of restoration and the increase of children (cf. Is 49:6; 51:4–5). Isaiah's prophecy certainly brought to Israel's mind the miraculous blessing of the once-barren Sarah. God promises that His people will be more numerous after their return than they were before the captivity. This promise was fulfilled in the Christian Church, whose number cannot be counted (Gn 15:5).

4:28 *Now you.* With an emphatic "you" Paul addresses the Gentiles. *of promise.* He applies the previously mentioned allegory to the Galatians who, like Isaac, are children of promise (cf. 3:8, 14). John the Baptist said to Jewish leaders: "God is able from these stones to raise up children for Abraham" (Mt 3:9). God's promise to Abraham did not fail. He promised to raise up children for Abraham from among the Gentiles to inherit His blessing.

4:29 *persecuted . . . now.* It is possible Paul is alluding to Gn 21:9, where during the weaning festivities Sarah saw the older Ishmael "laughing" at Isaac, that is, mocking him. This would explain Sarah's angry reaction in 21:10 (quoted in v. 30). Jewish tradition interpreted Ishmael's conduct as hostile against Isaac (e.g., that Ishmael shot arrows at Isaac; cf. Gn 16:12). *persecuted him who was born according to the Spirit.* Paul in effect is saying that history is repeating itself. Ishmael's mistreatment of Isaac foreshadowed the Jewish persecution of the Christian Church (the spiritual children of Abraham; cf.

1Th 2:14–15). The Galatians were under enormous pressure from the Judaizers to keep the Law (and undergo circumcision).

4:30 *Cast out.* The Judaizers held that uncircumcised Gentiles were excluded from God's covenant. Paul argues the opposite; they were not to be "cast out" but included as heirs of the Promise. Paul may be saying that the Galatians must exercise discipline, because a religion of bondage cannot coexist with the Gospel of freedom.

4:31 Cf. 3:29. Paul accents the fraternal tone of his conclusion ("brothers") by changing from "you" to "we" to include himself.

Devotion and Prayer in 4:21–31 The Jewish-Christian infiltrators would have argued that their position was firmly based on the OT Scriptures, and that Paul was the one in error. But he wants to know how they could read their Bible without really listening to it (v. 21)! Their interpretation of key OT texts was gravely deficient, for they had failed to see the greater realities fulfilled in Christ which OT historical events foreshadowed. No doubt using the same passages his opponents employed, Paul went to the heart of the matter by turning their definition of Abraham's true children upside down. The uncircumcised Gentile Christians are children of the free woman, Sarah. They are not children of Hagar, the slave woman. They are free, not slaves to be cast off unless circumcised. They belong to the covenant of Promise and to the heavenly Jerusalem by faith in Jesus Christ, the Seed promised to Abraham. Legalism (v. 21) imagines that a saving relationship with God depends on certain rules and regulations. It brings bondage, not freedom. The Christian religion sets people free, giving birth to heirs of eternal life in Christ. • We rejoice, O Lord, that through faith we are already members of Your heavenly kingdom. Lead us to share our joy by sharing the promise in Jesus. Amen.

Ch 5 Martin Luther taught, "By the Word [the Spirit] works and promotes sanctification, causing this congregation daily to grow and to become strong in the faith and its fruit, which He produces" (LC II 53). In ch. 5, Paul will explain more about the Spirit's work.

5:1 *freedom.* Christ has freed us from the Law, which places us under judgment because of our sins. He has forgiven our sins and thus freed us from an accusing conscience. How comforting this is for us as we lay our heads on pillows at night and go to sleep in peace! See the note on 2:4. *stand firm.* Paul often uses this expression meaning "hold your ground" (in the Lord, Php 4:1; in the faith, 1Co 16:13; in one Spirit, Php 1:27). *a yoke.* At the Apostolic Council (where Paul was present) Peter accused the Judaizers of "placing a yoke on the neck of the disciples" [i.e. circumcision], when both Jewish and Gentile believers are actually saved by grace (Ac 15:10–11). Melanchthon wrote, "Ordinances instituted as though they are necessary, or with the view that they merit grace, are contrary to the Gospel" (AC XXVIII 50; see FC Ep X 6).

First Argument about Living as a Justified Person (5:2–15): The Uselessness of Circumcision

Paul's direct command (5:2–6)

ESV	KJV
²Look: I, Paul, say to you that if you accept circumcision, Christ will be of no advantage to you. ³I testify again to every man who accepts circumcision that he is obligated to keep the whole law. ⁴You are severed from Christ, you who would be justified by the law; you have fallen away from grace. ⁵For through the Spirit, by faith, we ourselves eagerly wait for the hope of righteousness. ⁶For in Christ Jesus neither circumcision nor uncircumcision counts for anything, but only faith working through love.	**²Behold, I Paul say unto you, that if ye be circumcised, Christ shall profit you nothing. ³For I testify again to every man that is circumcised, that he is a debtor to do the whole law. ⁴Christ is become of no effect unto you, whosoever of you are justified by the law; ye are fallen from grace. ⁵For we through the Spirit wait for the hope of righteousness by faith. ⁶For in Jesus Christ neither circumcision availeth any thing, nor uncircumcision; but faith which worketh by love.**

5:2 *accept circumcision.* The Gk verb's form suggests that it be translated "have oneself circumcised." Paul, for the first time in the Letter, brings into the open this specific issue confronting the Galatians (cf. 2:3; 6:12–13). It is possible (note "if") that they were on the verge of getting circumcised but had not yet done so. *Christ will be of no advantage to you.* See the note on 2:21 and the principle set forth in this verse. Paul sees the issue as black and white. God's grace revealed in Jesus Christ ceases to be grace if requirements of the Law are added. For Galatians to acquiesce to the Judaizers' demands would render Christ superfluous. For Paul, therefore, the litmus test for a faithful proclamation of the pure Gospel is whether the message maintains that Christ alone is necessary for salvation.

5:3 *obligated to keep the whole law.* The decision to be circumcised had serious implications. Submission to this mandate necessitated keeping all the Law's precepts (3:10–14)—which not only is impossible to do but brings condemnation. The Galatians—as one commentator states—were saying by this action that Moses must be allowed to finish what Christ had begun. *whole.* Note what some were adding to the necessity of Gentile circumcision: " . . . and to order them to keep the law of Moses" (Ac 15:5). See the note on v. 14.

5:4 *severed from Christ.* The Galatians' attempt to be justified by the Law amounts to their wanting to have nothing to do with God's grace (cf. Rm 10:4). They would in effect become estranged or broken off from Christ. Paul uses the same Gk verb two more times in Galatians to underline the seriousness of appending the Law to justification by faith. To do so is tantamount to stamping "void" on the Promise (3:17) and removing "the offense of the cross" (5:11). *fallen away from grace.* If a person jettisons the "Christ alone" principle, he or she is throwing overboard "grace alone." The Gk term for "fallen away" could also be used to describe a ship drifting off course and running aground (Ac 27:17, 29) or withered flowers falling to the ground (Jas 1:11; 1Pt 1:24). One who is seeking righteousness before God on the grounds of merit is heading the opposite direction from access to the grace of God and from the glorious hope obtained through faith the Lord Jesus Christ (Rm 5:2; cf. 1:6; 1Pt 5:12). "Outside of this Christian Church where the Gospel is not found, there is no forgiveness, as also there can be no holiness" (LC II 56), Luther wrote.

5:5 *wait.* Believers eagerly await the full experience in heaven of the justification that is already theirs (Rm 5:1–2). The Gk term (*apekdechomai*) is an intensified form of "wait" and connotes an eager yearning (Rm 8:19, 23, 25; 1Co 1:7; Php 3:20; Heb 9:28). Such hope of salvation (1Th 5:8) must be kept alive, lest spiritual lethargy set in (1Th 5:1–7).

5:6 To Jewish ears this verse must have come across as one of Paul's most radical statements. He took what the Jews considered a matter of divine command and placed it into the category of "indifferent things," things neither commanded nor forbidden (adiaphora). He was putting circumcision into the realm of Christian freedom and individual discretion. Circumcised or not, Paul insists, one's physical condition has no impact on one's relationship to God. It is spiritually neither here nor there! *working.* If anyone is in Christ he is a "new creation" (2Co 5:17). The faith that justifies is a living faith which produces good works spontaneously by the power of the Holy Spirit (5:22–23). Far from being against the Law and encouraging a life morally barren and inactive, as some may have charged, Paul sees faith actively at work ("working"; Gk *energeo*). It issues forth in love (see v. 14), which stands at the head of the Spirit's fruit (v. 22). Luther wrote, "Faith . . . is a divine work in us which changes us and makes us to be born anew of God. . . . O it is a living, busy, active, mighty thing, this faith. It is impossible for it not to be doing good incessantly" (LW 35:370; cf. FC SD IV 11–12). Melanchthon wrote, "Love ought to follow faith" (Ap IV 111).

The Law divides the community (5:7–15)

ESV	KJV
[7]You were running well. Who hindered you from obeying the truth? [8]This persuasion is not from him who calls you. [9]A little leaven leavens the whole lump. [10]I have confidence in the Lord that you will take no other view than mine, and the one who is troubling you will bear the penalty, whoever he is. [11]But if I, brothers, still preach circumcision, why am I still being persecuted? In that case the offense of the cross has been removed. [12]I wish those who unsettle you would emasculate themselves! [13]For you were called to freedom, brothers. Only do not use your freedom as an opportunity for the flesh, but through love serve one another. [14]For the whole law is fulfilled in one word: "You shall love your neighbor as yourself." [15]But if you bite and devour one another, watch out that you are not consumed by one another.	[7]Ye did run well; who did hinder you that ye should not obey the truth? [8]This persuasion cometh not of him that calleth you. [9]A little leaven leaveneth the whole lump. [10]I have confidence in you through the Lord, that ye will be none otherwise minded: but he that troubleth you shall bear his judgment, whosoever he be. [11]And I, brethren, if I yet preach circumcision, why do I yet suffer persecution? then is the offence of the cross ceased. [12]I would they were even cut off which trouble you. [13]For, brethren, ye have been called unto liberty; only use not liberty for an occasion to the flesh, but by love serve one another. [14]For all the law is fulfilled in one word, even in this; Thou shalt love thy neighbour as thyself. [15]But if ye bite and devour one another, take heed that ye be not consumed one of another.

5:7 *running well.* Paul often pictured the course of his apostolic ministry and the believer's life in Christ as an athlete running a race (e.g., 2:2; Php 2:16; 3:14 [see commentary notes]; 1Co 9:26; 2Tm 4:7). Here the metaphor evokes imagery of a runner striding smoothly forward. *Who hindered you.* The Gk word (*enkopto*) means "cut in front of." The intention would be to break a runner's stride and impede progress (cf. 1Th 2:18). The Judaizers in effect tripped the Galatians, interrupting their stride and impeding their fruitful response to the truth of the Gospel (cf. 2:5, 14). Modern commuters may think of those who "cut in front of them" in heavy traffic.

5:8 The false teachers' rhetoric urging circumcision, however persuasive, did not originate with God. That is because God had originally "called [them] in the grace of Christ" (1:6), a persuasion not based on human merit.

5:9 Paul may be citing an ancient proverb. (In 1Co 5:6 the aphorism describes how moral failure has a corrupting influence on the Christian community.) Yeast's most basic property is that it spreads throughout the dough. The metaphor exhibits the insidiously corrupting power of a seemingly small error. Luther responded to those who accused him of making too much of a single doctrine: "In theology a tiny error overthrows the whole teaching . . . For doctrine is like a mathematical point. Therefore it cannot be divided; that is, it cannot stand either subtraction or addition" (LW 27:37).

5:10 *the one who is troubling you . . . whoever he is.* In Galatia Paul had more than one opponent (1:7; 5:12). The phrase "whoever he is" seems to indicate he is speaking generally. But it is probable that he had a particular person in mind who instigated and/or took the lead in the activities that unsettled the Galatians.

5:11 *still preach circumcision.* Opponents may have accused Paul of inconsistency, perhaps quick to point out that he did circumcise Timothy before taking him along on his first missionary journey (Ac 16:3; cf. 1Co 9:20). What the opponents could not accept was that Paul saw circumcision as no more than a custom and therefore something that could be permitted in some circumstances to avoid giving offense. But the custom was not allowable when required to make one righteous before God (Paul did not circumcise Titus; Gal 2:3). *why . . . persecuted?* Paul counters any false report that he preached circumcision. The Jews' continued harassment proves that he did not require circumcision of converts. He adds, at the end of this Letter, that his opponents scandalously wanted to force the Galatians to be circumcised "in order that they may not be persecuted for the cross of Christ" (6:12). *offense.* The Gk term in this context (*skandalon*) means "what arouses ridicule and opposition." (This is sometimes translated as "stumbling block"; cf. 1Co 1:23.) The cross offends human pride, which seeks to be justified by the Law (cf. 6:12–14). It brings people down to size. The cross removes the underpinnings of all religious systems advocating salvation by human merit (3:10–13; 6:14). Those who seek God must stop at the foot of the cross of Golgotha, where God meets human beings as their gracious and merciful Father.

5:12 *those who unsettle.* The advocates of circumcision turned things upside down in the churches (same Gk word in Ac 17:6). *emasculate.* Some see an allusion to the cult of Cybele, which originated in Pessinus in Galatia. The goddess's devotees practiced sacred castration. In Php 3:2 Paul called circumcision a mutilation. The allusion here may be to Dt 23:1 which bars a castrated person (eunuch; the same Gk word in the LXX as Paul uses here) from "the assembly of the Lord." The blunt language and bitter irony reveal the emotional intensity of Paul's disgust: it would serve the Judaizers right if with a slip of the knife they would "remove" themselves from fellowship with God's people, just as they sought to do with Gentile Christians.

5:13 *freedom.* See notes, 2:4; 5:1. *opportunity.* The word (Gk *aphorme*) signifies a set of circumstances favorable for a particular activity or endeavor. Freedom in Christ ought not become an occasion for doing as we please, following the desires of our fallen human nature. Luther summarizes the paradox of Christian freedom in his 1520 treatise on "The Freedom of A Christian": "A Christian is a perfectly free lord of all subject to none. A Christian is a perfectly dutiful servant of all, subject to all" (LW 31:344).

5:14 *whole.* Both this verse and v. 3 speak of "the *whole* law." The careful reader will note, however, that "whole" has a slightly different focus in each passage. In v. 3, "whole" defines Law as a total of individual precepts. Here in v. 14, "whole" describes Law as a unit, with emphasis on its spirit or intention. Paul intends to say that love for the neighbor perfectly brings to full expression the Law's very essence. In the NT, the command to love one's neighbor (Lv 19:18) is the most often cited passage in the first five books of Moses (Mk 12:31 [Mt 22:39; Lk 10:27]; 12:33; Mt 5:43; 19:19; Rm 13:9; Jas 2:8).

Freedom in Christ does not release us from responsibility to serve our neighbor, but heightens that responsibility.

5:15 *bite and devour.* Doctrinal controversies often produce bitter quarrels among Christians which have a tendency to degenerate into personal animosities and vindictiveness. They can become all-consuming. Evidently this was happening in Galatia. Paul uses the grotesque picture of animals viciously fighting one another, snapping at each other with bared fangs. The ugliness of partisan strife creates an atmosphere in which love for one's neighbor grows cold (Mt 24:12).

Devotion and Prayer in 5:1–15 It is now clearer than ever that circumcision was only the tip of a huge theological iceberg. Beneath the surface was the Judaizing requirement that Gentile Christians keep the Law of Moses in addition to faith in Christ. By agreeing to be circumcised the Galatians in principle submitted themselves to justification before God through obedience to the whole Law, a return to bondage. This departure from the truth of the Gospel endangered their relationship to Christ and produced bitter, corrosive division and tumult in the church. Their acceptance of the Judaizers' false gospel would wipe out Christ's benefits, in effect reducing Him to irrelevance. They would be rejecting God's grace and losing the freedom that Jesus brought through His cross. Congregational strife also today inevitably arises when issues in the area of Christian freedom are elevated to the level of biblical command. Such legalism always hinders progress in the Christian faith and life. Jesus loved us unto death on a cross so that He might lift the burden of guilt that troubles our consciences. He thus frees us to love one another as He has loved us. • Lord, as we eagerly await Your coming, free us from pettiness and self-indulgence so that we may love one another. Amen.

Second Argument about Living as a Justified Person (5:16–26): The Fruits of the Flesh and the One Fruit of the Spirit

The community living by the flesh is divided (5:16–21)

ESV	KJV
[16]But I say, walk by the Spirit, and you will not gratify the desires of the flesh. [17]For the desires of the flesh are against the Spirit, and the desires of the Spirit are against the flesh, for these are opposed to each other, to keep you from doing the things you want to do. [18]But if you are led by the Spirit, you are not under the law. [19]Now the works of the flesh are evident: sexual immorality, impurity, sensuality, [20]idolatry, sorcery, enmity, strife, jealousy, fits of anger, rivalries, dissensions, divisions, [21]envy, drunkenness, orgies, and things like these. I warn you, as I warned you before, that those who do such things will not inherit the kingdom of God.	[16]This I say then, Walk in the Spirit, and ye shall not fulfil the lust of the flesh. [17]For the flesh lusteth against the Spirit, and the Spirit against the flesh: and these are contrary the one to the other: so that ye cannot do the things that ye would. [18]But if ye be led of the Spirit, ye are not under the law. [19]Now the works of the flesh are manifest, which are these; Adultery, fornication, uncleanness, lasciviousness, [20]Idolatry, witchcraft, hatred, variance, emulations, wrath, strife, seditions, heresies, [21]Envyings, murders, drunkenness, revellings, and such like: of the which I tell you before, as I have also told you in time past, that they which do such things shall not inherit the kingdom of God.

5:16 *walk.* See the note on Eph 2:2. *flesh.* Here the "flesh" means the human being dominated by sin. See the note on 3:3.

5:17 *opposed to each other.* From the moment believers receive the Holy Spirit at Baptism, a lifelong struggle with the old Adam begins (see FC SD VI 7). Chemnitz wrote,

> True faith in Christ does not seek occasions or permission to sin, but seeks the remission of sin and deliverance from it. Likewise, where sin rules and there is no struggle against our corrupt desires, there it is certain that the Holy Spirit is not present. (Chemnitz 2:1172)

5:18 *led by the Spirit.* The Spirit "leads" us like a child is led who puts her hand into the hand of a beloved and trusted father. He brings freedom from the compulsion to sin and gently "prompts" us to follow our Lord (cf. 2Co 3:17). The Law can only "pressure" us. *under the law.* Instead of controlling the flesh, the Law increases sin (Rm 5; 8). It promises life but cannot deliver it to sinners (3:21).

5:19 Paul's list of the flesh's deeds begins with three descriptions of sexual sin prominent in society. "Sexual immorality" refers to all forms of unlawful sexual intercourse, including sex between an unmarried man and woman. "Impurity" is moral corruption especially in the area of sexual sins (Rm 1:24; Eph 5:3; Col 3:5). "Sensuality" denotes unbridled lack of restraint (e.g. 2Pt 2:7 applies this word to Sodom and Gomorrah). *works.* The flesh reveals its true colors in sinful actions (same Gk word as in "works of the Law").

5:20–21 *enmity . . . envy.* Of the 15 sins listed in vv. 19–21, eight have this in common: they are behaviors that disrupt Christian fellowship. The Galatians should have found this as self-evident (cf. "evident," v. 19). Similarly, the vices (17) listed in Rm 1:29–31 rend the fabric of society in general and make an agony of common life that God intended to be a blessing.

5:21 *things like these.* Paul's "catalog of vices" does not exhaust the sins that erupt from the flesh. Those aware of the flesh's powerful influence can certainly add to the list. *warned you before.* Paul repeats this teaching from previous instruction or an earlier Letter. The KJV's "tell you . . . told you" renders the Gk more literally but the present context favors the stronger "warn." *not inherit.* The Gk verb's present tense in "those who do such things" implies a habitual pattern of behavior typical of those who are "in the flesh." These are people whose impenitent lifestyle is controlled by sinful desires (Rm 7:5; 8:8). Paul intends to warn his readers that leading an unrepentant life will have eternal consequences (exclusion from God's heavenly kingdom; see note on Eph 5:5; cf. 1Co 6:9–10). Luther advised those who do not experience a need for the Lord's Supper:

> I know no better counsel than that they put their hand into their shirt to check whether they have flesh and blood. And if you find that you do, then go, for your good, to St. Paul's Epistle to the Galatians. Hear what sort of a fruit your flesh is. . . . [Galatians 5:19–21]. (LC V 75)

The community living by the Spirit is united (5:22–26)

ESV	KJV
[22]But the fruit of the Spirit is love, joy, peace, patience, kindness, goodness, faithfulness, [23]gentleness, self-control; against such things there is no law. [24]And those who belong to Christ Jesus have crucified the flesh with its passions and desires. [25]If we live by the Spirit, let us also walk by the Spirit. [26]Let us not become conceited, provoking one another, envying one another.	[22]But the fruit of the Spirit is love, joy, peace, longsuffering, gentleness, goodness, faith, [23]Meekness, temperance: against such there is no law. [24]And they that are Christ's have crucified the flesh with the affections and lusts. [25]If we live in the Spirit, let us also walk in the Spirit. [26]Let us not be desirous of vain glory, provoking one another, envying one another.

5:22 *fruit.* Gk *karpos.* The harvest of a life produced and guided by the one Holy Spirit is like a rich cluster (singular) of grapes (cf. Mt 13:23). In contrast, the flesh churns out products like a lifeless machine. The Spirit of life (Rm 8:2) causes fruit to flourish in our lives, bringing forth in us what enables us to "please God" (Rm 8:8; 1Th 4:1). The flesh manufactures dead works (Heb 6:1; 9:14). Its works pull people apart. The Spirit draws people together (Eph 4:3).

5:23 *there is no law.* Paul engages in rhetorical understatement, implying that the Spirit's fruit goes far beyond the Law's requirements. People who live by the Spirit do good without being badgered and forced (cf. 1Tm 1:9). The Law legislates and regulates conduct, but it does not have the power to provide a willing heart that produces fruit. As an act of Congress will do nothing to make a stand of wheat produce a bumper crop, likewise the demands of the Law will do nothing to cause a Christian to bear true fruit. The Lutheran confessional writings state,

> Faith must be the mother and source of works that are truly good and well pleasing to God, which God will reward in this world and in the world to come. This is why St. Paul calls them true fruit of faith, also fruit of the Spirit [Galatians 5:22–23]. (FC SD IV 9)

5:24 *crucified the flesh.* The Galatians participated in Christ's crucifixion when they were baptized (note the past tense of "crucified") and became believers in Christ (cf. Gal 2:19). St. Paul explains in Rm 6 that by being baptized into Christ's death, we Christians have made a decisive break with sin. We "died to sin" (6:2, 3), just as Christ "died to sin, once for all" (6:10). "Our old self was crucified with Him . . . so that we would no longer be enslaved to sin" (6:6). We must thus consider ourselves "dead to sin," severed from its lordship over us (6:11). Baptism is not merely a one-time event, but entails a daily crucifixion (cf. Col 3:5)—a killing of the sins of the flesh, so that sin may no longer be allowed to reign or have dominion over us (6:12, 14). Luther explained: "The Old Adam in us should, by daily contrition and repentance, be drowned and die with all sins and evil lusts" (SC IV; see also FC SD IV 19).

5:25 *live by . . . walk by.* The Spirit is the source and guide of our spiritual life. *walk.* As Paul now concludes the ethical section of the Epistle, he chooses a word that uniquely indicates putting into practice the new life that believers have through the Spirit. The term means literally "be in line with" or "keep in step with" (cf. 3:2; 4:6–7; Php 3:16). Paul may be countering the mistaken notion that freedom leads to license. Christ has set us free to "live to God" (2:19) and follow the leading of the Spirit, not to live as we please (which is a return to bondage).

5:26 *conceited.* This verse shows that how we treat others is determined by our opinion of ourselves. Christians who fall prey to feelings of self-importance can easily become demanding and testy toward others, and be filled with envy. Perhaps the Galatians had been parading their observance of the Law to show their superiority over others. See Paul's counsel in Rm 12:3–4.

Devotion and Prayer in 5:16–26 United with Christ's death and resurrection through Baptism and having received the gift of the Holy Spirit, believers now experience an inner, spiritual "civil war" going on within them. They are constantly battling their sinful flesh which works at odds with the Spirit's new life growing in them. Often they feel stymied and frustrated by sin's relentless pull. But Paul encourages us to follow the Spirit's leading in the confidence that He will enable us to break away from our selfish passions and desires. Paul encourages us to guard against spiritual pride, which causes envy and provocation harmful to others. We need to remember that Christ Jesus has nailed our sins to the cross and promises us daily forgiveness. The Spirit produces in us a Christ-like love, to the end that interpersonal tensions are set aside and the bond with our fellow Christians is strengthened. With the Spirit's power there is no limit to blessings He can channel to others through us • O Holy Spirit, give us daily victories over sin in our personal life and, above all, the power to love one another. Amen.

Third Argument about Living as a Justified Person (6:1–10): A Specific Application for the Community United by the Spirit

Bearing and restoring one another (6:1–5)

ESV	KJV
6 ¹Brothers, if anyone is caught in any transgression, you who are spiritual should restore him in a spirit of gentleness. Keep watch on yourself, lest you too be tempted. ²Bear one another's burdens, and so fulfill the law of Christ. ³For if anyone thinks he is something, when he is nothing, he deceives himself. ⁴But let each one test his own work, and then his reason to boast will be in himself alone and not in his neighbor. ⁵For each will have to bear his own load.	6 ¹Brethren, if a man be overtaken in a fault, ye which are spiritual, restore such an one in the spirit of meekness; considering thyself, lest thou also be tempted. ²Bear ye one another's burdens, and so fulfil the law of Christ. ³For if a man think himself to be something, when he is nothing, he deceiveth himself. ⁴But let every man prove his own work, and then shall he have rejoicing in himself alone, and not in another. ⁵For every man shall bear his own burden.

6:1 *spiritual.* The Gk *pneumatikos* means in its general sense one who possesses the Holy Spirit. All Christians have the Spirit (cf. 3:2–5, 14; 4:6), not just a select or elite few. Yet, Paul may specifically be addressing congregational leaders who are known to possess the requisite gifts for providing spiritual care in sensitive situations. For example, they would be able to deal gently with one who lapses into some sin, and to do so with a hold on themselves lest they be tempted to adopt an attitude of superiority (5:23). They would be humbly aware of their own vulnerability to temptation (note, "keep watch on yourself"; cf. 1Co 10:12). *restore.* The Gk (*katartizo*) carries the idea of putting something back into its former condition, and so "restore" (the word is used literally to describe fishing nets in Mt 4:21; Mk

1:19). In the words of the Lord Jesus, fellow Christians must seek to "gain" the brother who falls into some sin (Mt 18:15). Luther wrote,

> Even though we have sins, the ‹grace of the› Holy Spirit does not allow them to harm us. For we are in the Christian Church, where there is nothing but ‹continuous, uninterrupted› forgiveness of sin. This is because God forgives us and because we forgive, bear with, and help one another [Galatians 6:1–2]. (LC II 55)

Wesley wrote,

> By reproof, instruction, or exhortation [restore him]. Every one who can ought to help herein: only in the spirit of meekness. This is essential to a spiritual man. And in this lies the whole force of the cure. (Wesley 486)

6:2 *burdens.* The context suggests that Paul has in mind the heavy load that temptations and sin bring upon fellow Christians (v. 1). The passage may be applied, however, to all burdens people bear (worries, doubts, sorrows). We can be quite certain that "in every pew sits a broken heart." Luther wrote, "A Christian must have broad shoulders to carry . . . the weakness, of the brethren. . . . " (LW 27:113). Lifting the burdens of fellow Christians stands in bold contrast to legalists who lay heavy burdens on others and "are not willing to move them with their finger" (Mt 23:4). See the note on v. 5. *law of Christ.* Paul has just written, "through love serve one another, for the whole law is fulfilled in one word: 'You shall love your neighbor as yourself' " (5:13–14; see note on 5:14). Love, fulfilled through Christ's sacrificial death (1:4; 2:20), significantly, heads the list of the Spirit's fruit (5:22).

6:3 See the note on 5:26 (cf. 2Co 10:12). Those thinking they have fewer faults than others tend not to sympathize with others' shortcomings. Instead of reaching out to a brother or sister in Christ to restore a person caught in sin, they are prone to say, "it serves him or her right." We are here reminded of the parable Jesus told "to some who trust in themselves that they were righteous, and treated others with contempt" (Lk 18:9).

6:4 Paul urges his readers to examine their own performance before God instead of comparing themselves to others (cf. 1Th 5:21). He offers a similar warning to some Corinthians who were in the habit of commending themselves (cf. 2Co 10:17–18): "When they measure themselves by one another and compare themselves with one another, they are without understanding" (2Co 10:12). Chrysostom wrote,

> This he says . . . in the way of concession. . . . He that is wont to boast with reference to himself only, and not against others, will soon reform this failing [of self boasting] also. (*NPNF1* 13:44)

6:5 Verses 2 and 5 are not contradictory, but complementary. As Christians bear each others' burdens (v. 2, "burden," Gk *baros*) they are at the same time to bear their "own load" (Gk *phortion*; used literally of cargo on a ship in Ac 27:10). That is, they are to accept personal accountability for their own actions before God. We are not to condemn our fellow Christians, Paul writes to the Romans in a parallel passage, because each of us will have to give an account of ourselves to God (Rm 14:12). Playing the "blame game" is a way of avoiding accountability for one's actions.

Serving one another (6:6–10)

ESV	KJV
[6]One who is taught the word must share all good things with the one who teaches. [7]Do not be deceived: God is not mocked, for whatever one sows, that will he also reap. [8]For the one who sows to his own flesh will from the flesh reap corruption, but the one who sows to the Spirit will from the Spirit reap eternal life. [9]And let us not grow weary of doing good, for in due season we will reap, if we do not give up. [10]So then, as we have opportunity, let us do good to everyone, and especially to those who are of the household of faith.	[6]Let him that is taught in the word communicate unto him that teacheth in all good things. [7]Be not deceived; God is not mocked: for whatsoever a man soweth, that shall he also reap. [8]For he that soweth to his flesh shall of the flesh reap corruption; but he that soweth to the Spirit shall of the Spirit reap life everlasting. [9]And let us not be weary in well doing: for in due season we shall reap, if we faint not. [10]As we have therefore opportunity, let us do good unto all men, especially unto them who are of the household of faith.

6:6 *teaches.* "Taught" and "teaches" (ESV) translate the Gk verb (*katecheo*), giving us our word "catechize."

6:7 People should not be misled in thinking (cf. 3:1; 6:3) that they can turn up their noses at God and expect to get by with it. The immutable law built into creation, illustrated by sowing and reaping, is that actions have consequences (cf. Pr 22:8). A farmer does not plant wild oats expecting a bumper crop of wheat. As v. 8 will show, the "mocking" takes the form of foolish behavior. An old German proverb approximates the thought here: "That is a pitiful bird that messes up its own nest."

6:8 *corruption*. Pandering to our lower sinful nature leads to moral decay. Cf. 5:19–21. *sows to the Spirit*. The "Spirit of Him who raised Jesus from the dead" (Rm 8:11) also dwells in us so that we may avoid the corrupting influence of the flesh and live the resurrected life (Rm 6:4; 8:1–8). Paul has emphasized in Galatians that Christians live under the Holy Spirit's power and direction (5:5, 18, 25). *reap eternal life*. Cf. Rm 8:13.

6:9 The two Gk words for "grow weary" and "give up" form a pair to picture someone who has lost motivation or enthusiasm. Christians must not become discouraged when they do not see immediate or observable results from doing what is good (v. 10; sowing to the Spirit; cf. 2Co 9:8). Those who lose patience and are tempted to slack off (like a runner who gives up from exhaustion) can take a lesson from farmers who must wait patiently (see Jas 5:7–11). Cf. Lk 18:1; 2Co 4:1; 2Th 3:13; Eph 3:13.

6:10 In conclusion (this sense is indicated by the words "so then"), Paul encourages the Galatians to do good to the wider community around them as opportunities arise (see note on Eph 5:16). Merciful and generous acts can become a thankless task in a world that limits love to those who can reciprocate. In this regard, too, Christians must not grow weary or lose heart. Luther reminds us,

> But do good to all men [Galatians 6:10]. Help them and promote their interest—in every way and wherever you can—purely out of love for God and to please Him. Do this in the confidence that He will abundantly reward you for everything. (LC I 328)

Yet (Gk *de*, qualifies previous statement), helping those who are members of God's family through faith in Christ (Eph 2:19) is to be given priority. See the note on "The Collection" at 2:10. In the Greco-Roman world Christians who were poor could not expect help from a non-Christian state. Chrysostom writes, "The rule of life which Grace gives invited both land and sea to the [table] of charity, only it shows greater care for its own household" (*NPNF*1 13:45).

Devotion and Prayer in 6:1–10 Nine times in this Letter St. Paul calls the Galatians "brothers"! That is because he regards them as fellow members of "the household of faith." He sends them this stern Epistle precisely because he loves them. He seeks to correct the erring and restore faithfulness to the truth of the Gospel. He reminds them that as members of God's family they, too, have a responsibility to restore brothers caught in any sin. They are to do so in a spirit of gentleness, humility, and personal accountability before God. Self-centered attitudes and behavior cannot be expected to produce health and harmony in God's family. Rather, they lead to moral decay and threaten faith in Jesus Christ who has given us eternal life. Without losing heart, Christians patiently follow the Spirit's leading and demonstrate Christ's love by doing good to all people, both outside and within the Church (including Christian teachers). In all of this they are following the pattern of Jesus their Savior and His law of love (5:14; 6:2). The Son of God "loved me and gave Himself for me" (2:20), that I may be free to serve Him and my neighbor in need.
• Teach me to be patient with others, Lord, so I may not grow tired of doing good to all people, especially to the members of my family in the faith. Restore me with Your unfailing mercy. Amen.

The Reformers on the Role of the Law

Since the earliest days of the Church, Christians have pondered the role for the Law once one is declared righteous by grace through faith. They wonder, "Since God forgives my sins, do I really need to live by what the Law says? Can the Law really guide my life?" Because the reformers placed so much importance on the Gospel, they naturally also wrote often about the role of the Law as a counterpoint in Christian preaching and teaching. This article focuses on this contentious question of what use the Law has for the Christian.

Background

Early Church Fathers, following the writings of Paul, distinguished different roles for or "uses" of the Law of Moses. But they never arrived at specific and consistent wording for their thoughts. It was up to medieval theologians to provide this. In the thirteenth century, theologians at the University of Paris enumerated various uses of the Law of Moses, which became common. For example, Nicholas of Lyra distinguished the use of the Law (1) for threatening punishments, (2) for convicting someone under his sin, and (3) for prophesying the coming of Christ. Before the Reformation, theologians would have found such distinctions in the medieval commentaries on the Bible.

Although some of the medieval distinctions helped, others caused confusion since medieval theologians also commonly thought of "the Gospel" as a new law and not as a distinct doctrine of God's forgiveness through Christ.

Luther and Melanchthon

Luther learned the medieval distinctions and included them in his early lectures on Scripture. However, he eventually modified the distinctions in order to help others understand the role of the Law for Christians. Luther distinguished:

- The civil use of the Law, to curb sins by threats of punishment.
- The theological use of the Law, to show us our sins and need for repentance.

- The righteous man's use of the Law, when the Holy Spirit moves the believer to take up the commandments gladly and keep them to honor and praise God for His grace.

Perhaps most importantly, by refining the medieval distinctions, Luther showed that Christians are sinners and saints at the same time (*simul justus et peccator*). He also re-titled Lyra's prophetic use of the Law that proclaimed the coming of Christ by calling it "the Gospel."

To Luther, the Gospel was not a new law but a distinct message of salvation found in both the OT and NT. In this way, Luther distinguished "Law and Gospel" in reformation preaching and teaching as the two chief doctrines of the Bible. He also explained that throughout the Christian life, believers always need both the Law and the Gospel because they are still sinners who will need to practice daily repentance and exercise themselves in the good works taught by the Law. Luther's colleague, Melanchthon, built his famous theology textbook, the *Theological Commonplaces*, using Luther's distinctions. He defined what became known as the first, second, and third uses of the Law (cf. above) and the distinctions spread everywhere the Protestant Reformation spread.

Calvin

When Calvin wrote his famous 1536 *Institutes of the Christian Religion*, his comments on Law and Gospel were strongly influenced by Melanchthon's *Theological Commonplaces*. However, Calvin arranged the uses of the Law in a different order. He presented them as follows:

Theological use

Civil use

Righteous man's use

Calvin may have placed the theological use first to emphasize its role in conversion. He went on to describe the righteous man's use of the Law (the "third use") as the principal use. He described the Law and the Gospel not so much as distinct teachings but as one covenant of grace. For Calvin and later Reformed theologians, once the Gospel sets a person free, the principal thing for the Christian to do is to obey God.

Luther saw a historical and theological order of Law, then Gospel, in the teaching of the Bible. In contrast, Calvin emphasized theologically that grace preceded the Law; he preferred to emphasize a unifying theme of grace rather than a distinction. Whereas Lutherans wrote about "Law and Gospel," Reformed theologians came to write about

"Gospel and Law." Whereas Luther emphasized the Holy Spirit's work in the believer and the spontaneity of faith, which leads a believer to keep the Law, Calvin emphasized a duty to keep the Law and made this duty the principal matter of the Christian life. In these ways, both Luther and Calvin taught the importance and on-going role of the Law in the Christian life but with important differences that distinguished their views of the Christian life.

The Challenge of Antinomianism

Both the Lutheran and Reformed traditions were at times troubled by antinomianism, the belief that the Law no longer was necessary for the Christian life. Lutherans were affected most in the sixteenth century, Calvinists in the seventeenth century, although modern decisions about moral issues are perhaps affected by new expressions of antinomianism. For more on the doctrine of the Law during the Reformation, see Edward A. Engelbrecht, *Friends of the Law*, St. Louis: Concordia, 2011.

PART 6

SUMMARIZING CONCLUSION (6:11–18)

ESV	KJV
¹¹See with what large letters I am writing to you with my own hand. ¹²It is those who want to make a good showing in the flesh who would force you to be circumcised, and only in order that they may not be persecuted for the cross of Christ. ¹³For even those who are circumcised do not themselves keep the law, but they desire to have you circumcised that they may boast in your flesh. ¹⁴But far be it from me to boast except in the cross of our Lord Jesus Christ, by which the world has been crucified to me, and I to the world. ¹⁵For neither circumcision counts for anything, nor uncircumcision, but a new creation. ¹⁶And as for all who walk by this rule, peace and mercy be upon them, and upon the Israel of God. ¹⁷From now on let no one cause me trouble, for I bear on my body the marks of Jesus. ¹⁸The grace of our Lord Jesus Christ be with your spirit, brothers. Amen.	¹¹Ye see how large a letter I have written unto you with mine own hand. ¹²As many as desire to make a fair shew in the flesh, they constrain you to be circumcised; only lest they should suffer persecution for the cross of Christ. ¹³For neither they themselves who are circumcised keep the law; but desire to have you circumcised, that they may glory in your flesh. ¹⁴But God forbid that I should glory, save in the cross of our Lord Jesus Christ, by whom the world is crucified unto me, and I unto the world. ¹⁵For in Christ Jesus neither circumcision availeth any thing, nor uncircumcision, but a new creature. ¹⁶And as many as walk according to this rule, peace be on them, and mercy, and upon the Israel of God. ¹⁷From henceforth let no man trouble me: for I bear in my body the marks of the Lord Jesus. ¹⁸Brethren, the grace of our Lord Jesus Christ be with your spirit. Amen.

6:11 *large letters.* Some interpreters conjecture that Paul's "bodily ailment" (4:13) left him with poor eyesight requiring larger letters. One scholar speculates that when the Letter was read, Paul's handwritten closing could be easily read by all when held up. *with my* *own hand.* Paul's concluding words in 2 Thessalonians are instructive: "I, Paul, write this greeting with my own hand. This is the sign of genuineness in every letter of mine; it is the way I write" (cf. 1Co 16:21; Col 4:18). Although he likely dictated his Letters to secretaries, Paul added a handwritten postscript to authenticate the Letter and to emphasize the importance of what he is writing.

6:12 *persecuted.* If the Judaizers had actually preached the cross of Christ (central to the pure Gospel) like Paul, and dropped insistence on circumcision, they would have incurred the wrath of non-Christian Jews. It seems likely that the persecution would not have been occasioned by open opposition to a crucified Messiah as such. The message of the cross, the thematic thread running through the Letter (2:18–21; 3:1–2, 10–13; 5:2–6), was an offense to Jewish Christians because it excluded all works of the Law. By compelling circumcision, they may have appeased hard-line Jewish critics but they did so—Paul wants them to know—at the expense of the necessary and all-sufficient work of Jesus Christ on the cross (2:21).

6:13 *boast in your flesh.* To enhance their own standing in Jewish eyes, the circumcision party hypocritically bragged about their success in getting Gentile converts to accept circumcision (cf. Ti 1:10–11). What they could not honestly boast about, however, was their obedience to the Law (see the note on 3:10). The apostle James explains what it really means to be "under Law": "For whoever keeps the whole law but fails in one point has become accountable to all of it" (Jas 2:10).

6:14 *boast . . . in the cross.* In the first-century context, the very mention of "the cross" signified the height of foolishness and even madness. The cross symbolized a cruel, shameful, and humiliating death reserved for slaves and criminals. The word "cross" became a vulgar slur, but for Paul, the "word of the cross" was the "power of God" for salvation. He encapsulated the powerful message of salvation through Christ's death in this one word "cross." His Letter put his opponents on notice: individuals cannot boast in their ability to save themselves and simultaneously boast in Christ's cross. *crucified to me.* Today we use the term "kill" figuratively to mean "put an end to" or "defeat," as in "kill the deal" or "kill the amendment," or we might say that someone is "dead to me." Christ's crucifixion has terminated our relationship to the world (just as to the Law; 2:19; cf. Rm 6:9–10). That is, the Christian's relationship to the world—everything sinful, depraved, and hostile to God—has been severed. We owe it nothing, including any accommodation to it. The "big picture" of what Christ's death on the cross means has been described as follows. The world's basic values, assumptions, and operating procedures have been put on notice that they are passing away (1Co 7:31). Luther wrote that Christians regard the world as condemned, and the world "regards me as condemned in return" (LW 27:135). Because they are sinners, however, the struggle continues:

> Although believers are regenerate and renewed in the spirit of their mind, in the present life this regeneration and renewal is not complete. It is only begun. Believers . . . struggle constantly against the corrupt nature and character, which cleaves to us until death. (FC Ep VI 4)

6:15 *but a new creation.* A whole new order of existence has been inaugurated through Jesus' death and resurrection from the dead, through which we have the forgiveness of sins (Rm 4:25; Eph 1:7; 1Co 11:25). The old order, of which circumcision was a part, has thus been made obsolete—like a worn out and useless old garment (Heb 1:11; 8:13). Note that the "new creation" stands in sharp contrast with the world (v. 14), in which circumcision had its day but now is religiously insignificant. Those in Christ are already "a new creation" (2Co 5:17; cf. Is 65:17), though its fullness lies yet in the future (Rm 8:19–22; Rv 21:5; Is 43:19).

6:16 *walk.* See the note on 5:25. *this rule.* The Gk word (*kanon*) means standard or principle, and in this case the one just mentioned: the cross and the new creation. *Israel of God.* All believers in Christ, both Jew and Gentile, are the new Israel (cf. v. 10, "household of faith"). Calvin wrote,

> This is an indirect ridicule of the vain-boasting of the false apostles, who vaunted of being the descendants of Abraham according to the flesh. There are two classes who bear this name, a pretended Israel, which appears to be so in the sight of men,—and the Israel of God. Circumcision was a disguise before men, but regeneration is a truth before God. In a word, he gives the appellation of *the Israel of God* to those whom he formerly denominated the children of Abraham by faith, and thus includes all believers, whether Jews or Gentiles, who are united into one church. (Calvin, *Galatians* 166–67)

6:17 *marks of Jesus.* Explanations of this reference to "marks" (Gk *stigmata*) have varied (e.g., tattoos, as on a slave). Most likely, Paul is alluding to the physical wounds and scars he received in the service of Jesus, who bore the marks of suffering in His hands and side (Jn 20:25, 27; Ac 14:19; 2Co 11:23–25). Paul identified himself with the suffering Savior (cf. 2Co 4:8–10; see note on Php 3:10). The Judaizers boasted in circumcision as their "mark" of identity, but Paul took pride in the cross (v. 14).

6:18 *with your spirit.* This phrase is equivalent to "with you," which commonly occurs at the end of his other Letters (e.g., Rm 16:20; 1Co 16:23; 1Th 5:28). *brothers.* Paul wants to leave this affectionate address "ringing" in his readers' ears as he closes his stout words from a pastoral heart. He writes to them not as enemies, but as fellow-members of God's family. *Amen.* Here the word concludes a blessing, not a doxology, as in Paul's other Letters.

Devotion and Prayer in 6:11–18 We often add a handwritten note in greeting cards, conveying personal thoughts. Paul attaches a handwritten postscript to this Letter (dictated to a "secretary") to certify that it comes directly from him and to emphasize certain points. This personal conclusion can serve as an interpretive lens through which we may evaluate all Christian teaching and life: the message of the cross. For Paul "the cross," a symbol of shame in his day, signified the simple, powerful message that Christ died for our sins (1Co 15:3) and was raised to set us free (5:1) to serve Him (5:13). The cross first speaks a word of judgment against all self-righteous pride in spiritual accomplishments. Cursed is everyone who does not keep perfectly everything written in the Law (3:10). To us who believe, the cross is a precious symbol of God's gracious gift of salvation (1:6; 6:18). On the cross, Christ—who knew no sin—bore the curse we deserved (3:13). Together with Christians of every age, we take pride in the cross of Christ (v. 4), through which God has made all things new. • Lord Jesus, in Baptism, You put my old nature to death. By Your grace, I already am a new creation in You. Continue to renew me each day. Amen.

EPHESIANS

INTRODUCTION TO
EPHESIANS

Overview

Author

Paul the apostle

Date

c. AD 60

Places

Ephesus; Rome (from which Paul wrote)

People

Paul; Tychicus; "saints" and "brothers" at Ephesus

Purpose

Paul demonstrates that Baptism unites all Christians

Law Themes

Rivalry between believers; grieving the Spirit through unfaithfulness; marital unfaithfulness; spiritual warfare

Gospel Themes

Baptism; election by God's grace; justification by grace alone; the mystery of Christ revealed; unity in Christ's Body

Memory Verses

Election in Christ (1:3–10); saved by grace (2:8–10); unity through service (4:11–16); Bridegroom and Bride (5:22–33)

Reading Ephesians

At an early Christian Baptism, cool water would stream down people's heads and necks when they stepped away from the font. As they shivered through the baptismal prayers, droplets would fall from the tresses of their hair and land in puddles at their feet. The droplets would draw circles on the puddles' surfaces as the water slowly rolled across the floor, uniting with other droplets and puddles. Though the people baptized were different—and even from different ethnicities, ages, and social levels—the water and the Word of Baptism united them to share new life, sealing, enlightening, and washing in Christ.

At their Baptism, the Ephesians became something more than cold and damp. Baptism unites believers into one Body as easily as water meets and merges on a floor. Paul's Letter to the Ephesians shows that Baptism united Jews and Gentiles, leaders and followers, and all believers across all generations.

Setting

Ephesus was well situated as a trade center, with its harbor, access to the Cayster River, and location close to the Maeander Valley. It was a free city, famous for its temple to the Greek goddess Artemis and also for its thriving Jewish population, which enjoyed considerable privilege (see *Ant* 14:223–30). See map, p 000.

Central Issue

According to Ac 18–20, Paul spent nearly three years with the Ephesian congregation, more time than with any other mission congregation he served. He first visited a group of disciples at Ephesus during his third missionary journey (AD 52–55).

The depth of his relationship with the Ephesians shows through in the theological depth of this Pastoral Letter and its liturgical character. The key problem Paul addresses is division between the congregation's Jewish and Gentile members. His opening prayer, written in the traditional Jewish *Berakah* pattern (see note, 1:3–14), addresses the issue of unity and thanks God for His answer in Christ. Paul returns to the themes of unity, Baptism, and prayer repeatedly in the Letter (see Luther and the outline below).

After Paul wrote Ephesians in c. AD 60, he sent Timothy to Ephesus as a leader because false doctrine afflicted the congregation (1Tm 1:3). It eventually became a leading church in Asia Minor (Rv 2:1–7). According to the early Christian historian Eusebius, the apostle John settled in Ephesus for his final years of ministry (*NPNF2* 1:132).

Luther on Ephesians

In this epistle St. Paul teaches, first, what the gospel is, how it was predestined by God alone in eternity, and earned and sent forth through Christ, so that all who believe on it become righteous, godly, living, saved men, and free from the law, sin, and death. This he does in the first three chapters.

Then he teaches that false teachings and the commandments of men are to be avoided, so that we may remain true to one Head, and become sure and genuine and complete in Christ alone. For in him we have everything, so that we need nothing beside him. This he does in chapter 4.

Then he goes on to teach that we are to practice and prove our faith with good works, avoid sin, and fight with spiritual weapons against the devil, so that through the cross we may be steadfast in hope. (LW 35:385)

Calvin on Ephesians

The Ephesians had been instructed by Paul in the pure doctrine of the gospel. At a later period, while he was a prisoner at Rome, he was led by the accounts that reached him to write this Epistle, following up his former instructions in the manner that appeared to be necessary. The first three chapters are chiefly occupied with commending the grace of God. Immediately after the salutation in the commencement of the first chapter, he treats of God's free election. This affords him an opportunity of stating that they were now called into the kingdom of God, because they had been appointed to life before they were born. . . . But as the minds of men are ill fitted to receive so sublime a mystery, he betakes himself to prayer, that God would enlighten the Ephesians in the full knowledge of Christ. (Calvin, *Ephesians* 171–72)

Gerhard on Ephesians

For a two year period Paul had preached the Gospel in Ephesus, the chief city of Ionia in Asia Minor (Acts 19:1), and had gathered quite a large church for Christ (1 Cor. 16:9), which after his departure he had entrusted to his disciple Timothy (1 Tim. 1:3) and of which the evangelist John is said to have been in charge later. [Paul] directed his letter to the inhabitants of that city. No schisms had been stirred up there; no false doctrine had been sown there, as among the Galatians. Rather, the impelling cause for writing was the far-seeing concern of the apostle lest they become weak and weary of the Gospel because of the chains that were binding him at Rome. (Gerhard E 1.261)

Bengel on Ephesians

It appears from the records . . . that no city was mentioned by name in this inscription [Eph 1:1], whence some [scribes] have supplied Laodicea (although all that had a separate reference to the Laodiceans, was explained by Paul in the epistle written to the Colossians about the same time, Col. 4:15–16); others [supplied], Ephesus: either of them might be before the mind of the apostle; for Paul no doubt told Tychicus whither he should go,— to Laodicea, for example, and thence to Colosse, which was in the neighbourhood of Laodicea, and either first or last to Ephesus. Wherefore our annotations are now and then specially applicable to the Ephesians. . . . Paul, when writing to the churches planted by himself, generally mentions many circumstances concerning present and former events, having reference to himself or the churches; but he had been at Ephesus, and that too for a long time, not many years before. Acts xx. 31. Why then does he write as a person unknown, ver. 15, ch. iii. 2, 4? and why does he descend less to particulars in this epistle, than in any other? Why, at Eph 4:23–24, does he conclude in the third, and not in the second person, as he always does on other occasions? Why does he add no salutations, which, however, he does not omit even in the case of the Colossians? Why does he not mention Timothy, whom, however, he joins with himself. Col. 1:1? For, the close resemblance of the style of writing [the texture of composition] in both, the same mention in both of their bearer, Tychicus, and many other circumstances, confirm the fact, that each of these epistles, this and the one to the Colossians, was sent at one time. Why does he only call them brethren at 4:10? Answer. All these things are indeed proofs, that Paul so drew up the whole letter, that it might be publicly read, or privately perused, both at Ephesus and in many of the churches of Asia, to which, as having been perhaps pointed out to him by name, Tychicus would go, and that all might receive it as if it had been addressed to themselves; comp. Col. 4:16; 1 Thess. 5:27. (Bengel 61–62)

Wesley on Ephesians

EPHESUS was the chief city of that part of Asia, which was a Roman province. Here St. Paul preached for three years, Acts xx, 31, and from hence the Gospel was spread throughout the whole province, Acts xix, 10. At his taking leave of the Church there, he forewarned them both of great persecutions from without, and of diverse heresies and schisms, which would arise among themselves. And accordingly he writes this epistle (nearly resembling that to the Colossians, written about the same time) to establish them in the doctrine he had delivered, to arm them against false teachers, and to build them up in love and holiness, both of heart and conversation. (Wesley 494)

Challenges for Readers

Authorship. Though the early Christians uniformly believed that Paul wrote this Letter, critics have assumed that a disciple of Paul wrote it. They see significant differences from Paul's other Letters in the style of the sentences, some unique terms and expressions, and the Letter's general character, though all agree that this Letter bears great similarity to Colossians. They reject any relationship between the Ephesian congregation described in Ac 19–20 and the view of the church in the letter to the Ephesians. However, readers should note that the Ephesians had issues with the doctrine of Baptism (cf. Ac 19), and Paul shows great concern for strengthening leadership at Ephesus (cf. Ac 20). These are key themes in the Letter, pointing to Paul's authorship.

Address. Some early manuscripts and Church Fathers did not have copies of the Letter addressed specifically to the congregation "in Ephesus" (1:1). Critics have seen this as further evidence that Paul did not write it. However, early Christian letters were often copied to various congregations, which may explain why some copies lack the reference to Ephesus.

Date of Composition. Critics commonly date this letter to the last generation of the first century rather than the middle of the first century (cf. "Authorship" above). However, the Letter was always included in the collection of Pauline Epistles.

Blessings for Readers

Ephesians beautifully describes the important truths of the Christian faith that St Paul so eloquently emphasizes. The first chapter sees the entire Christian life in view of God's choosing His people in Christ. These words, rightly applied, offer incredible comfort in the midst of suffering and doubt. Likewise, no other place in the NT describes the relationship between grace, faith, and good works (justification and sanctification) quite so clearly as Eph 2. The entire Letter leads us to treasure our Baptism into Christ and into His Church, where a new way of life prevails.

As you study Ephesians, the Lord will equip you for victory over temptation and strife, over sin and Satan, so that you may serve Him and His people in all unity and joy. Read Ephesians as God's plan for your family, your pastor, and your congregation as you serve together according to God's eternal purposes.

Outline

I.   Salutation (1:1–2)
II. Prologue on Unity (1:3–23)
  A.   Prayer (1:3–14)
  B.   Thanksgiving (1:15–23)
III. Proofs for Unity (chs. 2–3)
  A.   New Creation by Grace Alone (2:1–10)
  B.   Gentiles and Israel (2:11–22)
  C.   Paul's Apostolic Mandate to the Gentiles (3:1–13)
  D.   Prayer and Doxology (3:14–21)
IV. Baptism Unites (4:1–5:21)
  A.   Baptism into One Body (4:1–16)
  B.   Baptism Clothes the Believer (4:17–32)
  C.   Baptism Directs the Believer's Walk (5:1–14)
  D.   The Liturgy of the Spirit (5:15–21)
V.   Baptism Reorders Relationships (5:22–6:9)
  A.   Husband and Wife (5:22–33)
  B.   Parents and Children (6:1–4)
  C.   Masters and Servants (6:5–9)
VI. Baptism Equips with Armor (6:10–17)
VII. Conclusion (6:18–24)
  A.   Exhortation (6:18–20)
  B.   Commendation to Letter-Bearer (6:21–22)
  C.   Final Greeting and Blessing (6:23–24)

PART 1

SALUTATION (1:1–2)

ESV	KJV
1 ¹Paul, an apostle of Christ Jesus by the will of God, To the saints who are in Ephesus, and are faithful in Christ Jesus: ²Grace to you and peace from God our Father and the Lord Jesus Christ.	1 ¹Paul, an apostle of Jesus Christ by the will of God, to the saints which are at Ephesus, and to the faithful in Christ Jesus: ²Grace be to you, and peace, from God our Father, and from the Lord Jesus Christ.

1:1 *apostle.* Paul begins his Letter to the Church at Ephesus by presenting his credentials as an apostle of Christ Jesus. "By the will of God" he became an apostle, an authorized representative of Christ (2Co 5:20) "set apart for the gospel of God" (Rm 1:1). The risen Christ appointed him to be His "servant and witness" (Ac 26:15–18), sending him to preach to the Gentiles "the unsearchable riches of Christ" (Eph 3:7–8). He did not volunteer for this office (his "apostleship in the Lord"; 1Co 9:2). *saints.* This is what Paul in all his Letters calls believers in Christ (1Co 1:2). They are separated for service to God, just as in the OT God graciously chose Israel from among the nations of the world as His own people (Ex 19:6; Dt 7:6–8; cf. 1Pt 2:9). Paul reminds the Ephesians that through Holy Baptism God has "sanctified" them (literally in Gk, "set [them] apart"), cleansing them and making them members of His one holy Church (5:26–27; 1Co 6:11).

1:2 *Grace . . . and peace.* The usual Hellenistic greeting in ancient letters was simply "greetings" (Gk *chairein*; see Ac 23:26). Ten of Paul's thirteen letters begin with this expanded greeting "grace and peace," signaling the content of the Gospel he proclaimed.

93

PART 2

PROLOGUE ON UNITY (1:3–23)

Prayer (1:3–14)

ESV	KJV
[3]Blessed be the God and Father of our Lord Jesus Christ, who has blessed us in Christ with every spiritual blessing in the heavenly places, [4]even as he chose us in him before the foundation of the world, that we should be holy and blameless before him. In love [5]he predestined us for adoption as sons through Jesus Christ, according to the purpose of his will, [6]to the praise of his glorious grace, with which he has blessed us in the Beloved. [7]In him we have redemption through his blood, the forgiveness of our trespasses, according to the riches of his grace, [8]which he lavished upon us, in all wisdom and insight [9]making known to us the mystery of his will, according to his purpose, which he set forth in Christ [10]as a plan for the fullness of time, to unite all things in him, things in heaven and things on earth.	[3]Blessed be the God and Father of our Lord Jesus Christ, who hath blessed us with all spiritual blessings in heavenly places in Christ: [4]According as he hath chosen us in him before the foundation of the world, that we should be holy and without blame before him in love: [5]Having predestinated us unto the adoption of children by Jesus Christ to himself, according to the good pleasure of his will, [6]To the praise of the glory of his grace, wherein he hath made us accepted in the beloved. [7]In whom we have redemption through his blood, the forgiveness of sins, according to the riches of his grace; [8]Wherein he hath abounded toward us in all wisdom and prudence; [9]Having made known unto us the mystery of his will, according to his good pleasure which he hath purposed in himself: [10]That in the dispensation of the fulness of times he might gather together in one all things in Christ, both which are in heaven, and which are on earth; even in him:

¹¹In him we have obtained an inheritance, having been predestined according to the purpose of him who works all things according to the counsel of his will, ¹²so that we who were the first to hope in Christ might be to the praise of his glory. ¹³In him you also, when you heard the word of truth, the gospel of your salvation, and believed in him, were sealed with the promised Holy Spirit, ¹⁴who is the guarantee of our inheritance until we acquire possession of it, to the praise of his glory.

¹¹In whom also we have obtained an inheritance, being predestinated according to the purpose of him who worketh all things after the counsel of his own will:
¹²That we should be to the praise of his glory, who first trusted in Christ.
¹³In whom ye also trusted, after that ye heard the word of truth, the gospel of your salvation: in whom also after that ye believed, ye were sealed with that holy Spirit of promise,
¹⁴Which is the earnest of our inheritance until the redemption of the purchased possession, unto the praise of his glory.

Introduction to 1:3–14 *Blessed be.* These words reflect the Jewish devotional language with which Paul grew up. Jewish prayers typically began with praise to God, containing the formula "Blessed art thou, O Lord our God" (the *Berakah*) followed by reasons for blessing God. Three times a day in the synagogue Jews were required to recite a prayer in which 18 Benedictions followed this pattern (common in the OT as well, especially in Psalms; e.g. Ps 73:18). Paul's outburst of praise in 1:3–4 blessing God for all spiritual blessings, resounds with distinctively Christian content. He praises the Father (Eph 1:3–6), Son (vv. 7–12), and Holy Spirit (vv. 13–14) for the plan of redemption conceived in eternity, carried out in history, and secured for all believers in Christ (note the word "us," embracing both Jews and Gentiles, in v. 3). Paul "brackets" the saving works of the Triune God that he extols with three phrases containing the noun "praise" (*epainos*; vv. 6, 12, 14). Remarkably, the term "blessed" with which Paul begins always refers to God in the NT! It will not be a surprise to us that Ephesians emphasizes throughout that our salvation depends completely on God's grace, not on human works or decisions.

1:3 *the God . . . of our Lord Jesus . . . in Christ.* When the risen Christ confronted the persecuting Paul on the road to Damascus, Paul asked, "Who are you, Lord?" "I am Jesus," came the immediate response. From that moment on, Paul's faith and worship became based on something radically new. The God of Abraham, Isaac, and Jacob was also "the Father of the Lord Jesus Christ." Saul [Paul's Jewish name] of Tarsus could only make such an extraordinary confession because he had seen Christ (Ac 9:11; 1Co 9:1; 2Co 11:31) and had become a Christian. *spiritual blessing.* All of the spiritual blessings in Paul's doxology centering "in Christ" (a phrase itself occurring 11 times in vv. 3–14) belong to us Christians right now. God has made them, and us, secure by His Spirit (our election, adoption, redemption and forgiveness, our knowledge of salvation, our hope, etc.). Though unseen and grasped only by faith (Heb 11:1; Rm 8:24), these blessings are not imaginary or illusory. *heavenly places.* The term here occurs in five passages in Ephesians for the unseen world of spiritual reality lying beyond the senses. It is the realm where both God or Christ exist (1:3, 20; 2:6) and also where evil forces are at work (3:10; 6:12). Wesley wrote,

> God's blessing us is his bestowing all spiritual and heavenly blessings upon us. Our blessing God is the paying him our solemn and grateful acknowledgments, both on account of his own essential blessedness, and of the blessings which he bestows upon us. (Wesley 489)

Calvin wrote,

> The lofty terms in which he extols the grace of God toward the Ephesians, are intended to rouse their hearts to gratitude, to set them all on flame to fill them even to overflowing with this thought. They who perceive in themselves discoveries of the Divine goodness, so full and absolutely perfect, and who make them the subject of earnest meditation, will never embrace new doctrines, by which the very grace which they feel so powerfully in themselves is thrown into the shade. The design of the apostle therefore, in asserting the riches of divine grace toward the Ephesians, was to protect them against having their faith shaken by the false apostles, as if their calling were doubtful, or salvation were to be sought in some other way. He shows at the same time, that the full certainty of future happiness rests on the revelation of his love to us in Christ, which God makes in the gospel. (Calvin, *Ephesians* 176)

1:4 *chose us.* God once chose Israel to be "a people for his treasured possession, out of all the people who are on the face of the earth" (Dt 14:2). So also God, before the creation of the world, chose believers to be His own and the heirs of eternal life (cf. 1:14; 1Pt 2:9–10). God was moved to choose Israel purely by His love for them, without any worthiness or merit on their part (Dt 7:7:6–8). Likewise, His elective choice of His saints flowed from His lavish grace revealed in Jesus Christ (vv. 6–7). The context here in which Paul mentions divine election (predestination) is all-important. God has revealed this precious doctrine to comfort believers in Christ and elicit their praise by what God has revealed to us. He does not want us to apply our thinking abilities to questions that lie hidden in the mind of God. The Lutheran reformers appropriately reminded us to "avoid speculating about God's bare, secret, concealed, mysterious foreknowledge," but to "think or speak about how God's counsel, purpose, and ordination in Christ Jesus—who is the true Book of Life—is revealed to us through the Word" (FC SD XI 13). *holy and blameless.* Paul uses this same expression one other time in Ephesians, which sheds some light on its meaning here. At 5:26–27 he teaches that Christ's sacrificial death, through Baptism, has cleansed us from sin. Since Christ is holy and blameless, the perfect sacrifice for our sins (Heb 7:26; 9:14), we, too, are made holy and blameless by forgiveness through His blood (Eph 1:7).

1:5 *predestined us.* The Gk word means "to decide beforehand or predetermine" (used in the NT at Ac 4:28; Rm 8:29f.; 1Co 2:7; Eph 1:5, 11). The verb's form (past participle) indicates that God's eternal election (v. 4) and decision are tied together. *adoption as sons.* The expression recalls God's gracious adoption of Israel in the days of the Exodus. God sent Moses to Pharaoh to tell him: "Thus says the LORD, Israel is My firstborn son, and I say to you, 'Let My son go that he may serve Me' " (Ex 4:22–23; cf. Hos 11:1; Rm 9:4). But Paul likely also alludes to the common Greco-Roman practice of adoption to describe the new status of the elect believers before God accomplished "through Jesus Christ" (cf. Gal 4:5). In the Greco-Roman world, adoption entailed four realities: (1) a person lost all old rights and gained new ones; (2) an individual became an heir of the father's estate; (3) the previous life with its debts and responsibilities ended; and (4) a person literally became the child of the new father. Thus, a person entered into a new status, with its rights and privileges. Through Baptism God adopts us into His family and makes us heirs of His eternal blessings (Gal 3:26–29). He takes great delight in this, just as loving parents receive a newborn child with joy.

1:6 *to the praise of His . . . glorious grace.* This refrain climaxes the first section of Paul's ascription of praise and moves smoothly to the second section extolling God's undeserved favor (grace) freely given in Christ (1:6; 12, 14). *Beloved.* The heavenly Father loves His Son (Jn 3:35; 5:20). He called Jesus "My beloved Son" both at His baptism (Mt 4:17; Mk 1:11; Lk 3:22) and at His transfiguration (Mt 17:5; Mk 9:7). Paul tells his brothers and sisters in Christ at Colossae that through Jesus God has "delivered us from the domain of darkness and transferred us to the kingdom of His beloved Son" (literally, "the son of His love"; Col 1:13). Just as God calls Israel "My beloved" in the OT (Is 5:1, 7; Jer 11:15; 12:7), God bestows the title "the beloved" (1Th 1:4; 2Th 2:13; Rm 9:25; Col 3:12) on those chosen in Christ, "the beloved one."

1:7 *redemption . . . the forgiveness of our trespasses.* In the first century context "redemption" often designated the "buying back" of slaves or captives by a ransom payment. This payment freed them from their captive condition. In the minds of Jewish readers, though, the term would recall OT texts about the release of slaves from bondage (Ex 21:8; cf. Lv 25:48), as well as God's deliverance of Israel from bondage in Egypt (Dt 7:8; 9:26; 13:5). In his writings Paul extends the term figuratively to mean the release from sin and its futile ways that comes through Christ. He boldly declares, in fact, that God made Christ "our redemption" (1Co 1:30). Thanks be to God that our redemption in Christ is not merely a deliverance to be expected in the future, but a present possession (note the verb "we have" at the beginning of v. 7)! Better yet, Paul equates our "redemption" with the "forgiveness of sins." Every time Christians announce God's forgiveness in Christ to each other, we are declaring the good news of our present release from the captivity of sin in our lives. *His blood.* Paul's mention of Christ's blood brings to mind the violent, sacrificial death He suffered for us. But it also points to the enormous cost of our redemption required because of sin and evil. The principle in the OT sacrificial system, "without the shedding of blood there is no forgiveness of sins" (Heb 9:22), takes on a whole new meaning as we learn that the blood of God's very own Son was shed. The apostle Peter expressly tell us that we were ransomed from the aimlessness of life under sin by the "precious blood of Christ, like that of a lamb without blemish or spot" (1Pt 1:18).

1:8 *all wisdom and insight.* God's superabundant grace takes effect in Christians' spiritual life as they use their spiritually renewed minds to grasp and apply what God has revealed in His Word. Paul prays that the Colossians "may be filled with the knowledge of His [God's] will in all spiritual wisdom and understanding so as to walk in a manner worthy of the Lord" (Col 1:9–10). He likewise urges Christians pressured to conform to worldly standards to "be transformed by the renewal of [their] mind" (Rm 12:2). They are to apply their new way of thinking to everything so that they "may discern what is the will of God, what is good and acceptable and perfect" (Rm 12:1–2).

1:9 *mystery.* In the OT, the term "mystery" occurs only in Daniel, where Daniel's dreams are called "mysteries" (2:18, 19, 27). (The Septuagint [Gk OT] translates the Aramaic word for "mystery" [*raz*]). Although there are some parallels with the term's meaning in the NT, Paul introduces something completely new. In 6:19 he speaks of "the mystery of the gospel" that he wants God to help him proclaim boldly. The gospel is "the mystery," the revelation of what has previously been hidden but now has been fully disclosed (Rm 16:25–26). The gospel of which he was made a minister (3:7), in other words, is an "open secret." God's saving plan for humankind and for the restoration of all things (1:10), conceived in eternity, can now be known but only by divine disclosure (1:9; 3:3). Philosophies and cults of Paul's day promised to reveal mysterious truths, too, but this was to enable their initiates to climb to higher levels of knowledge and spirituality. For Paul, however, the revealing of God's mystery came in the person and work of Jesus Christ. He explicitly calls Jesus "God's mystery . . . in whom are hidden all the treasures of wisdom and knowledge" (Col 2:2–3). Paul later exposes the heart of the mystery he proclaims, that the Gentiles are "fellow heirs, members of the same body, and partakers of the promise in Christ Jesus through the gospel" (Eph 3:6). God intended that both Jew and Gentile belong to a new community made possible through the reconciling work of Jesus on the cross (2:16).

1:10 *fullness of time.* The KJV's "fullness of the *times*" (plural form in Gk) provides an important nuance. God has ordered or arranged (ESV, "set forth . . . a plan" [Gk *oikonomia*]; cf. 3:9) the various periods of history to implement the salvation of the world. This plan reached its climax in the coming of His Son (Gal 4:4; Lk 2:6; Jn 12:23). Christian historians have often pointed to various factors of the Greco-Roman world (e.g., cultural, political, and economic aspects) to show how the "time was ripe" for the Savior to be born ("the right time," Rm 5:6). *Unite.* The word (Gk, *anakephalaio*) means "to sum up, recapitulate" (see Rm 13:9). In some way beyond our human understanding, the entire universe is on its way to being fully "summed up" in Christ. The fragmentation and disunity caused by the fall is being set in reverse and everything will be brought into harmony or "reset," with Christ as "head over all things" (v. 22; cf. Col 1:16, 20). God's eternal plan includes the reconciliation of human beings not only to God (2Co 5:18–20) but to each other (2:14–16; cf. Col 1:21–22; Gal 3:26–29) through Christ in whose name we are baptized. See comments on v. 9.

1:11 Paul now begins the final section of his opening prayer (vv. 11–14). He describes the Holy Spirit's work as believers await the final goal of their liberation (vv. 13–14). Note Paul's movement from the "we" of v. 11 to the "you also" of v. 13. This hardly noticeable change anticipates what will become a centerpiece of Paul's message in Ephesians—how not only Jewish Christians, but also Gentile believers share equally in the spiritual blessings guaranteed to the elect. *obtained an inheritance.* These words translate a single Gk word that in this passage means literally "obtain by lot." Again Paul draws from a key OT theme. Not only was the Promised Land allotted to the Israelite tribes (Nu 25:55–56), but God's chosen people were themselves His "allotted heritage": "The LORD's portion is His people" (Dt 32:9). Peter declares of Christians who are "chosen and precious," "you are . . . a people for His [God's] own possession" (1Pt 2:9). No wonder Paul begins this Epistle with a song of praise; what belongs to the Lord belongs also to His people, the heirs of His eternal inheritance (see v. 14; Col 1:12)! *predestined.* The apostle repeats what he has previously affirmed. Those whom God predestined before the foundation of the world (v. 5) bear the title of those who "have been predestined." *purpose . . . counsel.* In his opening song of praise (vv. 3–14) Paul amasses a series of terms to depict the intent, unfolding, and fulfillment of God's saving work in Christ. "Purpose" denotes something planned in advance, as according to a blueprint (see also

3:11). "Counsel" (*boule*; only occurrence in Ephesians) refers to what one decides, thus "decision." As the Lutheran reformers remind us,

> In [Christ] we are to seek the eternal election of the Father, who has determined in His eternal divine counsel [Ephesians 1:11–12] that He would save no one except those who know His Son Christ and truly believe in Him. Other thoughts are to be ‹entirely› banished. . . . We know ‹assuredly› that out of pure grace, without any merit of our own, we have been elected in Christ to eternal life. (FC Ep XI 13)

1:12 *first to hope.* Paul is probably thinking here of Jewish Christians. The verb he uses means, literally, "to be prior in hoping." He recognizes a certain priority in the proclamation of the Gospel: "to the Jew first and also to the Greek" (Rm 1:16). In Ephesians the Gentiles prior to their conversion were "alienated from the commonwealth of Israel and strangers to the covenants of promise" (2:12). But they are now "fellow heirs, members of the same body, and partakers of the promise in Christ Jesus through the gospel" (3:6). Thus, the apostle returns to the pronoun "our" in 1:14. The Gentiles who once had "no hope" (2:12) have been called to the one hope (4:4) shared with Jewish believers. *to the praise of His glory.* See the notes on v. 6.

1:13 *you also.* See the note on v. 11. *the word of truth.* Throughout his writings Paul emphasizes the apostolic gospel as God's truth (2:5, 14; 5:7; 2Co 4:2; 6:7; Col 1:5; 2Tm 2:15). It is not only completely reliable but it is also the very means through which God works faith and brings salvation to people (Rm 10:14–17; Rm 1:16). Paul therefore regards it as crucial to say in v. 13 that the Ephesians have heard it. Calvin wrote,

> Nothing is more earnestly attempted by Satan than to lead us either to doubt or to despise the gospel. Paul therefore furnishes us with two shields, by which we may repel both temptations. In opposition to every doubt, let us learn to bring forward this testimony, that the gospel is not only certain truth which cannot deceive, but is, by way of eminence, *the word of truth* as if, strictly speaking, there were no truth but itself. If the temptation be to contempt or dislike of the gospel, let us remember that its power and efficacy have been manifested in bringing to us salvation. (Calvin, *Ephesians* 187)

sealed. In the ancient world sealing served as a mark of ownership that had legal significance. Objects, animals, and human beings (specifically slaves) were identified and protected as the property of their owner. This practice and image, commonly found also in the OT (e.g., Gn 4:15; 17:11), enables Paul to say that it is none other than God's Holy Spirit Himself who marks us as God's own. That means we are guaranteed to receive in full the final inheritance reserved for us in heaven (v. 14). With a possible reference to Baptism, Paul writes in 2 Corinthians that God "has put His seal on us and given us His Spirit in our hearts as a guarantee" (1:22). In modern times, many Coptic Christians in Egypt have a custom of tattooing a cross on their right forearms, signifying their identification as Christ's own. With an allusion to Ezk 9:4ff., Revelation speaks of "the seal of the living God" placed on the foreheads of "the servants of God," a sign of God's possession and protection (7:2; 9:4). It may be noted that in a summary of the doctrine of election, the Lutheran confessional writings speak of the Sacraments (Baptism and the Lord's Supper) as a "seal" of God's promises: "Christ causes the promise of the Gospel not only to be offered in general, but He also seals it through the Sacraments. He attaches them like seals of the promise, and by them He confirms the Gospel to every believer in particular." (FC SD XI 37).

1:14 *guarantee.* In Hellenistic Gk an *arrabon* ("guarantee") was a regular commercial term for a "payment of part of a purchase price in advance," that is, a first installment, deposit, or pledge. An installment was a promise that the whole payment was coming. For Paul the Holy Spirit who dwells in Christians is God's "down payment" guaranteeing the salvation to come—the resurrection and eternal life (2Co 1:22; 5:4–5; Rm 8:23). *possession.* In the OT God calls Israel "My treasured possession" (Ex 19:5; see note, v. 4). The one community of Jews and Gentiles together ("our," "we") fulfills God's loving intention in eternity. God, "the Creator of Israel," (Is 43:15) has now formed a new people for Himself "that they may declare [His] praise" (v. 21; 1Pt 2:9). These thoughts stirred such excitement in the apostle Paul that he could not contain a final outburst of praise.

Devotion and Prayer in 1:3–14 Paul's opening doxology praising God, for His glorious grace expands our vision of God's redemptive plan centering in Jesus Christ. God's love embraces everything He has made, including especially us whom He has chosen and redeemed to be His own through His Son. Ephesians lifts our eyes away from ourselves. It teaches us to trust in His promises in Christ and to give Him our praise. Our sinful pride continually tempts us to focus only on ourselves and trust in our achievements as a way of keeping in "good graces" with God. Pride can also lead to a spiritual elitism, causing us to think that we are better than others. An inflated view of self-importance among Christians usually leads to divisions among them. Paul's song of praise moves us to put away our sinful pride, to place our trust in Christ alone, and to rejoice in the many spiritual blessings that we have because of Him. Through the Holy Spirit God assures us that He is gracious toward us and forgives our sin. We thank God that He has embraced us as His treasured possession. • Heavenly Father, forgive my self-centeredness, and teach me to rely on Your grace alone; through Jesus Christ. Amen.

The Doctrine of Election among the Reformers

One of the more controversial issues that affected churches of the Reformation is the doctrine of election or predestination. Discussions of similar ideas in classical writers, who argued for the freedom of the human will or its control by fate, influenced Christian understandings of the doctrine. Among early Christian theologians, Augustine held the greatest influence. He sought to harmonize the apostle Paul's teaching about God's election with classical ideas of free will. Luther, as an Augustinian friar, was influenced by Augustine and medieval consideration of Augustine's views. He wrote a treatise on *The Bondage of the Will*, since he concluded from Scripture that the human will was bound by sin. Luther also emphasized the grace of God, who chose to save the saints. After careful study of Scripture, Luther emphasized more and more God's desire to save all people. For Luther, the doctrine of election was a mystery that human reason could not solve.

Augustine's views likewise influenced Calvin. He emphasized not only election by grace but also the idea that God chose some people for destruction. In a most famous summary of his teaching, Calvin wrote,

> We say, then, that Scripture clearly proves this much, that God by his eternal and immutable counsel determined once for all those whom it was his pleasure one day to admit to salvation, and those whom, on the other hand, it was his pleasure to doom to destruction.[1]

Calvin's statement that it was God's "pleasure" to doom people continues to shock readers today.

Unlike Luther who sought to approach the doctrine by Scripture alone (sola scriptura), Calvin ultimately drew his views from Scripture texts as well as human reason, concluding that if God chose to save

---

[1] John Calvin, *Institutes of the Christian Religion,* Henry Beveridge, translator (Edinburgh, 1845–46), Book III, ch. 21.7.

some, He must have chosen to damn others. Calvin even held that God predestined mankind to fall into sin, making God in some sense responsible for sin and evil.

Melanchthon reacted sharply to Calvin's views, regarding them as a new form of Greek Stoicism. Melanchthon wrestled with the matter by noting that condemnation is truly self-chosen by willful rejection of God's love in Christ. While trying to distance Protestant teaching on election from Calvin, Melanchthon ultimately also went beyond Scripture by attributing certain powers to the human will, which led to controversies among the Lutheran churches. These controversies were settled in 1580 with publication of the Book of Concord.

While the Lutheran churches reached a lasting settlement on the issue of election, the Reformed churches erupted into controversy when Jacob Arminius, a Dutch Reformed professor, tried to sort out the matter. Like Calvin, Arminius appealed to both Scripture and reason. But unlike Calvin, who emphasized God's sovereign will to choose and damn, Arminius concluded that God elected people to salvation because He knew in advance that they would repent and believe. In other words, Arminius concluded that there was something in a person that led to his salvation rather than something in God. Although several Reformed confessions of faith spoke in support of Calvin and against Arminius, the latter's views spread and influenced popular preachers such as John Wesley. The Reformed tradition has never recovered fully from this controversy over election, resulting in numerous views on the topic as theologians of each generation explore the issue.✎

Thanksgiving (1:15–23)

ESV	KJV
[15]For this reason, because I have heard of your faith in the Lord Jesus and your love toward all the saints, [16]I do not cease to give thanks for you, remembering you in my prayers, [17]that the God of our Lord Jesus Christ, the Father of glory, may give you a spirit of wisdom and of revelation in the knowledge of him, [18]having the eyes of your hearts enlightened, that you may know what is the hope to which he has called you, what are the riches of his glorious inheritance in the saints, [19]and what is the immeasurable greatness of his power toward us who believe, according to the working of his great might [20]that he worked in Christ when he raised him from the dead and seated him at his right hand in the heavenly places, [21]far above all rule and authority and power and dominion, and above every name that is named, not only in this age but also in the one to come. [22]And he put all things under his feet and gave him as head over all things to the church, [23]which is his body, the fullness of him who fills all in all.	[15]Wherefore I also, after I heard of your faith in the Lord Jesus, and love unto all the saints, [16]Cease not to give thanks for you, making mention of you in my prayers; [17]That the God of our Lord Jesus Christ, the Father of glory, may give unto you the spirit of wisdom and revelation in the knowledge of him: [18]The eyes of your understanding being enlightened; that ye may know what is the hope of his calling, and what the riches of the glory of his inheritance in the saints, [19]And what is the exceeding greatness of his power to us-ward who believe, according to the working of his mighty power, [20]Which he wrought in Christ, when he raised him from the dead, and set him at his own right hand in the heavenly places, [21]Far above all principality, and power, and might, and dominion, and every name that is named, not only in this world, but also in that which is to come: [22]And hath put all things under his feet, and gave him to be the head over all things to the church, [23]Which is his body, the fulness of him that filleth all in all.

1:15 *For this reason.* The splendid panorama of God's saving plan (vv. 3–14) leads Paul to offer a prayer of thanksgiving. *heard.* News and information among Christians in Paul's day could spread fairly quickly, due to frequent travel on Roman roads and merchant vessels on busy sea lanes. Ephesus was a major center of commerce—a situation no doubt Paul utilized often to keep in touch with the churches he founded (see Ac 18:24–28; 1Th 3:1–5; Phm).

1:16 *Ceaseless.* Many pious Jews prayed several hours a day, a custom Paul undoubtedly continued in spite of his rigorous schedule as missionary traveler (see, e.g., 1Th 1:2; 2Th 1:3; 2:13; 1Co 1:4; Php 1:4; Col 1:3; Phm 4). He also often encouraged his readers to "pray without ceasing" (1Th 5:17) and to devote themselves to a life of prayer (Rm 12:12). Believers have the comforting promise that when they pray the Spirit constantly intercedes in their behalf "according to the will of God." This happens especially when they are at a loss for words in difficult circumstances (Rm 8:26–27). *give thanks.* The Gk verb (*eucharisteo*) appears 38 times in the NT. Twenty-four of these occurrences are in Paul's writings. He uses the noun 12 of the 15 times that it appears in the NT (cf. Eph 5:4).

1:17 *God of glory.* In the OT "glory" tells us something important about God. It denotes the splendor of His divine presence and power (cf. Ac 7:2). *a spirit of wisdom.* Commentators are divided on whether "a spirit" (no definite article in Gk) means the human spirit (reflected in ESV, KJV, RSV), or is a reference to the Holy Spirit (NIV). On balance, the context seems to favor the Holy Spirit. At 3:5 Paul says that the mystery of Christ was revealed to the apostles and prophets "by the Spirit" (cf. Col 1:9; 1Co 2:6–16; Jn 14:26; 16:13). Notably, in the OT the Spirit of God is called "the Spirit of wisdom" (Ex 28:3; 31:3; 35:31; Is 11:2, etc.).

1:18 *eyes of your hearts enlightened.* The OT expression "the eyes of your heart" (Ps 13:3; 19:8) fits perfectly into Paul's prayer that the Ephesians gain spiritual insight into God's purposes (Ps 119:18). Spiritual illumination affects the heart, the whole inner life of human beings in whom the Spirit works. The "heart" in the Bible describes the center of the human desiring, willing, and thinking. Apart from Christ, people are "darkened in their understanding" (Eph 4:18). Paul even calls people in this condition "darkness" (5:8). Christians "have been enlightened" (literally in Gk) as God gives to them the Spirit of wisdom and of revelation in the knowledge of Him. Paul writes in Colossians that God has qualified them "to share in the inheritance of the saints in light" and has "delivered [them] from the domain of darkness" (Col 1:12–13; cf. Ac 26:18). Some interpreters see this latter passage as a reference to Baptism. In fact, early Christians spoke of Baptism as enlightenment. Justin Martyr wrote: "This washing [Baptism] is called illumination, because those who learn these things are illuminated in their understandings" (*ANF* 1:183). *hope*. The Ephesians once had no hope (2:12), but now they have the "one hope" that belongs to their call—that is, God's call through the Gospel. The Gospel is all about hope (Col 1:23, 27). *riches*. Based on Ephesians, you have to say that God is extremely wealthy and exceedingly generous! Everywhere we hear of the extravagant outpouring of His blessings in Christ (Eph 1:7, 18; 2:7; 3:8, 16; cf. Col 1:27; 2:2). *inheritance*. See note on v. 11. *saints*. See note, v. 1.

1:19 Paul emphasizes God's great power by piling up a series of synonyms (four, in Gk). In their struggle to "be strong in the Lord," believers must know that they face evil forces beyond their strength to resist (6:12). Only by God's extraordinary power can they withstand their foes.

1:20 God exerted and publicly displayed His extraordinary power by raising His Son from the dead and exalting Him to a position of supreme honor and authority. Scripture clearly teaches that in Baptism Christians "were also raised with Him [Christ] through faith in the powerful working of God, who raised Him from the dead" (Col 2:12). That is, in Baptism God unites us with Christ and the power of His resurrection. Miraculously, it creates the faith by which we receive new life. The power displayed in Christ's resurrection not only guarantees our own future resurrection (1Co 6:14; Php 3:10–11, 21), but also now produces in us a new way of living (Rm 6:4). *seated . . . right hand*. God has enthroned Jesus at His right hand and the subjugated under His absolute authority all the powers opposed to God. This is the messianic fulfillment of Ps 110:1: "The LORD says to my Lord: Sit at My right hand, until I make your enemies your footstool." (The NT quotes or alludes to this Psalm over thirty times!) The spatial metaphor "right hand," the Lutheran reformers taught, "is no set place in heaven" but "nothing other than God's almighty power, which fills heaven and earth." Thus, Christ in both His divine and human natures is "present everywhere" (FC SD VIII 27–28). In the OT the expression "right hand" pictures God's conquering, saving, and sustaining power (Ex 15:6; Ps 48:10; Is 41:10). Astonishingly, Paul says that we Christians are exalted together with Christ (2:6). We are literally drawn into Christ's divine, spiritual, heavenly status and life!

1:21 *rule and authority and power and dominion*. Paul's readers may have been familiar with Jewish speculation about the spiritual

109

forces that were thought to occupy heavenly regions. The four terms found here occur in a Jewish apocalyptic writing (2En 20–22; AD 1–50) that imagines a hierarchy of angels controlling human affairs. The Ephesians (and the Colossians) were probably familiar with pagan superstitions about supernatural spiritual forces. In this Letter Paul does not engage in speculation. He is speaking of real spiritual forces at work "behind the scenes." All such spiritual powers, which affect earthly life and structures, are purposefully opposed to "the mystery of [God's] will" (1:9), the Gospel (6:12; cf. 3:10). The powers mentioned are illustrative (note "every name that is named") of all the entities that were originally created by and through Christ (Col 1:16) but at some point came under the power of evil. Christ has conquered these evil agencies and reigns "far above" them. He has disarmed them (Col 2:15). They therefore cannot separate us from "the love of God in Christ Jesus our Lord" (Rm 8:38–39). *this age . . . one to come.* Christians receive solid comfort that Christ reigns in their behalf both in the present and in the future.

1:22 *all things under His feet.* The apostle applies these words from Ps 8:6 to Christ. The first half of that verse recalls God's creation of Adam who was given dominion over "the works of [God's] hands" (cf. Gn 1:26–28). The resurrected and exalted Christ is the Second Adam to whom the entire universe and everything in it is subordinated. God's victorious Son has dominion over "all things" (cf. 1Co 15:27–28). Nothing is left outside His control (Heb 2:6–9). What a great comfort this is when we feel that things in our life seem "out of control"! *church.* God's Church consists of all those who in every place believe in the Lord Jesus Christ (all those "who believe" (v. 19; 1Co 1:2). The "Church universal" is a good way to refer to it. Christians confess in the Apostles' Creed that we believe in the "one holy Christian Church." Paul uses the term in this way elsewhere in Ephesians (3:10, 21; 5:23ff, 27, 29, 32). The Church in this broader meaning, though present locally, transcends geographical location: " . . . the church throughout all Judea and Galilee and Samaria had peace and was built up" (Ac 9:31).

1:23 *His body.* As elsewhere in the Pauline epistles (Rm 12:4–5; 1Co 12:12–27), the Church is not only compared to a body; it is said *to be* "the body of Christ" (Eph 4:12; Col 1:24; 1Co 12:27). God wants us to think of His Church as an organic unity with many members having differing functions. Christians have become members of the one body of Christ through Baptism (1Co 12:13) and are nurtured by receiving His true body and blood in the Lord's Supper in which they jointly participate (1Co 10:16–17). It is amazing what Paul tells us about Christ's body in this Letter alone! Christ is the head of His body (5:23; cf. Col 1:18); Jews and Gentiles are reconciled "in one body" through Christ's death (2:16; 4:4; cf. 1Co 12:13; Col 3:15); the body is built up when God provides servants in the ministry (4:12); the body grows when its parts work properly (4:16; cf. Col 2:19); and the body and its members in relation to Christ are a model for marriage (5:23, 28, 30). *fullness.* The word probably refers to the immediately preceding word "body." Interpretations differ as to how exactly the word should be understood. Taken in a passive sense, "fullness" signifies that the Church is filled by Christ in whom "the whole fullness of deity dwells bodily" (Col 2:9). Read with an active meaning, "fullness" suggests that the Church fills or completes Christ in some way. The passive sense seems most likely, in light of Paul's prayer in 3:19 that his readers "know the love of Christ that surpasses knowledge, that [they] may be filled with all the fullness of God." Further, not only is Christ the one in whom all the fullness of God dwells (Col 1:19; 2:8), but believers "have been filled in Him" (2:10). Indeed, He "fills all in all" (v. 23).

Devotion and Prayer in 1:15–23 Paul has praised God for all the spiritual blessings belonging to those whom He has chosen by grace (vv. 3–14). God has worked mightily in Christ, raising Him from the dead and exalting Him to the highest position in heaven. The apostle now gives thanks and prays that we may know and understand more fully the riches of Christ. A lazy prayer life, neglecting to study God's Word, and poor worship habits threaten to draw us away from Christ. What a great comfort it is to know that Christ Jesus, who lives and reigns in heaven, does not abandon us! In His everlasting love He forgives us and strengthens our faith. • Gracious Lord, open our eyes to see the depth of Your grace that we may rejoice in the hope of our calling each day. Amen.

PART 3

PROOFS FOR UNITY (CHS. 2–3)

New Creation by Grace Alone (2:1–10)

ESV	KJV
2 ¹And you were dead in the trespasses and sins ²in which you once walked, following the course of this world, following the prince of the power of the air, the spirit that is now at work in the sons of disobedience— ³among whom we all once lived in the passions of our flesh, carrying out the desires of the body and the mind, and were by nature children of wrath, like the rest of mankind. ⁴But God, being rich in mercy, because of the great love with which he loved us, ⁵even when we were dead in our trespasses, made us alive together with Christ— by grace you have been saved—⁶and raised us up with him and seated us with him in the heavenly places in Christ Jesus, ⁷so that in the coming ages he might show the immeasurable riches of his grace in kindness toward us in Christ Jesus. ⁸For by grace you have been saved through faith. And this is not your own doing; it is the gift of God, ⁹not a result of works, so that no one may boast. ¹⁰For we are his workmanship, created in Christ Jesus for good works, which God prepared beforehand, that we should walk in them.	**2** ¹And you hath he quickened, who were dead in trespasses and sins; ²Wherein in time past ye walked according to the course of this world, according to the prince of the power of the air, the spirit that now worketh in the children of disobedience: ³Among whom also we all had our conversation in times past in the lusts of our flesh, fulfilling the desires of the flesh and of the mind; and were by nature the children of wrath, even as others. ⁴But God, who is rich in mercy, for his great love wherewith he loved us, ⁵Even when we were dead in sins, hath quickened us together with Christ, (by grace ye are saved;) ⁶And hath raised us up together, and made us sit together in heavenly places in Christ Jesus: ⁷That in the ages to come he might shew the exceeding riches of his grace in his kindness toward us through Christ Jesus. ⁸For by grace are ye saved through faith; and that not of yourselves: it is the gift of God: ⁹Not of works, lest any man should boast. ¹⁰For we are his workmanship, created in Christ Jesus unto good works, which God hath before ordained that we should walk in them.

2:1 *And you.* In view of *"we all* once lived" in v. 3, the "you" in the present verse refers to Paul's Gentile readers in Asia Minor. But Paul's thought quickly moves to a description of the universal human condition. *dead in . . . sins.* God's Word reveals what is impossible to know through self-diagnosis, however perceptive a person may imagine himself or herself to be. In the spiritual realm all human beings are dead even while they seem alive (cf. 1Tm 5:6)—like "dead men walking." "Trespasses and sins" realistically describes the closed circle in which all humans now exist (see Col 2:13). The image of a lifeless corpse suggests itself:

> Now, a person who is physically dead cannot from his own powers prepare or make himself come back to life again. So the person who is spiritually dead in sins cannot by his own strength make or apply himself to acquire spiritual and heavenly righteousness and life. (FC SD II 11)

"Dead" people cannot bring themselves to life again.

2:2 *walked.* Even today this imagery, a Hbr idiom common especially in the Psalms and Proverbs (e.g., Ps 1:1; 15:2; 128:1l; Pr 1:2; 20:7), indicates a habit of conduct or ethical behavior ("walk the talk"). Paul speaks this way in his writings when he details the "lifestyle" of those who believe and are baptized—also in Ephesians (4:1; 5:2, 8, 15). *prince of the . . . air.* Most Jews in Paul's day believed that evil spirits occupied the lowest realm of the heavens (the heavenly regions; cf. 3:10; 6:12)—something like our "atmosphere." The title "prince" fits the Devil, for he is the chief ruler or authority of evil (4:27; 6:11, 16). Elsewhere in the NT he is called the "prince of demons" (by Jewish scribes, Mk 3:22), "ruler of this world" (Jn 12:31), and "god of this world" (2Co 4:4). He sits at the command center of evil, so to speak. Melanchthon wrote, "World history itself shows how great is the strength of the devil's rule. Blasphemy and wicked teachings fill the world, and in these bonds the devil holds enthralled those who are wise and righteous in the eyes of the world" (Ap II 49). *sons of disobedience.* "Disobedient" is just the right adjective for fallen humankind. Whether they realize it or not, people are born rebels against God. They are held captive to attitudes and lifestyles behind which the devil is the driving force.

2:3 *we all . . . once.* We may call the term "once" in Ephesians a "marker." It usually points to a description of the readers' pre-Christian past (2:2, 2, 11, 13; 5:8). Jews and Gentiles alike "by nature"

114

are under sin's power (Rm 3:9, 23). *flesh*. This word often in Paul signifies the total human being as dominated by sin, to the point that wherever flesh is, all forms of sin are likewise present. Sin, so to speak, makes its "headquarters" in the flesh. See note, Gal 3:3. *children of wrath*. This Hebraic expression means that humans are deserving of God's wrath and condemnation (Rm 1:18; Col 3:5–6).

2:4–10 Against the dark background of sin and judgment the Gospel now shines, like the stars appear against the blackness of the night sky.

2:5 *even when . . . dead*. The repetition of "dead" (v. 1) sets up a sharp contrast with the life that Christ brings. In Rm 6 especially Paul concentrates on the powerful transition from spiritual death to life through Baptism "into Christ Jesus." Prior to union with Christ sin enslaved us. We desperately needed to be "set free." But in Christ Christians now live as persons brought from "death to life" (Rm 6:13). God has acted in mercy despite human rebellion and spiritual impotence (cf. Rm 5:6). *made us alive . . . with*. A single compound verb used here occurs only in this verse and in Col 2:13 A combination of "with" and "make alive" (synonym for "raise"), the word describes beautifully how people who were once dead in their sins have now been made alive by God through union with Christ. *by grace . . . saved*. Verses 8–9 below expand on what is said in this parenthetical comment. The verb form emphasizes both God's action (see "but God . . . " in v. 4!) and the continuing reality of His divine rescue.

2:6 *raised us up with . . . seated us with*. Paul likes compound verbs when he explains how much Christ means to us. He adds two more here for God's action in Christ (see comments on "made us alive . . . with," v. 5). This is his way of saying that we, incredibly, are linked to three saving events in our Savior's life: resurrection, ascension, and session at God's right hand. Since we are "fellow heirs with Christ" (Rm 8:17), we have what He has (1Co 1:21) and the benefits of His saving acts belong to us.

2:7 *coming ages*. "Ages" in Ephesians appears to be a general description of history as a succession of periods or generations, stretching from the past and on into eternity (cf. 1:21; 3:9, 11; 3:21). The verse resumes a thought of the opening doxology in 3:14. The "coming" ages will be filled with what God is still planning to do for us (cf. Mk 10:30): "When Christ who is your life appears, then you also will appear with Him in glory" (Col 3:3–4).

115

2:8–9 *by grace.* If all of Ephesians were a song, the keynote would most assuredly be God's "grace," His generous mercy toward undeserving human beings. Paul sounded the note in his opening "hymn" of praise (1:6–7). This rich phrase (literally, "by this grace") conveys not only the cause but also the basis of salvation. We simply cannot wrap our minds around the inexhaustibly rich grace that God has lavished upon us (on the theme of God's wealth toward us see especially 1:18; 2:7; 3:8, 16; Col 1:27; 2:2–3). Luther properly called God's gracious work a treasure:

> So you see plainly that there is no work done here by us, but a treasure, which God gives us and faith grasps [Ephesians 2:8–9]. It is like the benefit of the Lord Jesus Christ upon the cross, which is not a work, but a treasure included in the Word. It is offered to us and received by faith. (LC IV 37)

saved. God has rescued us from power of the world (v. 2), the devil (v. 2), and our sinful flesh (v. 3). Most importantly, the holy and just God has delivered us from His terrifying wrath on the Day of Judgment (cf. Rm 1:18; 2:5, 8; see comments on 2:3). In the hope of our final liberation, says Paul to the Romans, "we were saved" (Rm 8:24). But for Paul salvation involves not only our future deliverance; it remains a present reality (1Co 1:18; 2Co 6:2). *through faith.* This carefully chosen prepositional phrase shows that faith functions as the instrument that receives Christ the Savior—the hand that grasps Christ and thus the salvation He brings (Rm 3:22, 28; Gal 2:16; Php 3:9; 2Tm 3:15). "But as a wooden box which contains a costly gem becomes a precious box, so our faith also becomes something precious only because it holds Jesus in hand" (C. F. W. Walther, Convention Essay, Western District Convention Proceedings [1875], 110). God Himself through the Word and sacraments creates the very faith that trusts His promises and receives the salvation accomplished through Christ (Rm 1:17; 10:17; Gal 2:16; 3:23–4:7). Melanchthon wrote,

> The faith that justifies is not merely a knowledge of history. It is to believe in God's promise. In the promise, for Christ's sake, forgiveness of sins and justification are freely offered . . . it is to want and to receive the offered promise of forgiveness of sins and of justification. (Ap IV 48)

this is not your own doing. The Gk grammar suggests that the word "this" refers back to the preceding phrase taken as a whole— God's gracious plan of salvation that becomes ours through faith—

and not just faith itself. Everything belonging to our salvation is pure gift, apart from and independent of any human initiative. *not a result of works.* Neither Jews who obey the Law, nor Gentiles who heed "the work of the law [that] is written on their hearts" (Rm 2:15), may claim a reward from God on the basis of their moral achievements (Rm 3:19–31). Luther wrote, "Christ's merit is obtained not by our works or pennies, but from grace through faith, without money and merit" (SA II II 24).

2:10 *His workmanship.* Paul now gives an additional reason (the verse begins with "for") why no one has grounds for boasting. He chooses two powerful words, "workmanship" (Gk "what is made," "creation"—used elsewhere only at Rm 1:20) and "created," to drive home another central Christian truth. Believers are not a refurbished or renovated version of an "older model" (cf. Mt 9:16–17)! They are a new creation (2Co 5:17; Gal 6:15), with God alone the Creator (note "His"). From eternity, God set in motion His grand design that those whom He redeemed may by His creative work "be conformed to the image of His Son" (Rm 8:29; cf. Eph 1:4). The contrasts in this chapter could not be more stark: an evil lifestyle (vv. 1–3) versus a lifestyle of good deeds; the devil (v. 2) as the prince of evil versus God the Creator of the good. *good works.* Our works do not cause or contribute to our salvation (vv. 5–9); they are the result or consequence of it. We cannot even take credit for them because God created them for us to do in Christ. Martin Luther captured well what Paul is saying:

> Faith, however, is a divine work in us that changes us and makes us to be born anew of God, John 1[:12–13]. . . . O, it is a living, busy, active, mighty thing, this faith. It is impossible for it not to be doing good works incessantly. It does not ask whether good works are to be done, but before the question is asked, it has already done them, and is constantly doing them. (FC SD IV 10–11)

walk. See the comments on v. 2.

Devotion and Prayer in 2:1–10 In this section Paul teaches that people who are "in trespasses and sins" are completely lifeless and "dead," not merely weak and sick. All human beings are conceived and born into this condition. Apart from Christ they live under the evil control and influence of the world, the devil, and their own sinful flesh. They are by nature spiritually unresponsive, just like a deceased person is unable to make himself or herself alive or do the things living people do. Self-help experts and their writings galore issue grand promises of spiritual enlightenment and "new life." In testimonials of success people boast about their accomplishments. But God alone can and does truly deliver us from our sinful predicament and make us truly alive. By His rich grace He sent our Savior Jesus Christ to die for sin, rise up to life, and ascend into heaven. As we embrace Him by faith He gives us a new life and the power to do what pleases God. • Lord, lead me to abandon sinful self-confidence and rejoice in Your grace alone. Amen.

Gentiles and Israel (2:11–22)

ESV	KJV
[11]Therefore remember that at one time you Gentiles in the flesh, called "the uncircumcision" by what is called the circumcision, which is made in the flesh by hands— [12]remember that you were at that time separated from Christ, alienated from the commonwealth of Israel and strangers to the covenants of promise, having no hope and without God in the world. [13]But now in Christ Jesus you who once were far off have been brought near by the blood of Christ. [14]For he himself is our peace, who has made us both one and has broken down in his flesh the dividing wall of hostility [15]by abolishing the law of commandments expressed in ordinances, that he might create in himself one new man in place of the two, so making peace, [16]and might reconcile us both to God in one body through the cross, thereby killing the hostility. [17]And he came and preached peace to you who were far off and peace to those who were near.	[11]Wherefore remember, that ye being in time past Gentiles in the flesh, who are called Uncircumcision by that which is called the Circumcision in the flesh made by hands; [12]That at that time ye were without Christ, being aliens from the commonwealth of Israel, and strangers from the covenants of promise, having no hope, and without God in the world: [13]But now in Christ Jesus ye who sometimes were far off are made nigh by the blood of Christ. [14]For he is our peace, who hath made both one, and hath broken down the middle wall of partition between us; [15]Having abolished in his flesh the enmity, even the law of commandments contained in ordinances; for to make in himself of twain one new man, so making peace; [16]And that he might reconcile both unto God in one body by the cross, having slain the enmity thereby: [17]And came and preached peace to you which were afar off, and to them that were nigh.

¹⁸For through him we both have access in one Spirit to the Father. ¹⁹So then you are no longer strangers and aliens, but you are fellow citizens with the saints and members of the household of God, ²⁰built on the foundation of the apostles and prophets, Christ Jesus himself being the cornerstone, ²¹in whom the whole structure, being joined together, grows into a holy temple in the Lord. ²²In him you also are being built together into a dwelling place for God by the Spirit.	¹⁸For through him we both have access by one Spirit unto the Father. ¹⁹Now therefore ye are no more strangers and foreigners, but fellow-citizens with the saints, and of the household of God; ²⁰And are built upon the foundation of the apostles and prophets, Jesus Christ himself being the chief corner stone; ²¹In whom all the building fitly framed together groweth unto an holy temple in the Lord: ²²In whom ye also are builded together for an habitation of God through the Spirit.

Introduction to 2:11–22 In eternity God conceived a plan "for the fullness of time, to unite all things in Him [Christ], things in heaven and things on earth" (1:10; Col 1:20). Disharmony reigns throughout the entire universe. Evil powers oppose the will of God—including the master of division, Satan himself (Eph 6:11–12). On earth fierce enmity exists, separating people from God (Rm 8:7) and from each other. An historic rift between Jews and Gentiles was present in the communities where Paul founded churches. He himself "persecuted the church of God" (1Co 15:9). Paul now shows how God has healed this longstanding division between Jews and Gentiles.

2:11 *you Gentiles in the flesh.* Since Gentiles were not circumcised they did not bear the distinguishing physical mark of membership in God's chosen people given to Abraham by God (Gn 17). *the uncircumcision.* Jews stigmatized the Gentiles by attaching this term collectively to them. *made . . . by hands.* Paul does not deny the importance of the physical circumcision in the history of our salvation (Php 3:4). But it pointed to something radically new, a *real* circumcision "made without hands," that is, a circumcision that is a matter of the heart and the working of the Spirit (Rm 2:28–29). Through Baptism God unites us with Christ and the power of His resurrection (Col 2:11). Thus circumcision "by hands" belongs to the old order that is obsolete (Gal 6:15). Baptism belongs to the new spiritual order that has arrived in Christ.

2:12 *commonwealth of Israel.* The Gk for "commonwealth" (*politeia*; used 2 times in the NT) can mean simply "citizenship," as in Ac 22:28 of Paul's Roman citizenship. But in this context it describes Israel as a people to whom belong certain religious advantages (cf. Rm 3:1–2). In Rm 9 Paul lists them: "the adoption, the glory, the covenants, the giving of the law, the worship, and the promises . . . the patriarchs" (v. 4). Most importantly, "from their race, according to the flesh, is the Christ, who is God over all, blessed forever. Amen" (v. 5). *covenants of promise.* Israel received the promise of the coming Messiah which was given and renewed throughout Israel's history (Abraham [Gn 15, 17], Isaac [Gn 26], Jacob [Gn 28]; Israel ([Ex 24], and David [2Sm 7]). Through Christ, the Gentiles are now included (v. 19; 3:6). *without God.* The Gentiles worshipped many gods, but they did not worship the one true God (1Co 8:5–6). Calvin wrote,

> Why, then, are they styled *Atheists*? for an *Atheist*, strictly speaking, is one who does not believe, and who absolutely ridicules, the being of a God. That appellation, certainly, is not usually given to superstitious persons, but to those who have no feeling of religion, and who desire to see it utterly destroyed. I answer, Paul was right in giving them this name, for he treated all the notions entertained respecting false gods as nothing; and with the utmost propriety do godly persons regard all idols as "nothing in the world." Those who do not worship the true God, whatever may be the variety of their worship, or the multitude of laborious ceremonies which they perform, are without God: they adore what they know not. (Calvin, *Ephesians* 214–215)

2:13 *brought near.* In the OT, Gentiles are "far off" (1Ki 8:41; Is 5:26), but Israel is near to God (Ps 148:14). The gap between Jews and Gentiles, between the so-called "advantaged and disadvantaged," was not removed by turning Gentiles into Jews (as in Judaism when Gentiles became proselytes). "In Christ" God created a new people, all of whom have access to the Father through Him (v. 18). *blood of Christ.* See the note on 1:7.

2:14 *peace.* Hbr *shalom* in the OT was truly a loaded term. Like no other concept, it conveyed the promise of well-being and prosperity for those who experienced God's salvation. In Ps 85 the psalmist prays for God's steadfast love and salvation, and then in the same breath cries "speak peace to His people, to His saints" (vv. 7–8). The forward thrust of "peace" in its fullest sense becomes clearest in Isaiah. The prophet promises an everlasting state of peace to arrive when "the Prince of Peace" comes (9:6–7; cf. Mi 5:5). This promise of eternal peace is fulfilled in Christ, in whom true, spiritual well-being is found (v. 15; Jn 14:27; 20:19). For this reason Paul calls Christ Himself "our peace." *made us both one.* In 4:3 Paul urges the Ephesians to preserve "the unity of the Spirit in the bond of peace." The unity (*henotes*; only occurrence in NT) between Jews and Gentiles exists as a new reality created by Christ's saving work. *dividing wall.* In Herod's temple in Jerusalem, a five-foot stone fence separated the (inner) court of the Jews from the (outer) court of the Gentiles (*Ant* xv, 11). In 1871 an archeologist discovered a white limestone slab that served as notice to any Gentile contemplating entry beyond this fence. It reads: "No foreigner may enter within the barrier and enclosure round the temple. Anyone who is caught doing so will have himself to blame for his ensuing death." Paul was falsely charged with taking a non-Jew into the temple beyond this boundary (Ac 21:27–29). Notices of this kind were a vivid reminder of what really separated Gentiles from Jews: the Law (Eph 2:15). In the "gospel of peace" (6:15) that he proclaimed, Paul declared that Gentiles are no longer barred from true worship of God or the reception of His gifts (cf. Jn 4:21–24).

2:15 *abolishing the law.* Some interpreters have argued that God abrogated only ceremonial laws, not the moral Law. Others say Paul rejected only a legalistic use of the Law. The added phrase "expressed in ordinances" suggests, however, that Paul likely had in mind the hundreds of regulations that Jewish tradition had erected as a kind of fence around the Law (613 regulations, to be exact; cf. Col 3:11). These regulations guaranteed that Gentiles would keep their distance from Jews. They formed a true "dividing wall of hostility" (v. 14). Paul's basic principle was that the Law in general had lost its power to condemn us (Rm 8:1–4). The Gk word for "abolish" means literally "render powerless or ineffective." That includes all the humanly established precepts that separated Jews from Gentiles. They have lost all power to condemn and divide. In fact, Christ also overcame the entire Law's ability to condemn believers by redeeming them from the curse of the law, having become a curse for them (Gal 3:13). *one new man.* Christ has created something that did not exist before: a new humanity. Christ, the Second Adam (Rm 5:12–21; 1Co 15:21–22), has created in Himself one new corporate entity. External distinctions of ethnic origin, social status, custom, etc. count for nothing when it comes to becoming a member of God's new people in Christ.

2:16 *reconcile.* Deep-seated hostility between opposing parties is not easily removed. It took Christ's death on the cross to "kill" enmity in two directions at the same time. Christ not only reconciled (in Gk, an intensified form) Jews and Gentiles to each other. He also removed the estrangement between God and human beings, all of whom are by nature under His wrath (2:23; 2Co 5:17–20). *in one body.* With one exception (5:28), "body" in Ephesians refers to the Church (1:23; 2:16; 4:4, 12, 16; 5:23, 30). Paul's call to preserve "the unity of the Spirit in the bond of peace," coupled with the sevenfold "ones" of 4:4–6, reveals that the church's unity in Christ is of paramount importance to him (cf. 1:10).

2:17 *He came and preached.* Isaiah told of a messenger who "publishes peace, who brings good news of happiness, who publishes salvation, who says to Zion, 'Your God reigns' " (Is 52:7). Again, " 'Peace, peace, to the far and to the near,' says the LORD, and 'I will heal him' " (Is 57:19). Paul combines thoughts in these verses and applies them to God's salvation in Christ of both Jews and Gentiles. Jesus our peace (vv. 14–16) came to proclaim "the gospel of peace" (6:15). An allusion again to Is 52:7 in 6:15 indicates that Paul regarded these Isaiah texts as messianic prophecies (see Rm 10:15).

2:18 *access.* As noted above, Gentiles did not have access to the temple, let alone entry into the sacred areas of the sanctuary. But through Christ all believers now have full and direct access to God the Father by one Spirit (Gal 4:6). Like a person granted admission into the "presence chamber" of an ancient monarch, we are led into God's presence by Christ. Indeed, "through him [Christ] we have also obtained access by faith into this grace in which we stand" (Rm 5:2).

2:19 *fellow citizens.* Paul alludes to Roman citizenship, which was a prized possession in his day and carried with it significant privileges under the laws and governance of the Roman empire (see Ac 22:22–29). Just as there is a "body of citizens," so also the Church is a "body" of which Christians are members. The allusion could be readily understood by Paul's readers. The comparison would have been especially apt in light of the tension often existing between

Jews and Gentiles in the Pauline churches. As Acts and Paul's Letters show, Paul labored continuously to make the Gentile believers welcome in the largely Jewish-Christian churches of the first century. The Gentiles together with their fellow Jewish Christians are full-fledged citizens of God's Church (Php 3:20), with all of the rights and privileges that Christ has gained for His people. Christians no longer live on a passport as travelers without permanent residency. They have their "new birth" certificate (Baptism) and can be certain of their citizenship in God's heavenly kingdom together with all of God's saints. *saints.* See the notes on 1:1. Knox wrote,

> The apostle, speaking of the vocation of the Gentiles. . . . Here we find men, who before were strangers, made citizens with the saints and of the household of God; we find them builded upon the foundation of the apostles and prophets; we find Jesus Christ to be the chief corner-stone. (Knox 283)

2:20 *built on the foundation.* The Church resembles a building that has been erected upon a foundation (cf. 1Co 3:10–11). A foundation provides the basis for the structure to come into being. Believers in Christ, the members of God's family, come into being as the Holy Spirit works faith through the preaching and teaching of the apostles and prophets (see notes at 3:5; 4:11; Rm 10:14–17). The Gospel they proclaimed and taught has been preserved in the authoritative writings of the NT. For us these writings are the normative source for the church's proclamation and teaching (1Co 15:1–3; cf. Rm 15:20) *cornerstone.* The term (combination of the two words "extreme" and "corner") occurs elsewhere in the Bible only in Is 28:16 and 1Pt 2:6. Paul alludes to Is 28:16 where the text speaks, literally, of a stone "for the foundations." This implies a cornerstone that supports and joins together walls of an edifice. Calvin wrote,

> *Foundation* in this passage, unquestionably means doctrine; for no mention is made of patriarchs or pious kings, but only of those who held the office of teachers, and whom God had appointed to superintend the edification of his church. . . . In the strict sense of the term, Christ is the only foundation. He alone supports the whole church. He alone is the rule and standard of faith. But Christ is actually the foundation on which the church is built by the preaching of doctrine; and, on this account, the prophets and apostles are called builders. (Calvin, *Ephesians* 223)

2:21 *grows.* Christ's body, the Church, as a living organism grows to maturity "into Christ" (4:15–16). In this text God's Church as a structure grows into a holy temple in the Lord. Whether "body" or "structure," God gives the growth (1Co 3:7; Col 2:19). The apostle Peter develops the picture of a building being constructed by God when he writes, "you yourselves like living stones are being built up as a spiritual house. . . . (1Pt 2:5). Growth takes place when members of the church speak the truth in such a way that love is maintained (Eph 4:15).

2:22 *dwelling place.* These words translate a term that occurs quite frequently in the OT for the temple as the place where God dwells (e.g., 1Ki 8:13). Paul now calls the Church God's "dwelling place," just as the temple was the place where God was present in the midst of His people. "We are the temple of the living God," writes Paul to the Corinthians (2Co 6:16; 1Co 3:16).

Devotion and Prayer in 2:11–22 Paul writes that the Gentiles were once "far off." They were a long way from being accepted as members of God's chosen people. Jews posted "No Trespassing" signs blocking them from entering temple areas. A host of laws had been created that spoke volumes: Gentiles were "outsiders." Christian congregations today also can seem wary of outsiders. By their attitudes and actions they can in effect restrict access to the Gospel of Jesus Christ who commanded His Church to make disciples of "all nations." We rejoice that God in Christ has reconciled the whole world to Himself, not counting our sins against us. Paul urges all of us to remember who we were apart from Christ and that in Him God has made us members of His family. • Lord, forgive my prejudices and teach me to reach out to all those I meet and know with the message of Your grace. Amen.

Paul's Apostolic Mandate to the Gentiles (3:1–13)

ESV	KJV
3 ¹For this reason I, Paul, a prisoner for Christ Jesus on behalf of you Gentiles—²assuming that you have heard of the stewardship of God's grace that was given to me for you, ³how the mystery was made known to me by revelation, as I have written briefly. ⁴When you read this, you can perceive my insight into the mystery of Christ, ⁵which was not made known to the sons of men in other generations as it has now been revealed to his holy apostles and prophets by the Spirit. ⁶This mystery is that the Gentiles are fellow heirs, members of the same body, and partakers of the promise in Christ Jesus through the gospel. ⁷Of this gospel I was made a minister according to the gift of God's grace, which was given me by the working of his power. ⁸To me, though I am the very least of all the saints, this grace was given, to preach to the Gentiles the unsearchable riches of Christ, ⁹and to bring to light for everyone what is the plan of the mystery hidden for ages in God who created all things, ¹⁰so that through the church the manifold wisdom of God might now be made known to the rulers and authorities in the heavenly places. ¹¹This was according to the eternal purpose that he has realized in Christ Jesus our Lord,	3 ¹For this cause I Paul, the prisoner of Jesus Christ for you Gentiles, ²If ye have heard of the dispensation of the grace of God which is given me to you-ward: ³How that by revelation he made known unto me the mystery; (as I wrote afore in few words, ⁴Whereby, when ye read, ye may understand my knowledge in the mystery of Christ) ⁵Which in other ages was not made known unto the sons of men, as it is now revealed unto his holy apostles and prophets by the Spirit; ⁶That the Gentiles should be fellowheirs, and of the same body, and partakers of his promise in Christ by the gospel: ⁷Whereof I was made a minister, according to the gift of the grace of God given unto me by the effectual working of his power. ⁸Unto me, who am less than the least of all saints, is this grace given, that I should preach among the Gentiles the unsearchable riches of Christ; ⁹And to make all men see what is the fellowship of the mystery, which from the beginning of the world hath been hid in God, who created all things by Jesus Christ: ¹⁰To the intent that now unto the principalities and powers in heavenly places might be known by the church the manifold wisdom of God, ¹¹According to the eternal purpose which he purposed in Christ Jesus our Lord:

¹²in whom we have boldness and access with confidence through our faith in him. ¹³So I ask you not to lose heart over what I am suffering for you, which is your glory.	¹²In whom we have boldness and access with confidence by the faith of him. ¹³Wherefore I desire that ye faint not at my tribulations for you, which is your glory.

Introduction to 3:1–13 As a result of Paul's missionary journeys large numbers of Gentiles became members of the Early Church. This situation led to tensions between Gentile and Jewish Christians in the churches that Paul established. Paul even spent time in prison because of his call to preach Christ to the Gentiles. Jewish believers insisted that Gentiles must be circumcised to become full-fledged members of Christ's body, the Church. This led to the Apostolic Council in Ac 15 which resolved the issue in large part. However, the ongoing work of "maintaining the unity of the Spirit in the bond of peace" (4:3) continued. The Gentiles at Ephesus lived in a strongly pagan environment and experienced its pressures, but they also needed assurance that they were full members of God's new people. They were part of an eternal plan much bigger than they could have imagined.

3:1 *prisoner*. During his career Paul suffered numerous imprisonments (2Co 11:23), some of which are mentioned in Acts. To protect him from a Jewish mob in the temple at Jerusalem, a Roman military commander arrested him, ordered him to be bound with two chains, and brought him to the barracks (Ac 21:27–36). Paul spent a year and a half in prison in Caesarea (Ac 23:23–26:32), and toward the end of his ministry, two years under house arrest in Rome (Ac 28:30). At the end of Ephesians he calls himself "an ambassador in chains" because of the Gospel of peace that he proclaimed. Evidently the Ephesians had become dispirited because of his imprisonment—most likely while he was at Rome (3:13). In his final words of encouragement he asked them to pray for him, that he might be able boldly to proclaim "the mystery of the gospel" (6:20, 22). Paul's wrists and ankles may have been chained and his body confined. But his heart and mind were firmly attached to the Lord and His purposes for his life in the interest of others (note, "on behalf of you Gentiles"). Being "bound with chains as a criminal" was no setback; he was willing to "endure everything for the sake of the elect, that they also may obtain the salvation that is in Christ Jesus with eternal glory" (2Tm 2:9–10; cf. Col 1:24).

3:2 The word "assuming" (ESV) introduces a digression that extends to v. 14 where Paul again repeats the phrase, "for this reason" and resumes his originally intended point. The Gk expression implies the certainty of an underlying assumption (see 4:21, where the KJV has "if so be"). *heard.* See note on 1:13. *stewardship.* Paul borrows a concept no doubt very familiar to his readers—the activity and responsibility of a household manager charged with the administration (Gk *oikonomia*) of his master's goods (Lk 12:42; 16:1–4). In Eph 1:10 and 3:9 the word designates God's plan of salvation (ESV, "plan"; KJV, "dispensation, fellowship"), the arrangements God made in eternity and carried out in history. Paul focuses on his apostolic office and the administration of God's grace assigned to him (3:2; Col 1:25; 1Co 4:1–2; Gal 2:7, 9; cf. Ti 1:7).

3:3 *mystery.* See the note on 1:9. *by revelation.* Paul's opponents often questioned his apostolic authority, charging that his message was of human origin (e.g., 2Co 10–13). In Galatians he made a special point of saying that it came by divine revelation and was not "man's gospel": "I received it through a revelation of Jesus Christ" (Gal 1:11–12; see notes). Therefore he was in God's business of divine disclosure. He preached "according to the revelation of the mystery that was kept secret for long ages" but now "disclosed" (Rm 16:25) and through the prophetic writings made known (v. 26). *written.* This probably refers to the first part of this Letter (1:9–10; 2:11–22).

3:4 *When you read.* Public reading of the OT Scriptures took place in synagogue worship on the Sabbath (Ac 15:21). Likewise, Paul intended that his Letters be read aloud to the assembled congregations to whom they were addressed (Col 4:16; 1Th 5:27; 1Tm 4:13). Thus his Letters had authority and he considered them normative for what was to be taught. *mystery.* See the note on 1:9.

3:5 *revealed.* God unveiled a mystery that was not made known to previous generations: the incorporation of Jews and Gentiles into the body of Christ. Without a new revelation, people could otherwise have no knowledge of it. "Was made known" and "has been revealed" are usually called "divine passives," which is a way of stressing that God alone is the Revealer or Author. Calvin wrote,

> Paul does not mean that this subject had been altogether unknown. There had always been some of the Jewish nation who acknowledged that, at the advent of the Messiah, the grace of God would be proclaimed throughout the whole world, and who looked

forward to the renovation of the human race. The prophets themselves, though they spoke with the certainty of revelation, left the
time and manner undetermined. They knew that some communication of the grace of God would be made to the Gentiles, but
at what time, in what manner, and by what means it should be
accomplished, they had no information whatever. This ignorance
was exemplified in a remarkable way by the apostles. (Calvin,
Ephesians 231–32)

holy apostles and prophets. We now know why Paul considered
the apostles and prophets the foundation of God's "holy temple," the
Church (2:20). The apostles and prophets spoke as they were moved
by the Holy Spirit, also when they wrote biblical books in which
God has preserved their message for all times (2Pt 1:21; 1Jn 1:3–4;
2Th 2:15). The apostles were holy, not because they were sinless, but
because they were "set apart for the gospel of God" (Rm 1:1).

3:6 *mystery.* See the note on 1:9. *fellow . . . same body . . . partakers.* Paul uses a number of Gk words in Ephesians that are prefixed
with the word "with" to show that the Jewish and Gentile Christians
are united with Christ, and that they are united with each other
because of what Christ has done (see the notes on 2:5–6 and vv.
19–22). He now summarizes what he has said previously. Together
with Jews, the Gentiles are co-heirs of a heavenly inheritance (1:14),
co-members of the same body (2:16, 19–22), and co-participants in
the promise fulfilled in Christ Jesus (2:12–13). *the gospel.* The Gospel
is God's creative Word through which He brings this new situation
into being.

3:7 *a minister.* Paul was intensely aware of his apostolic office as
a ministry of service, which God gave to him according to His grace
(Rm 15:16; 1Co 3:5; 15:10; 2Co 3:6; 6:4). Through the Risen Christ,
Paul tells the Romans, he "received grace and apostleship" (Rm 1:5).
In language of worship, he regarded his ministry to the Gentiles as a
"priestly service of the gospel of God" (Rm 15:16).

3:8 *least of all the saints.* Paul, whose Roman name literally meant
"little," considered himself the least likely candidate for the office of
apostle especially because he fiercely opposed the Christian movement (1Co 15:9; Gal 1:13; 1Tm 1:15). He consented to the stoning of
Stephen (Ac 7:58; 8:1; 22:20) and persecuted the Jerusalem Church
(Ac 9:1). He aggressively pursued Christians—who were likely flee-
ing from Jerusalem—to "bring them bound to Jerusalem" (Ac 9:2).
Paul was not trying to brag about his humility! He wanted to mag-

nify God's abundant grace. *grace was given.* God extended His grace through the good news proclaimed to the Gentiles.

3:9 *bring to light.* These words reflect exactly what Jesus said to Paul at his conversion on the road to Damascus (Ac 26:18; see comments on 1:18).

3:10 *through the church.* The very existence of the Church serves as a kind of object lesson "to the rulers and authorities in heaven places." Paul declares in Colossians that on the cross of Christ God "disarmed the rules and authorities . . . triumphing over them in him" (Col 2:15). These divisive powers would do well to study how God's saving wisdom is displayed in full color in the Church, where Jews and Gentiles have been made one in Christ (see note on 1:21). A Christian writer once remarked that the Church now serves as a "graduate school" for heavenly beings!

3:11 *the eternal purpose.* The creation of "one new man in place of two" (one body; 2:15–16) forms a distinctive pattern in the unfolding tapestry of God's eternal purpose. *Christ Jesus our Lord.* "Lord" for Jesus occurs 24 times in Ephesians. Converts to Christianity were expected to confess "Jesus is Lord," an early creedal statement (see Php 2:11 and note).

3:12 *access.* Luther explained,

> By these words ["Our Father who art in heaven"] God would tenderly encourage us to believe that He is our true Father and that we are His true children, so that we may ask Him confidently with all assurance, as dear children ask their dear father. (SC III)

See the note on 2:18.

3:13 *suffering . . . your glory.* In light of God's glorious inheritance to be fully revealed (1:18; 3:16), Christ-like suffering becomes for Christians a momentary burden to be endured with joy and patience (Rm 5:3; 8:17–18; Col 1:24; 2Co 4:17). Paul saw his sufferings as a source of comfort and strength for others. In 2Co 1:3–7 he explains how God comforts us in our afflictions so that we may be able to comfort others in their distresses. Christians therefore experience God's comfort through people who have gone through similar pressures in life. Suffering teaches us "to rely not on ourselves, but on God who raises the dead" (2Co 1:9). See the note on v. 1. Paul's positive view of suffering and its salutary effects runs counter to popular views of suffering as a sign of God's judgment and displeasure. See the notes on 3:1.

Devotion and Prayer in 3:1–13 Paul expands on God's revelation to him that the Gentiles are full beneficiaries and participants in God's eternal plan of salvation in Jesus Christ. God called him to make known the unsearchable riches of Christ to the Gentiles, who now together with all the saints have full access to God's saving grace. God makes His eternal purpose known through us who are members of His Church. Despite Christ's triumphant victory on the cross, powers opposed to God's purposes are continually attempting to obstruct our witness to His grace. Christ's enemies put pressure on us and so seek to stifle the proclamation of His Gospel. But Christ has triumphed over them and gives us His power to bear His name to others. • Lord, enlighten my heart with renewed understanding and courage to share Your love in Christ. Amen.

Prayer and Doxology (3:14–21)

ESV	KJV
¹⁴For this reason I bow my knees before the Father, ¹⁵from whom every family in heaven and on earth is named, ¹⁶that according to the riches of his glory he may grant you to be strengthened with power through his Spirit in your inner being, ¹⁷so that Christ may dwell in your hearts through faith—that you, being rooted and grounded in love, ¹⁸may have strength to comprehend with all the saints what is the breadth and length and height and depth, ¹⁹and to know the love of Christ that surpasses knowledge, that you may be filled with all the fullness of God.	¹⁴For this cause I bow my knees unto the Father of our Lord Jesus Christ, ¹⁵Of whom the whole family in heaven and earth is named, ¹⁶That he would grant you, according to the riches of his glory, to be strengthened with might by his Spirit in the inner man; ¹⁷That Christ may dwell in your hearts by faith; that ye, being rooted and grounded in love, ¹⁸May be able to comprehend with all saints what is the breadth, and length, and depth, and height; ¹⁹And to know the love of Christ, which passeth knowledge, that ye might be filled with all the fulness of God.
²⁰Now to him who is able to do far more abundantly than all that we ask or think, according to the power at work within us, ²¹to him be glory in the church and in Christ Jesus throughout all generations, forever and ever. Amen.	²⁰Now unto him that is able to do exceeding abundantly above all that we ask or think, according to the power that worketh in us, ²¹Unto him be glory in the church by Christ Jesus throughout all ages, world without end. Amen.

3:14–15 The phrase "for this reason" in v. 14 indicates that Paul, after a digression (vv. 2–12), is returning to what he originally intended to say in v. 1 on the basis of his previous discussion on the unity of the Church. See the note on v. 2. *bow my knees.* Normally both Jews and Christians stood when they prayed (Mt 6:5; Mk 11:25; Lk 18:11; cf. 1Ki 8:22). Kneeling for prayer suggested humble reverence and submission (Php 2:10), and sometimes expressed emotional intensity (Ac 7:60; Mk 14:35). In the Greco-Roman world people often prostrated themselves before rulers. Calvin wrote,

> The bodily attitude is here put for the religious exercise itself. Not that prayer, in all cases, requires the bending of the knees, but because this expression of reverence is commonly employed, especially where it is not an incidental petition, but a continued prayer. (Calvin, *Ephesians* 241)

Father . . . family. The ESV's "every family" is a more literal translation of the Gk than the KJV's "the whole family" (in the Gk there is no definite article "the"). Although "family" (*patria*) and "Father" (*pater*) (see ESV note) are related terms, throughout Ephesians God is the Father of our Lord Jesus Christ (e.g., 1:17). Only through Him do we have access to the Father (2:18). In a general sense, of course, all family groupings (in heaven and on earth) derive from God the Father as the Creator (cf. Ac 17:24–29).

3:16 *strengthened.* Paul's prays that God will strengthen believers with power that far exceeds human ability, the same power that God "worked in Christ when He raised him from the dead. . . . " (1:19–20). *inner being.* The Holy Spirit works in the very depths of the human being (equivalent to "heart," v. 17). In contrast to what Paul calls "our outer nature," renewal takes place "day by day" in our inner nature (2Co 4:16), so that in our "inner being" we delight in God's Law (Rm 7:22).

3:17 *dwell.* Paul prays that Christ may permanently reside in the hearts of those who believe (cf. Gal 2:20). His language suggests the image of settling down in a home as opposed to a brief stay, let's say, in a motel. In fact, the noun form of this verb "dwell" occurs in 2:20 as the permanent "dwelling place" for God by the Spirit. Since baptized Christians are in Christ (Gal 3:27), Christ dwells by the Spirit in them (Rm 8:10; Gal 2:20). Paul prays that He will continue to dwell in them by faith, and as a result that they be deeply rooted and grounded in love. See the note on 2:22. *hearts.* See the note on 1:18.

3:18–19 *breadth and . . . surpasses knowledge.* The Bible uses spatial imagery in descriptions of the immensity and immeasurability of God's wisdom and knowledge (Jb 11:5–9; Rm 11:33). The same is true of God's love in Christ for it, too, exceeds all limits of human measurement (2:7; 3:8). The full dimensions of Christ's love, stretching out infinitely in every direction, cannot be grasped by the human mind (cf. Php 4:7). Yet Paul fervently prays that God will give his readers the faith and strength (Gk, "be strong enough") to know and experience the love of Christ. In fact, "to come to know God," Paul tells the Galatians, is actually "to be known by [Him]" (see note on Gal 4:9). Luther wrote,

> The whole world with all diligence has struggled to figure out what God is, what He has in mind and does. Yet the world has never been able to grasp ‹the knowledge and understanding of› any of these things. But here [in the Apostles' Creed] we have everything in richest measure. (LC II 63)

fullness of God. The Church already now shares in God's fullness (1:22). At the same time, God's fullness is yet to be fully realized—something that Paul prays will happen (3:19). We can sense here the tension between the "already" and the "not yet" which runs through the NT. What Christians now fully possess they will possess in full (1:14). See the note on 1:23.

3:20–21 Paul packaged God's redemptive plan initiated in eternity, carried out through Christ and sealed in us by the Spirit, in three songs of praise (1:6, 12, 14). As a musical composition grows in intensity, the Letter's first half now reaches its crescendo in a doxology. Paul's prayer that his readers experience personally the revelation of God's saving love flows spontaneously into praise. *more abundantly.* A Greek-English dictionary concludes that the word Paul uses here is "the highest form of comparison possible" and can best be translated "infinitely more than." Paul's point is that humans simply cannot mentally take in what God has done and is doing among us. God's love and power are so immense that we cannot even adequately pray. We need the Spirit's help (Rm 8:26–27). Luther said,

> But because he is God, he also claims the honor of giving much more and more abundantly than anyone can understand [Ephesians 3:20]. He is like an eternal, unfailing fountain. The more it pours forth and overflows, the more it continues to give. (LC III 56)

power. See the notes on 1:19, 20. *glory in the church*. This is the only NT doxology that combines the Church and Christ Jesus (cf. Rm 16:25–27; Jude 24–25). Paul prays this way because he believes that the Church is the place were God is present (2:20; see note). Yes, God is present everywhere, but He is present in grace only among His people, who assemble around Word and Sacrament (cf. Mt 18:20; 2Co 6:16–18).

Devotion and Prayer in 3:14–21 As Paul contemplates God's wisdom and the immeasurable riches of His glory among those who are in Christ Jesus, he breaks out in prayer and praise. He prays that we Christians may be strengthened in faith and grounded in love as we grow in our understanding of God's grace. He praises God for His extraordinary power at work in the Church, a power that surpasses all human understanding. Compressed in these verses is the essence of Christian worship. We worship as we receive God's saving gifts through Word and Sacrament. In them God reveals His power and grace through the death and resurrection of Christ. But we also worship as we respond in prayer and praise. • O God of glory, dwell deeply within my heart through faith, that I may offer You acceptable praise and practice Your love in my daily life. Amen.

PART 4

BAPTISM UNITES (4:1–5:21)

Baptism into One Body (4:1–16)

ESV	KJV
4 ¹I therefore, a prisoner for the Lord, urge you to walk in a manner worthy of the calling to which you have been called, ²with all humility and gentleness, with patience, bearing with one another in love, ³eager to maintain the unity of the Spirit in the bond of peace. ⁴There is one body and one Spirit—just as you were called to the one hope that belongs to your call—⁵one Lord, one faith, one baptism, ⁶one God and Father of all, who is over all and through all and in all. ⁷But grace was given to each one of us according to the measure of Christ's gift. ⁸Therefore it says, "When he ascended on high he led a host of captives, and he gave gifts to men." ⁹(In saying, "He ascended," what does it mean but that he had also descended into the lower regions, the earth? ¹⁰He who descended is the one who also ascended far above all the heavens, that he might fill all things.) ¹¹And he gave the apostles, the prophets, the evangelists, the shepherds and teachers,	4 ¹I therefore, the prisoner of the Lord, beseech you that ye walk worthy of the vocation wherewith ye are called, ²With all lowliness and meekness, with longsuffering, forbearing one another in love; ³Endeavouring to keep the unity of the Spirit in the bond of peace. ⁴There is one body, and one Spirit, even as ye are called in one hope of your calling; ⁵One Lord, one faith, one baptism, ⁶One God and Father of all, who is above all, and through all, and in you all. ⁷But unto every one of us is given grace according to the measure of the gift of Christ. ⁸Wherefore he saith, When he ascended up on high, he led captivity captive, and gave gifts unto men. ⁹(Now that he ascended, what is it but that he also descended first into the lower parts of the earth? ¹⁰He that descended is the same also that ascended up far above all heavens, that he might fill all things.) ¹¹And he gave some, apostles; and some, prophets; and some, evangelists; and some, pastors and teachers;

¹²to equip the saints for the work of ministry, for building up the body of Christ, ¹³until we all attain to the unity of the faith and of the knowledge of the Son of God, to mature manhood, to the measure of the stature of the fullness of Christ, ¹⁴so that we may no longer be children, tossed to and fro by the waves and carried about by every wind of doctrine, by human cunning, by craftiness in deceitful schemes. ¹⁵Rather, speaking the truth in love, we are to grow up in every way into him who is the head, into Christ, ¹⁶from whom the whole body, joined and held together by every joint with which it is equipped, when each part is working properly, makes the body grow so that it builds itself up in love.	¹²For the perfecting of the saints, for the work of the ministry, for the edifying of the body of Christ: ¹³Till we all come in the unity of the faith, and of the knowledge of the Son of God, unto a perfect man, unto the measure of the stature of the fulness of Christ: ¹⁴That we henceforth be no more children, tossed to and fro, and carried about with every wind of doctrine, by the sleight of men, and cunning craftiness, whereby they lie in wait to deceive; ¹⁵But speaking the truth in love, may grow up into him in all things, which is the head, even Christ: ¹⁶From whom the whole body fitly joined together and compacted by that which every joint supplieth, according to the effectual working in the measure of every part, maketh increase of the body unto the edifying of itself in love.

4:1 *therefore.* Usually at the beginning of a sentence, the Gk three letter word *oun* introduces the result of what has preceded (cf. Rm 12:1). Paul now prepares to spell out the consequences of our unity with Christ and our fellow Christians. *prisoner.* See the note on 3:1. *walk.* See the note on 2:2. *the calling.* "Those whom He predestined, He also called," Paul wrote to the Christians at Rome (Rm 8:30). Specifically, God has called us "into the fellowship of His Son, Jesus Christ, our Lord" (1Co 1:9).

4:2 These qualities are of great value for preserving unity in the Church. Consider how they measure up against their opposites (which are all self-centered): humility vs. condescending pride, gentleness vs. self-assertive rudeness, patience vs. short-tempered intolerance, forbearance vs. impatient faultfinding. With the inner strength the Spirit provides, we are faithful to our calling when we follow Christ's example. He set aside self-interest for the sake of others (Mt 11:29; 21:5; 2Co 10:1; Php 2:5–8). Inter-personal relationships are a matter of first importance (4:13–16; Col 3:12–15).

4:3 *maintain the unity.* The Holy Spirit creates the unity of the Church. Through one Baptism He calls us to one faith in one Lord. The virtues mentioned in v. 1 do not create this unity. Rather, it is through them that the unity which already exists among believers is expressed. Divisions caused by pride and lovelessness obscure this precious treasure. *bond of peace.* In love Christians are to pursue peace and harmony, which keeps them from splintering into factions and cliques that belie their unity in the Lord. The ESV's "eager" ("endeavor to" in the KJV) is actually an imperative verb that means "take pains" or "make every effort." Overcoming contentions in a congregation requires a good deal more effort than an occasional handshake!

4:4–6 The sevenfold structure of these verses has led some to suggest that Paul has drawn from an early Christian hymn or creed (see also 1Tm 3:16). It is important to note that this unit of seven "ones" contains an allusion to the three persons of the Trinity: "one Spirit" (v. 4), "one Lord" (v. 5), and "one God and Father of all" (v. 6). The poetic form of Paul's affirmation, together with its Trinitarian frame of reference, strongly reinforces his previous exhortation to preserve and manifest the Church's unity. It is also possible that the number seven itself (signifying completeness and perfection) caught the attention of some ancient readers familiar with its widespread use in the OT.

4:4 *one body.* "Body" is a central unity concept in the Letter. The whole epistle revolves around the good news that God has reconciled to Himself "in one body" both Jews and Gentiles through the cross of Christ (2:16). See the notes on 1:10, 23. *one Spirit.* The one Spirit and the one body are linked together because "in one Spirit we were all baptized into one body. . . . " (1Co 12:13; cf. Rm 12:5).

4:5 *one Lord.* In the first half of the Letter Paul calls Jesus "Lord" several times. That is because in "His great might" God raised Him from the dead and seated Him at His right hand . . . far above every rule and authority," now and in the age to come (1:20–21). Jesus is therefore "head over all things" (1:22). Luther explained what it means to call Jesus "Lord":

> But what does it mean to become Lord? It is this. He has redeemed me from sin, from the devil, from death, and from all evil. For before I did not have a Lord or King, but was captive under the devil's power. (LC II 27)

See the note on 3:11. *one faith*. In the NT "faith" can refer to the act of believing, or that which is believed (e.g., Gal 1:23; 1Tm 4:10). Paul appears to be using the term in the second sense (cf. v. 13). *one baptism*. The risen Lord Jesus Christ instituted and commanded Baptism in the name of the Triune God (Mt 28:18–20). This Baptism unites Christians with the "one Lord" Jesus Christ and with the power of His resurrection (Rm 6:1–4). Since there is only one Baptism, it is unrepeatable. Moreover, God gives His one Spirit in this one Baptism (1Co 12:13; Gal 3:26–27; 4:6–7). (Hence, what some call the "Spirit baptism" may not be separated from "water baptism," as if to say there are two Baptisms.) Christians have confessed in the Nicene Creed throughout the centuries, "I acknowledge one Baptism for the remission of sins."

4:6 *Father.* The question arises whether God's Fatherhood applies to all things (including unbelievers) or whether Paul is referring to all persons—implying in the context of Ephesians that only Christians can call God Father (note the KJV's "in you all," the believers in Ephesus). The Scriptures certainly teach that God the Father created all things (see notes on 3:14–15; also, Rm 10:12; 11:36; 1Co 8:6). But only through Christ can we know Him as, and call Him, our Father (Gal 4:6).

4:7 *the measure of Christ's gift.* Paradoxically, a family is one and many at the same time. A unity exists through marriage and parenthood, yet the family is made up of individuals with specific gifts. Similarly, a congregation is one body and many members at the same time (1Co 12:12). The one Spirit gives gifts "to each one" for the common good (1Co 12:4–11; cf. Rm 12:3–8). When each part works properly the body grows (4:16). See the note on 1:10.

4:8 Paul applies Ps 68:18 to Christ's ascent on high to give gifts to His Church. The Psalm passage refers to God's victorious ascent on Mt. Zion to receive gifts after He delivered His people from slavery in Egypt. A tradition in Judaism, with which Paul was no doubt also familiar, applied the Psalm to Moses' ascent on Mt. Sinai to receive the Law and give it to the people. On Pentecost Judaism commemorated the giving of the Law (Ps 68 was read). In light of its original intent and use, Ps 68:18 according to Paul was fulfilled in Jesus Christ who freed those captive to sin and ascended into heaven to give gifts to His people (Ac 1:8–9; 2:33). "For the law was given through Moses; grace and truth came through Jesus Christ" (Jn 1:17).

4:9 Employing a rabbinic interpretive technique, Paul comments on Ps 68:18. One element of his interpretation is difficult to interpret: that Jesus *"descended into the lower regions."* Various explanations have been put forward for these words. These include seeing a description of the descent into hell, an expression of His incarnation, or an allusion to the giving of the Spirit. A general reference to Christ's lowering Himself to become a human being seems most probable, i.e., His descent to take on the form of a servant at His incarnation (Php 2:7; Jn 3:13).

4:10 *ascended far above.* "Far above" occurs also at 1:21, where all powers in the universe are subordinated to the exalted Christ (cf. "on high," v. 8). See the notes on 1:20, 23; 2:6.

4:11 *He gave.* Paul applies Ps 68 (see note, v. 8) in a further direction. The risen and ascended Lord gives men who serve in the Office of the Public Ministry to His Church. This one Office is a divine institution, not a human arrangement. It was established by the risen Christ before His Ascension (Mt 28:18–20; Ac 20:28; 1Co 12:28; Ti 1:5). The titles and functions of those who occupy this office vary. The terminology often points to the functions assigned, even though there is no detailed list of these responsibilities. In some instances the functions or roles of these callings seem to have overlapped (cf. 1Tm 2:7; 4:13; 5:17). Paul's coupling of the first two callings (apostles and prophets) in 2:20 and 3:5 as the foundation on which the Church is built reveal that these offices were limited to the apostolic age. The apostles' teachings, which are preserved in the Holy Scriptures, are normative for the Church of all times and places. *apostles.* See the notes on 1:1; 2:20. *prophets.* The reference here is probably not to the OT prophets, but to those in the apostolic age who had received special revelation from God (Ac 11:27–28; 1Co 14:3–6, 22–32). *evangelists.* The NT mentions this office only three times (here and at Ac 2:8; 2Tm 4:5). Philip "the evangelist," one of the seven chosen to serve (Ac 6:1–6), distinguished himself by his devotion to preaching the good news (Ac 8:12, 35, 40). The early church historian Eusebius (AD 260–340) seems to have believed that evangelists assisted and followed the apostles in the work of mission preaching and founding churches. *pastors.* Although this is the only NT passage where the noun "pastor" itself (meaning "shepherd") occurs, pastors in local churches ("overseers," "elders") were assigned the responsibility of "shepherding" or "pastoring" (related verb form) the portion of God's flock placed in their charge (Ac 20:17, 28; 1Pt 5:2; cf. Ac 14:23; 1Tm 4:14; 5:17, 19). Following the model of "the Chief Shepherd" Jesus, they were to care for God's flock as they exercised oversight and administered affairs in the local congregation (1Pt 5:1–5; Jn 10:11–16; Ac 20:28). Already in the OT God is pictured as a shepherd (Gn 49:24; Ps 23:1; 80:1; 40:11) whose leaders in Israel cared for His people like shepherds (2Sm 5:2; Ezk 34:11). *teachers.* Pastors of local congregations were responsible for the authoritative transmission of apostolic doctrine (e.g., 1Tm 2:12; 3:2; 5:17; Ti 1:9; 2Tm 1:13–14). The Gk grammar raises the possibility that "pastors and teachers" refers to the same office. But the specific category of "teacher" (1Co 12:28) can also be taken to mean that some exercised a calling specifically for this task in the Church (Ac 13:1; 2Tm 1:11; Jas 3:1). St. Augustine writes, "He added teachers [to the list] that pastors might understand that teaching—*doctrina*—belongs to their office" (*Church* 158). Calvin wrote,

> It may excite surprise, that, when the gifts of the Holy Spirit form the subject of discussion, Paul should enumerate offices instead of gifts. But when men are called by God, gifts are necessarily connected with offices. God does not confer on men the mere name of Apostles or Pastors, but endows them with gifts, without which they cannot properly discharge their office. He whom God has appointed to be an apostle does not bear an empty and useless title. (Calvin, *Ephesians* 259)

4:12 *equip the saints.* God has given servants of the Word to His saints to equip them for their calling (4:1). As a soldier needs preparation for battle (6:10–17), so the saints need disciplined training for their work. Note: Some translations include a comma after this phrase to distinguish it from the following "the work of [the] ministry" (Gk has no "the") as the function of clergy (cf. KJV). Others have no comma, indicating preparation of the saints for works of service (ESV; cf. NIV). (The original Gk text had no commas.) Cogent reasons have been given for both options. *the work of ministry.* The term "ministry" (*diakonia*) or "servant" (*diakonos*) in the NT can refer to service in general (Lk 10:40; 1Co 16:17), and to the specific ministry of the Word (1Tm 1:12; Ac 6:4; Rm 11:13). While either meaning is possible in this verse, it should be noted that both Paul (4:6–7) and Tychicus (6:21) are ministers in the specific sense. *building . . . body.* See the notes on 1:10, 23.

4:13 *unity of the faith.* All believers in Christ are one with Him and each other through the faith created in their hearts by the Spirit through the Gospel. Though invisible to the human eye, Christians believe that this unity is a present reality (cf. Apostles' Creed). Paul calls on Christians as Christ's body to "maintain" (4:3) this unity by "attaining" to the unity of the faith and of the knowledge of the Son of God. They are to seek external unity in the Church through confession of the faith (apostolic teaching; see note on v. 5). Pastors play a crucial role in the quest for external unity "in the bond of peace" (4:3). Their faithful teaching promotes unity in the confession of the apostolic faith given in the Scriptures (Ti 1:9; 2:1). See the notes on vv. 2–6. *mature . . . measure . . . of Christ.* Paul moves from the preceding building imagery, "for the building up of the body of Christ" (4:12), to the dynamic image of a body growing to maturity. Christ's body grows to maturity in Him and His fullness through faithful proclamation of Law and Gospel (Col 1:28). Lutheran reformers noted, "This healing is only begun in this life. It will not be perfect until the life to come" (FC SD I 14).

4:14 *children.* No doubt Paul has in mind the immaturity, instability and vulnerability of little children—not their childlike humility (Mt 18:3)—as he makes his comparison. *tossed . . . schemes.* Studies have shown that Ephesus and surrounding cities (such as Colossae) were hotbeds of divergent philosophies and cultic beliefs. The Christians there may already have come under the deceptive influence of teachings dangerous to their new faith (note, "no longer"). Wholesome teaching counteracts susceptibility to religious trends contrary to the biblical faith. It equips Christians to recognize subterfuge and trickery when they see it (1Tm 4:6–10). Satan always plays with loaded dice and is ready to do anything to stunt the growth of Christ's body (6:11; 2Co 2:11).

4:15 *speaking the truth in love.* Truth, unity, and love are interrelated. When Christians speak the truth so that love is shown, the unity of Christ's body grows and the body "builds itself up in love" (v. 16). What does Paul mean by "speaking the truth"? Certainly in this Letter he is intent on sharing "the word of truth, the gospel of [your] salvation" (1:15), for "the truth is in Jesus" and is part of the defensive equipment Christians have in their stance against "the schemes of the devil" (6:14). Christ's love for us is to be reflected in a life that distinguishes itself by love for others (5:1–2). In this way the credibil ity of our witness to God's truth is enhanced (1Pt 1:22; 3:15). *grow.* See 2:20. When love increases in the Christian congregation you can readily see that faith is growing (2Th 1:3). Luther said,

> Through this congregation [the Holy Spirit] brings us to Christ and He teaches and preaches to us the Word [John 14:26]. By the Word He works and promotes sanctification, causing this congregation daily to grow and to become strong in the faith and its fruit, which He produces [Galatians 5]. (LC II 53)

See the note on 2:21 *head.* See the notes on 1:10, 23.

4:16 *every joint.* "Joint" translates a Gk word meaning "ligament" (cf. Col 2:19). The images of a building (2:21) and of the body (bound together and energized by joints and ligaments) both picture members of Christ's Church—pastors and people—working together so that the growth may happen. *body.* See the notes on 1:10, 23.

Devotion and Prayer in 4:1–16 In chs. 1–3 Paul has proclaimed the good news of God's grace revealed in Jesus Christ. God reconciled both Jew and Gentile in one body through the cross. He now urges believers to live a life worthy of their calling into the fellowship of God's Son. He calls on all Christians to preserve and manifest their unity with Christ and each other. To equip them for this task the victorious and ascended Lord has given to them servants of the Word. God wills that through their ministry the body of believers remain faithful to the truth, grow to maturity in Christ, and be built up in love. The Church's unity is threatened by attempts to undermine the truth of the Gospel through which our oneness in Christ is preserved, deepened, and extended. False teaching leads away from Christ, not to Him, thus endangering unity. God enables us to speak the truth in love to each other and thus strengthens us in the one faith that binds us together. • Lord teach us to love another just as You have loved us. Amen.

Baptism Clothes the Believer (4:17–32)

ESV	KJV
¹⁷Now this I say and testify in the Lord, that you must no longer walk as the Gentiles do, in the futility of their minds. ¹⁸They are darkened in their understanding, alienated from the life of God because of the ignorance that is in them, due to their hardness of heart. ¹⁹They have become callous and have given themselves up to sensuality, greedy to practice every kind of impurity. ²⁰But that is not the way you learned Christ!—²¹assuming that you have heard about him and were taught in him, as the truth is in Jesus, ²²to put off your old self, which belongs to your former manner of life and is corrupt through deceitful desires, ²³and to be renewed in the spirit of your minds, ²⁴and to put on the new self, created after the likeness of God in true righteousness and holiness. ²⁵Therefore, having put away falsehood, let each one of you speak the truth with his neighbor, for we are members one of another. ²⁶Be angry and do not sin; do not let the sun go down on your anger, ²⁷and give no opportunity to the devil. ²⁸Let the thief no longer steal, but rather let him labor, doing honest work with his own hands, so that he may have something to share with anyone in need.	¹⁷This I say therefore, and testify in the Lord, that ye henceforth walk not as other Gentiles walk, in the vanity of their mind, ¹⁸Having the understanding darkened, being alienated from the life of God through the ignorance that is in them, because of the blindness of their heart: ¹⁹Who being past feeling have given themselves over unto lasciviousness, to work all uncleanness with greediness. ²⁰But ye have not so learned Christ; ²¹If so be that ye have heard him, and have been taught by him, as the truth is in Jesus: ²²That ye put off concerning the former conversation the old man, which is corrupt according to the deceitful lusts; ²³And be renewed in the spirit of your mind; ²⁴And that ye put on the new man, which after God is created in righteousness and true holiness. ²⁵Wherefore putting away lying, speak every man truth with his neighbour: for we are members one of another. ²⁶Be ye angry, and sin not: let not the sun go down upon your wrath: ²⁷Neither give place to the devil. ²⁸Let him that stole steal no more: but rather let him labour, working with his hands the thing which is good, that he may have to give to him that needeth.

²⁹Let no corrupting talk come out of your mouths, but only such as is good for building up, as fits the occasion, that it may give grace to those who hear. ³⁰And do not grieve the Holy Spirit of God, by whom you were sealed for the day of redemption. ³¹Let all bitterness and wrath and anger and clamor and slander be put away from you, along with all malice. ³²Be kind to one another, tenderhearted, forgiving one another, as God in Christ forgave you.

²⁹Let no corrupt communication proceed out of your mouth, but that which is good to the use of edifying, that it may minister grace unto the hearers.
³⁰And grieve not the holy Spirit of God, whereby ye are sealed unto the day of redemption.
³¹Let all bitterness, and wrath, and anger, and clamour, and evil speaking, be put away from you, with all malice:
³²And be ye kind one to another, tenderhearted, forgiving one another, even as God for Christ's sake hath forgiven you.

4:17 *walk.* See the note on 2:2. *Gentiles . . . futility.* Life without Christ is spiritually pointless, empty of purpose and meaning. In Rm 1 Paul gives a similar analysis of the pagan mindset, which manifests itself most crassly in idolatry (1:21–23).

4:18–19 *darkened.* See the note on 1:18. Deep darkness, as in an underground cave, has fallen heavy on the pagan mind. It is completely incapable of spiritual and moral perception (1Co 2:14). *hardness of heart.* The pagan lifestyle reveals willful ignorance stemming from a closed and obtuse mind. Hardened unbelief stubbornly resists God's revelation of Himself in nature and in His Word (Rm 1:19–21; 2:5; cf. 11:25; Mk 3:5). *callous.* Morally insensible persons have reached the point where they are not bothered by what they are doing wrong (cf. 1Tm 4:2).

4:20–21 *learned Christ!* A disciple of Jesus learns not only about Him and His salvation, but by the Spirit is drawn into His entire way of life (note the immediate context; cf. 5:1–2; Col 2:6–7; Lk 10:16). (The Gk term for "learn" is *manthano,* from which "disciple" is derived.) *heard . . . were taught.* Paul's Gospel was all about Christ. He literally embodies the truth (Jn 14:6; Col 1:5–6; 1Co 1:23).

4:22–24 *old self.* Paul views human beings not as merely a composite of distinct parts, but as whole persons. When he refers to the "old" person, body and soul, he means the unregenerate human being as conceived and born in sin and therefore "enslaved to sin"

(Rm 6:6). Through Baptism we are united with Christ, in His death and His resurrection. Because our "old self" has been "crucified with Christ" (Rm 6:6, 10) and we have "put on" Christ (Gal 3:27; cf. Col 2:12), we have become new persons freed from the dominion of sin. Through daily repentance we can actually now "put off" our old sinful and corrupt habits, as if we are shedding an old garment and putting on a new one (Col 3:9–10). *renewed . . . minds.* Spiritual renewal is happening every day in the baptized Christian's life (the Gk verb implies continuous or ongoing action)! The "new person" created in Christ (2Co 5:17) is simultaneously and continually becoming new (2Co 4:16; cf. v. 24). This renovation occurs in our inner being (3:16), that part of us that thinks and makes decisions (Rm 12:1–2). The Lutheran reformers taught that this renewal remains incomplete in this life:

> [The Holy Spirit] renews and sanctifies them [the righteous before God through faith in Christ] and works in them love for God and for their neighbor. But the beginning of renewal is imperfect in this life. Sin still dwells in the flesh, even in the regenerate. Therefore, the righteousness of faith before God comes from the free crediting of Christ's righteousness, without the addition of our works. So our sins are forgiven us and covered and are not charged against us (Romans 4:6–8). (FC SD III 23)

put on the new self. In the Early Church, candidates for Baptism stripped and were baptized naked, after which they were clothed in white. This pictured the removal of the sinful nature and the re-clothing with Christ in Baptism (Gal 3:27; Rv 7:13–14). This early baptismal practice of removing clothing and being re-clothed acted out "being buried with Christ" (Rm 6:4; Col 2:12) and "being raised with Christ" (Col 2:12; 3:1). *likeness of God.* In keeping with what Paul had previously taught, God desires to renew or restore in fallen human beings the image in which He originally created them (Col 3:10; Gn 1:26–27). The image of God consists in "true righteousness and holiness," attributes of God Himself which were characteristic of Adam and Eve before their fall into sin. Melanchthon wrote, "Paul shows in Ephesians 5:9 and Colossians 3:10 that the image of God is the knowledge of God, righteousness, and truth" (Ap II 20). As in the beginning (Gn 1), the new self comes into being as a result of God's creative act (2:10).

4:25 *having put away falsehood.* Paul now answers the prover-
bial "what does this mean?" question. That is, what does it mean for
Christians to discard the old way of life (note "therefore")? He zeroes
in on specific behavior that threatens to tear the fabric of their common life. Having "put off" the old self through Baptism into Christ,
the individual believer must get rid of (same verb as v. 22) conduct
the old self likes to do. First on the list is lying, which undermines
trust. Many marriages fall apart when one lie is stacked on top of another. Lying has a similar effect on other relationships as well. *neighbor.* Paul applies the OT exhortation in Zec 8:16 (where "neighbor"
means fellow Israelite) to the fellow Christian.

4:26 Ps 4:4 serves Paul well to show that anger, a common human emotion, can easily lead to sin (Jas 1:19–20). "Don't go to bed
angry" is biblically grounded advice for those who tend to let their
anger simmer like a glowing ember. Calvin wrote,

> There are three faults by which we offend God in being angry. The
> first is, when our anger arises from slight causes, and often from
> no cause whatever, or at least from private injuries or offences.
> The second is, when we go beyond the proper bounds, and are
> hurried into intemperate excesses. The third is, when our anger,
> which ought to have been directed against ourselves or against
> sins, is turned against our brethren. (Calvin, *Ephesians* 281)

4:27 Do not give the devil a chance to exert his influence. Paul
exposes the devil's methodology (6:11), whereby he uses anger as an
incubator to hatch other sins in a person's life (v. 31; 1Pt 5:8).

4:28 Evidently "the former manner of life" (v. 22) of some included the habit of stealing and its accompanying vice, indolence or
habitual laziness. The opposite of thievery is productive work, which
enables a person to carry out social responsibilities beneficial to others (1Th 4:11; 2Th 3:6–13; Ti 3:1).

4:29 Rotten food (Gk *sapros*) does not contribute positively to a
person's health (Mt 7:17–18)! Unwholesome speech does damage to
relationships. People become soured on one another. What comes
out of the mouth not only defiles the person speaking (Mt 15:18), but
contaminates other hearts. *give grace.* Good and appropriate speech,
as opposed to unkind and vulgar talk, builds people up. It reflects
"the goodness and kindness of God our Savior" (Ti 3:4; v. 32) and
edifies the Church (v. 16).

4:30 *grieve the Holy Spirit.* As noted earlier, the Holy Spirit creates the Church's unity, which is to be manifested in the bond of peace (vv. 3–4). Christians "are being built together into a dwelling place for God by the Spirit" (2:20). Both Jews and Gentiles, who are members of Christ's body, have access to the Father "in one Spirit" (2:18). Conduct like that previously mentioned works directly at cross-purposes with the Spirit's gracious work. Sins that divide and alienate Christians from one another therefore cause Him great sadness and distress. Paul may be alluding to Is 63:10 where Israel by her rebellion in the wilderness "grieved his Holy Spirit." As the Lutheran reformers remind us, "When the baptized act against their conscience, allowing sin to rule in them, they grieve the Holy Spirit in them and lose Him" (FC SD II 69). *sealed for the day of redemption.* See the notes on 1:13–14.

4:31–32 God's forgiveness in Christ is the best antidote against sins that poison relationships among Christians. Anger especially endangers harmony because it so easily mounts up in the sinful heart. It typically begins with brooding resentment and finally can explode in unrestrained, heated outbursts of rage—fed by mean-spiritedness. Christ's forgiveness becomes the power and model for the Christ-like life. The verbs Paul uses vividly portray the life-pattern of a Christian touched by God's kindness: "put away" (v. 31; remove or extract the sin) and "be" (Gk "become," what you are, a forgiven sinner). Perhaps the main point of Paul's summary in vv. 31–32 can be best illustrated by the similarity of sound when Greeks pronounced the words "Christ" (*christos*) and "kindness" (*chrestos*). Nothing "binds everything together in perfect harmony" (Col 3:14) like the tenderheartedness we have come to know in our Lord Jesus.

Devotion and Prayer in 4:17–32 The Ephesians had "learned Christ" from Paul (v. 21). He taught them God's truth about the unsearchable riches of God's grace in Jesus Christ that transformed their lives. With the tenderheartedness of Jesus, Paul urges Christians to make their sinful habits a thing of the past and to become the new persons that they already are in Christ. God is restoring His image in them by the Spirit. We Christians know well that our sinful nature still hangs on to us during our entire life. Thus we need daily to repent, to "put off" the sins of our "old self" and to "put on" the "true righteousness and holiness" of the "new self" (v. 24). Luther wrote:

[Baptism] signifies that the old Adam in us should, by daily contrition and repentance, be drowned and die with all sins and evil lusts. And also it shows that a new man should daily come forth and arise, who shall live before God in righteousness and purity forever. (SC IV)

To God's good pleasure (Php 2:13), the new life in Christ preserves and restores harmony in the church. • Father, forgive us our sins, that we may forgive those who sin against us. Amen.

Baptism Directs the Believer's Walk (5:1–14)

ESV	KJV
5 ¹Therefore be imitators of God, as beloved children. ²And walk in love, as Christ loved us and gave himself up for us, a fragrant offering and sacrifice to God. ³But sexual immorality and all impurity or covetousness must not even be named among you, as is proper among saints. ⁴Let there be no filthiness nor foolish talk nor crude joking, which are out of place, but instead let there be thanksgiving. ⁵For you may be sure of this, that everyone who is sexually immoral or impure, or who is covetous (that is, an idolater), has no inheritance in the kingdom of Christ and God. ⁶Let no one deceive you with empty words, for because of these things the wrath of God comes upon the sons of disobedience. ⁷Therefore do not become partners with them; ⁸for at one time you were darkness, but now you are light in the Lord. Walk as children of light ⁹(for the fruit of light is found in all that is good and right and true),	5 ¹Be ye therefore followers of God, as dear children; ²And walk in love, as Christ also hath loved us, and hath given himself for us an offering and a sacrifice to God for a sweetsmelling savour. ³But fornication, and all uncleanness, or covetousness, let it not be once named among you, as becometh saints; ⁴Neither filthiness, nor foolish talking, nor jesting, which are not convenient: but rather giving of thanks. ⁵For this ye know, that no whoremonger, nor unclean person, nor covetous man, who is an idolater, hath any inheritance in the kingdom of Christ and of God. ⁶Let no man deceive you with vain words: for because of these things cometh the wrath of God upon the children of disobedience. ⁷Be not ye therefore partakers with them. ⁸For ye were sometimes darkness, but now are ye light in the Lord: walk as children of light: ⁹(For the fruit of the Spirit is in all goodness and righteousness and truth;)

¹⁰and try to discern what is pleasing to the Lord. ¹¹Take no part in the unfruitful works of darkness, but instead expose them. ¹²For it is shameful even to speak of the things that they do in secret. ¹³But when anything is exposed by the light, it becomes visible, ¹⁴for anything that becomes visible is light. Therefore it says, "Awake, O sleeper, and arise from the dead, and Christ will shine on you."	¹⁰Proving what is acceptable unto the Lord. ¹¹And have no fellowship with the unfruitful works of darkness, but rather reprove them. ¹²For it is a shame even to speak of those things which are done of them in secret. ¹³But all things that are reproved are made manifest by the light: for whatsoever doth make manifest is light. ¹⁴Wherefore he saith, Awake thou that sleepest, and arise from the dead, and Christ shall give thee light.

5:1 *imitators of God.* Paul now summarizes the previous verses. With attentive eyes children observe what their parents do and imitate them (at times even to their parents' dismay!). God's adopted sons (1:5; Gal 4:5) not only do what He says but also what He does—unlike the parent who says to a child, "do as I say not as I do." Jesus taught: "Be merciful, even as your Father is merciful" (Lk 6:36). The Father's love shines through us. Paul was even bold to say that the Thessalonians "became imitators" of him and "of the Lord" (1Th 1:6; 1Co 11:1; cf. Eph 4:24).

5:2 *walk.* See the note on 2:2. Jews trained in rabbinic schools (like Paul) followed their teacher in word and deed ("walk after," in Hbr *halak achare*). *as Christ loved us.* Believers are to forgive each other "as God in Christ forgave [them]" (4:32). Thus to imitate God is to imitate Christ. But believers do not simply emulate Christ's exemplary loving behavior—which most moralists would likely be willing to urge. Much more, Christians are enabled to love because of what Christ has done for them (Gal 2:20). "We love *because* He [God] loved us" (1Jn 4:19). *offering and sacrifice.* Christ loved us by sacrificing Himself once and for all (unlike OT sacrifices) to "put away" our sin (Heb 9:26).

Introduction to 5:3–14 In Paul's ethical appeal self-sacrificial love (vv. 1–2) and self-indulgence—especially in various forms of sexual immorality—stand in sharp opposition (note the word "But" in v. 3 signifying a contrast). Sexual immorality and vulgar talk about it (cf. 1Th 4:3–7) lie in the background of the darkness/light discussion in vv. 8–14.

5:3–4 *covetousness.* When Paul catalogues pagan vices, he often associates sexual immorality and greed (1Co 5:10–1; 6:9–10; Col 3:5). Lust and avarice pair up in the sinful heart to seek to have a "neighbor's wife" (or husband; cf. the Tenth Commandment). *not even be named . . . talk.* Christians, in their attitudes and conversation, should not regard such sins as acceptable in their midst. Obscene and boorish talk as well not only exceeds the bounds of propriety among Christians but can create a toxic atmosphere for further sin (v. 12; 4:29; Mt 15:18–19; Jas 3:2–8). *thanksgiving.* Before addressing marriage in vv. 22–33, Paul caps vv. 1–21 with a call to thanksgiving. We have here the hallmark of the Christian life (5:20). Lust and greed are forms of idolatry (v. 5), for they entail worship of the creation rather than the Creator (Rm 1:21, 25). But thanksgiving recognizes God as the Giver of every good and perfect gift (Jas 1:17; including sex and possessions).

5:5 *sexually immoral . . . covetous . . . idolater.* Paul did not relax God's standards to accommodate the surrounding culture. Instead, he warned that those locked into the lifestyle described by these words cannot inherit the kingdom of God. This is not an isolated warning in the Pauline Letters (e.g., 1Co 6:9–10; Gal 5:21). Paul appeals to Christians to avoid the oft-listed pagan vices, so that they don't slip back into their old ways. In the words of 1 Corinthians, Christians are "washed [baptized]. . . . sanctified . . . justified" (1Co 6:11). Their "virtues" come under the title "the fruit of the Spirit" (Gal 5:22ff.). *inheritance.* See the notes on 1:5, 11.

5:6 *empty words.* Deceivers use plausible-sounding arguments to justify immoral conduct and diminish the seriousness of sin. However persuasive these arguments may seem, Paul calls them "empty" because they are without substance and, worse still, not based on God's truth. *sons of disobedience.* See the note on 2:2.

5:7 *do not associate with them.* The Gk word for "associate with" (in NT, only here and 3:6) means to have a share with someone in some possession or relationship. We are not to participate in someone's sinful deeds, that is, "throw in" with them. Paul recognizes, of course, that we cannot completely remove ourselves from contact with immoral persons, "since then you would need to go out of the world" (1Co 5:10).

5:8 *darkness . . . light.* See the note on 1:18. Christians "are" light because of their relation to Jesus ("in the Lord"), who is "the light of the world" (Jn 8:12). *Walk.* See the note on 2:2. *children.* See the note on 1:5.

5:9 *fruit.* In this verse "fruit" and "light" are joined together as "product" is to "power." Similarly, in Gal 5:22 the Spirit produces the product or fruit (note the singular, like a cluster of grapes). Truly, Christians have a productive life filled with good words and deeds that flow naturally from their union with Christ (Jn 15:1–8; Col 1:10).

5:10 *discern.* Those who have "learned Christ" make it their aim to please Him (2Co 5:9) by consciously determining a course of action in keeping with the standards set forth in God's Word (Rm 12:2; Php 1:9–10; 1Th 5:21).

5:11 *Take no part.* See the note on v. 7. *unfruitful works of darkness.* Such works (e.g., immorality) are of no use. The Spirit produces good "fruit" yielding beneficial results (Mt 7:17; Gal 5:19–21; 22–23). *expose them.* The term (Gk *elengcho*) usually means "convince" or "convict" (e.g., Ti 1:9, 13). Sinful deeds are to be exposed and confronted for what they are in order to bring about repentance (v. 13; Jn 3:20; 16:8).

5:12 See the note on v. 3. All you have to do is mention that there are secret sins to show how shameful they are.

5:13–14a *visible is light.* Cf. v. 8. Light exposes sin, but it also gives life and enlightenment (cf. Jn 1:4, 6–9; 3:19–21; 8:12). The words and deeds of Christians reveal the ugly reality of sin. But the light of the Gospel also shines through them (cf. 2Co 4:4, 6).

5:14b We do not know this quotation's source. Some commentators suggest that it may have been part of an early baptismal hymn (cf. v. 19) echoing OT themes (Is 26:19; 60:1–2). Perhaps it was a call to a baptismal candidate. *Awake.* The immediate context suggests sinners are being called to rise up from the sleep of sin and death. Through Baptism, Christ has already raised us up from death to life (Rm 6:4; Eph 2:1–6). Now we must remain awake as we await the our Lord's coming. Since Christians are "children of light . . . not of the night or of the darkness," they must not sleep as others do, but "keep awake" (1Th 5:5–6). *shine on you.* God has "shown in our hearts to give us the light of the glory of God in the face of Jesus Christ." That is a saving knowledge of Christ (2Co 4:6; see note, 1:18; Is 9:2; Lk 2:32). Calvin wrote, "The allusion . . . is to the prophecies which

relate to Christ's kingdom; such as that of Isaiah [60:1], 'Arise, shine; for thy light is come, and the glory of the Lord is risen upon thee' "
(Calvin, *Ephesians* 296).

The Liturgy of the Spirit (5:15–21)

ESV	KJV
[15]Look carefully then how you walk, not as unwise but as wise, [16]making the best use of the time, because the days are evil. [17]Therefore do not be foolish, but understand what the will of the Lord is. [18]And do not get drunk with wine, for that is debauchery, but be filled with the Spirit, [19]addressing one another in psalms and hymns and spiritual songs, singing and making melody to the Lord with your heart, [20]giving thanks always and for everything to God the Father in the name of our Lord Jesus Christ, [21]submitting to one another out of reverence for Christ.	[15]See then that ye walk circumspectly, not as fools, but as wise, [16]Redeeming the time, because the days are evil. [17]Wherefore be ye not unwise, but understanding what the will of the Lord is. [18]And be not drunk with wine, wherein is excess; but be filled with the Spirit; [19]Speaking to yourselves in psalms and hymns and spiritual songs, singing and making melody in your heart to the Lord; [20]Giving thanks always for all things unto God and the Father in the name of our Lord Jesus Christ; [21]Submitting yourselves one to another in the fear of God.

5:15 *walk.* See the note on 2:2. Living wisely requires close attention to God's will (v. 10, 17).

5:16 *best use of the time.* Time is a precious commodity not to be wasted. Paul is saying, "take advantage of the opportunities that come your way" as you live wisely (unlike an "unwise" life full of missed opportunities; cf. Gal 1:4). *days are evil.* Although Christ has given Himself for our sins to "deliver us from the present evil age" (Gal 6:10), Christians are to make the most of the time they have because the "forces of evil" are still actively set against them (6:12; 2Tm 3:1). Bengel wrote,

> The days, says Paul, are evil, and are in the power of wicked men, not in your own power. Wherefore, since you see that you are hard pressed, endeavour, until the hostile intervals of this unhappy period pass away, to pass through and spend your time,

if not with profit, at least without loss, which is done by keeping quiet, or at least by acting with moderation. (Bengel 105)

5:17 *foolish.* Foolish persons lack good judgment when it comes to the consequences of their actions. The "foolish virgins" in Mt 15:1–13 did not consider in advance the result of not taking with them a supply of oil for their lamps and therefore were unwise. Wise Christians give careful thought to how God's will applies to them.

5:18 *drunk.* Like sexual immorality and greed, drunkenness belongs among the "unfruitful works of darkness" (v. 11; 1Th 5:1–8). Drunkenness appears in NT lists of the sins notoriously present among pagans. Christians must dissociate themselves from such conduct (Rm 12:12–13; 1Co 5:9–11; 6:9–11; 1Pt 4:1–6; cf. 1Tm 3:8; Ti 2:3). There is no indication that this problem existed specifically in the congregation at Ephesus, or surrounding churches. But drunkenness could and did occur in a Christian gathering. Paul had to sternly address the issue in 1 Corinthians in connection with the way the Lord's Supper was being celebrated (1Co 11:20–22). *debauchery.* Excessive use of alcohol leads to a loss of good sense and to reckless and unbridled behavior (Ti 1:6; 1Pt 4:4). *filled . . . Spirit.* Paul exhorts all Christians to be filled with the Holy Spirit. In the present context he means that they should live Christian lives by the Spirit's power. Christians are already filled with the fullness of Christ (1:23; 3:19), and sealed by the Spirit (1:13); now they must manifest His presence in them (2:22) in their life and worship (vv. 19–20).

5:19 Boisterous and unruly parties, as well as crude language (v. 4), must give way instead to wholesome and edifying worship under the Spirit's influence. Those who attend Christian worship services can expect to find an atmosphere entirely different from what one would find in taverns and banquets where excessive drinking takes place. *psalms . . . hymns . . . songs.* Attempts have been made to distinguish between these terms, but they are virtually synonymous. They all belong to the general category "songs of praise." "Psalm" would be very familiar to those accustomed to OT forms of worship rooted in the Book of Psalms (cf. Lk 20:42; 24:44; Ac 1:20; 13:33). "Hymns" and "songs," though also recalling OT worship (e.g., Is 42:10), have a distinctively Christian content in the NT (cf. 5:14b; Col 3:16; Rv 5:9–10; 14:3). *spiritual.* Those "filled with the Spirit" (v. 18) worship with Spirit-inspired ascriptions of praise (cf. 1:3–14). When gathered for worship, Christians "speak" from the bottom of their hearts in two directions: to "one another" and "to the Lord." In a parallel Colossians text Paul writes that singing can serve as a means of teaching and admonishing in the Christian assemblies (3:16).

5:20 *giving thanks.* Thanksgiving not only permeates public worship. It is a constant attitude of the heart expressed in all circumstances.

5:21 *submitting.* This is the fifth in a series of five "—ing" words explaining what it means to "be filled with the Spirit" (v. 19). "Submitting" serves as a "hinge" or link to v. 22 (which in Gk does not contain the verb "submit"). Translators have rightly supplied the word "submit" in v. 22, where Paul proceeds to explain what submission means within the divinely arranged relationship of husband and wife (see note on v. 22). Spouses honor their God-given responsibilities in marriage by looking out for each others' interests (Gal 5:13; Php 2:2; cf. 1Pt 5:5).

Devotion and Prayer in 5:1–21 Mindful of Christ's self-giving love and their new status as God's "children of light," Christians must resist pressures to take part in sinful behavior. Sexual immorality, greed, drunkenness and crude language are also among the public sins in our society. These vices not only are commonplace, but they receive public approval (cf. Rm 1:32). Conduct regarded as "mainstream" becomes "the new normal." Sadly, such sins make an agony of life with others. Through His Word God enables us to recognize evil when we see it. He helps us to make wise choices with the help and guidance of His Spirit. We are moved to thank God continually in all circumstances. We join our fellow-Christians in public worship as we praise God our Father for the grace and forgiveness we have in Christ Jesus. In our struggle against temptation, we can rely on Christ's Word and Spirit to lead us. • Lord, strengthen me to speak and act according to what pleases You. Amen.

PART 5

BAPTISM REORDERS RELATIONSHIPS (5:22–6:9)

Husband and Wife (5:22–33)

ESV	KJV
22Wives, submit to your own husbands, as to the Lord. 23For the husband is the head of the wife even as Christ is the head of the church, his body, and is himself its Savior. 24Now as the church submits to Christ, so also wives should submit in everything to their husbands. 25Husbands, love your wives, as Christ loved the church and gave himself up for her, 26that he might sanctify her, having cleansed her by the washing of water with the word, 27so that he might present the church to himself in splendor, without spot or wrinkle or any such thing, that she might be holy and without blemish. 28In the same way husbands should love their wives as their own bodies. He who loves his wife loves himself. 29For no one ever hated his own flesh, but nourishes and cherishes it, just as Christ does the church, 30because we are members of his body.	22Wives, submit yourselves unto your own husbands, as unto the Lord. 23For the husband is the head of the wife, even as Christ is the head of the church: and he is the saviour of the body. 24Therefore as the church is subject unto Christ, so let the wives be to their own husbands in every thing. 25Husbands, love your wives, even as Christ also loved the church, and gave himself for it; 26That he might sanctify and cleanse it with the washing of water by the word, 27That he might present it to himself a glorious church, not having spot, or wrinkle, or any such thing; but that it should be holy and without blemish. 28So ought men to love their wives as their own bodies. He that loveth his wife loveth himself. 29For no man ever yet hated his own flesh; but nourisheth and cherisheth it, even as the Lord the church: 30For we are members of his body, of his flesh, and of his bones.

[31]"Therefore a man shall leave his father and mother and hold fast to his wife, and the two shall become one flesh." [32]This mystery is profound, and I am saying that it refers to Christ and the church. [33]However, let each one of you love his wife as himself, and let the wife see that she respects her husband.	[31]For this cause shall a man leave his father and mother, and shall be joined unto his wife, and they two shall be one flesh. [32]This is a great mystery: but I speak concerning Christ and the church. [33]Nevertheless let every one of you in particular so love his wife even as himself; and the wife see that she reverence her husband.

Introduction to 5:22–6:9 In the Greco-Roman world a form of moral instruction called the "household code" appears quite often in the literature. These household rules outlined the duties of husbands and wives, parents and children, and masters and slaves. Paul employed similar household codes in his instruction (here and at Col 3:18–4:1; cf. 1Pt 2:13–3:7). For Paul the Gospel did not overturn the various structures that order our life in this world but reinterpreted and gave new meaning to them. In his "tables of duties" Paul uses phrases like "as to the Lord" (v. 22), "in the Lord" (6:1; cf. Col 3:18), "pleases the Lord" (Col 3:20), "fearing the Lord" (Col 3:22), and "serving the Lord" (Col 3:23). Indeed, it is "reverence for Christ" (5:21) that governs how Christians regard, and serve in, their various callings. For Christ's sake it is an honor for them to accept willingly the duties and responsibilities of their positions in life. They also humbly follow their Lord who ranked His interests beneath the needs of others (Php 2:3–5). See Luther's Table of Duties (*Haustafeln,* "house tables") in the SC.

5:22 *submit.* The Gk term *hypotasso* means literally "to place under." It occurs 38 times in the NT, each occurrence of which must be read carefully within its context. In this passage it means "subject oneself to" or "be subjected to," and involves recognition of an ordered structure (cf. 1Pt 3:1–6). Wives are to submit themselves to their husbands *as to the Lord.* This is not a submission imposed by the man on the woman from a position of superior authority or power. Significantly, nowhere does Scripture say that power or authority or rule is given to the man over the woman. Their relationship is grounded in an arrangement instituted by God to which both of them are subject (Gn 3:16 is a reference to the arrangement and not a command for the husband to dominate his wife by force). This creational pattern is not abrogated by the general principle of Christian conduct in the church in v. 21. It is important to distinguish our assigned roles in life from the manner and spirit in which we carry them out—willingly and with concern for another's well-being.

5:23 *head.* The term "head" occurs two other times in Ephesians. Christ is declared to be "head over all things" (1:22). To grow "into Christ" is to grow into "the head" of the Church, which is His body (4:15). Christ's headship involves rule over all things. As the Church's Head, He is its Savior and Leader whom His disciples follow (Ac 5:31; Jn 8:12). Christ's headship of the Church is the reason (note the word "for") why wives submit to their husbands. Paul is saying that the husband's "headship" in marriage, in keeping with God's design in creation, is to reflect the Lord's headship of His body the Church (1Co 11:3). Although only Christ is the Savior, the husband follows Christ's example when he "nourishes and cherishes" his wife (v. 29). It should not be inferred from Paul's words that the husband is superior to his wife or intrinsically better than her.

5:24 *church submits to Christ.* The Church willingly and whole-heartedly submits herself to Christ, for He gave Himself in love for her (vv. 2, 24) and continues to sustain and nourish her as His very own body (v. 29). The risen and reigning Lord has done and continues to do everything for the benefit of His Church (1:22). The Church's willing and unforced submission to Christ serves as a model for the wife's voluntary submission to her husband. An autocratic and domineering attitude on the husband's part—which stems from the fall into sin, not from God's design in creation—erodes and can even destroy a wife's loving relationship to her husband.

5:25 *love.* Ancient household codes did not list love for one's wife as a husband's duty. They only told husbands to make their wives submit to them. Paul radically qualifies and subverts the surrounding culture's values by going far beyond them. He directs Christian husbands to love their wives. Conspicuously absent is any command that the husband rule over his wife (cf. Col 3:19). *as Christ loved the church.* The OT depicts God's covenant relationship with His people Israel as a marriage in which He is devoted to them with steadfast love (e.g., Is 54:5; Jer 2:1–3; 31:31–32; Hos 1–3). Christ, the Bridegroom (Mk 2:18–20; cf. Jn 3:29; 2Co 11:2; Rv 21:9), loved His bride the Church so much that He gave up His life for her. The term "give up" occurs numerous times in the NT, not only to describe the betrayal of Christ (e.g., Mt 26:15, 25, 46, 48; Ac 3:13), but also His voluntary submission to suffering and death on behalf of His bride (Rm 4:25; 8:32; Gal 2:20; Ti 2:14). Christ's love was no mere emotion, but an act of the will. Paul applies to marriage his general appeal that Christians love one another (3:17; 4:2, 15, 16; 5:2). God commands husbands to be imitators of Christ and walk in His kind of love. The husband who loves his wife with a Christ-like love will be willing to give up his very life for her (1Jn 3:16). Calvin wrote,

> This is intended to express the strong affection which husbands ought to have for their wives, though he takes occasion, immediately afterwards, to commend the grace of Christ. Let husbands imitate Christ in this respect, that he scrupled not to die for his church. One peculiar consequence, indeed, which resulted from his death,—that by it he redeemed his church,—is altogether beyond the power of men to imitate. (Calvin, *Ephesians* 302)

5:26 *washing of water with the word.* Other NT texts refer to Baptism as a "washing." Ananias tells Paul after his conversion, "Rise and be baptized and wash away your sins, calling on His [Jesus'] name" (Ac 22:16). God saved us, writes Paul to Titus, "by the washing of regeneration and renewal of the Holy Spirit" (Ti 3:5). In a close parallel with 5:26, Paul recalls in 1Co 6:11 that the Christians at Corinth "were washed . . . sanctified . . . justified in the name of the Lord Jesus Christ and by the Spirit of our God" (cf. Ac 2:38). In an unmistakable reference to Baptism, Paul presents the purpose of Christ's self-sacrifice: that Christ's bride, the Church be sanctified and cleansed through Baptism (cf. Jn 3:3–6; 1Pt 3:21). *word.* Luther wrote,

> It is not the water indeed that does them, but the Word of God, which is in and with the water, and faith, which trusts this Word of God in the water. For without the Word of God the water is simple water and no Baptism. But with the Word of God it is a Baptism, that is, a gracious water of life and a washing of regeneration in the Holy Spirit. (SC IV; cf. Ti 3:5–8)

See Mt 28:19.

5:27 *holy and without blemish.* Through Christ's reconciling work on the cross, God has presented believers to Himself "holy and blameless and above reproach" (Col 1:22). Through Baptism God has cleansed them, forgiving their sins (Ac 2:28). They are blameless and without fault, brilliant in their purity like a bride adorned in splendor (cf. Ezk 16:8–14; Rv 21:2, 9–11). What believers already are in Christ they are now to become. God has "redeemed" His people from "all iniquity" and purified (Gk, "cleansed") them for Himself "zealous for good works" (i.e., for a life of sanctification; Ti 2:14; 3:4–7; Eph 2:10). See the note on 1:4.

5:28 *as their own bodies.* The "body" (and "flesh"; v. 29) equals "self." People are embodied persons. When husband and wife become "one flesh" in marriage (Gn 2:24), their union is not merely physical; it is a union of two persons (though yet distinct). Hence, when a husband loves his wife he loves himself by virtue of this personal union (cf. v. 33).

5:29 *nourishes.* The husband who imitates Christ's loving care for the Church seeks to fulfill his wife's needs. He does not harm her or neglect her, just as he does not harm or neglect his own body.

5:30 *members.* Christ cares for His body (the Church), of which each of us is a member. In 4:25 "we are members of one another" obligates us to speak the truth with our neighbor. See also the notes on 1:23.

5:31–32 Referring to Gn 2:24, which describes the institution of marriage, Paul says expressly that in the first instance he has in mind the unity of Christ and the Church (v. 32). The oneness of Christ and His body the Church is central to the mystery that God has revealed in the Gospel (see note on 1:9). In marriage God has created an institution that pictures profoundly the union of Christ and His body, whose members are one with Him and each other. At the same time, unity of Christ and the Church serves as a model for the relationship of husband and wife.

5:33 Paul now summarizes the main point of the preceding discussion. Addressing each husband first, he commands him to love his wife. He then exhorts each wife to respect her husband. When both husband and wife love and respect each other their oneness grows and deepens. Christian spouses are thus putting into practice the foundational principle of the Second Table of the Law (which includes the Sixth Commandment): "You shall love your neighbor as yourself" (Lv 19:18; Mt 22:39). Luther said, "Everyone should live chaste in thought, word, and deed in his condition—that is, especially in the estate of marriage. But also everyone should love and value the spouse God gave to him" (LC I 219).

Devotion and Prayer in 5:22–33 Paul taught the churches he founded that marriage is a divine institution designed by our Creator to be a blessing to humankind and to be held in honor by all. In these verses—the most extended discussion of marriage in the NT—he presents God's will for the proper relationship of husband and wife according to the Creator's intent. He urges Christian wives to submit themselves to their husbands and to respect them. He urges husbands to love their wives as themselves and to follow the example of Christ who loved the Church and gave Himself up for her. God's design for marriage is subverted when spouses fail to love and respect each other as persons and pursue only their selfish interests. The apostle begins ch. five by urging his readers to "be imitators of God" and to "walk in love, as Christ loved us and gave Himself up for us" (5:1–2). Christ's steadfast and forgiving love enables husbands and wives to fulfill God's intent for marriage. With God's help spouses can carry out their responsibilities toward each other by not looking out only for themselves but by caring for one another as Christ nourished and cherished His bride, the Church. • Heavenly Father, teach all husbands and wives to love and honor each other, as Your Son loved and gave Himself up for us all. Amen.

Parents and Children (6:1–4)

ESV	KJV
6 ¹Children, obey your parents in the Lord, for this is right. ²"Honor your father and mother" (this is the first commandment with a promise), ³"that it may go well with you and that you may live long in the land." ⁴Fathers, do not provoke your children to anger, but bring them up in the discipline and instruction of the Lord.	6 ¹Children, obey your parents in the Lord: for this is right. ²Honour thy father and mother; which is the first commandment with promise; ³That it may be well with thee, and thou mayest live long on the earth. ⁴And, ye fathers, provoke not your children to wrath: but bring them up in the nurture and admonition of the Lord.

6:1 *obey*. Paul addresses children directly as Christians. They are to obey their parents (Gk *hypakouo*), defining their responsibility within the family structure. *in the Lord*. See the note on 5:22–6:9. *right*. Jewish and Greco-Roman writers were unanimous in prescribing that children honor and obey their parents. But for Paul a child's obedience is not just the right thing to do. This "pleases the Lord" (Col 3:20).

6:2 *promise.* Christian children can expect God's blessings on earth when they obey God's commandment to honor their parents (Ex 20:12; Dt 5:16; cf. 1Tm 4:8). Luther explained how this promise extends beyond individual well-being or prosperity:

> Here, then, you have learned the fruit and the reward, that who-ever keeps this commandment shall have happy days, fortune, and prosperity. . . . For to have long life in the sense of the Scriptures is not only to become old, but to have everything that belongs to long life: health, wife, children, livelihood, peace, good gov-ernment, and so on. Without these things this life can neither be enjoyed in cheerfulness nor long endure. . . . Experience teaches that where there are honorable, old families who do well and have many children, they certainly owe their origin to the fact that some of them were brought up well and were full of regard for their parents. (LC I 134, 138)

6:3 *live long in the land.* When quoting the Fourth Command-ment from the LXX Paul omits the words "that the LORD your God is giving you" (Ex 20:12; Dt 5:16). The "promise" in the OT context was tied to the land of Israel. By omitting these words Paul intentionally applies the promise of well-being to earthly life in general. Christians enjoy this life (and its blessings) not merely for its own sake, but in light of their eternal inheritance as they give praise to God (1:14; 3:6; see note on 1:11).

6:4 In Paul's day Greco-Roman fathers had absolute power and control over their children. Children's' education often included ex-cessively harsh discipline. Training and discipline of children that is distinctively Christian requires parental self-control and restraint (especially of one's temper). Parents must realize that they represent the Lord ("of the Lord"). *provoke.* Parental vindictiveness, unfair de-mands, incessant nagging, arbitrariness, cruel outbursts of anger, sar-casm and ridicule—and even fawning over-indulgence—are among the several ways that children become disheartened and filled with resentment (Col 3:21; cf. Rm 10:19). *discipline and instruction.* Rais-ing children requires a proper mix of correction and godly training (cf. 2Tm 3:16; Ti 2:12; 2Co 6:9). The words "bring them up" (Gk *trepho*, literally, "feed") can mean "nourish" (cf. 5:29). Christian par-ents are to see their children above all as members of God's family.

The Lord, one might say, "cherishes and nourishes" them through their parents (5:29). And, just as the Lord disciplines His children for their good because He loves them, so Christian parents discipline their children out of loving concern for them (Pr 3:11–12; Heb 12:5, 7, 8, 11). Again, Luther reminded parents,

> . . . [W]e must spare no diligence, time, or cost in teaching and educating our children, so that they may serve God and the world. We must not think only about how we may amass money and possessions for them. God can indeed support and make them rich without us, as He daily does. But for this purpose He has given us children and issued this command: we should train and govern them according to His will. (LC I 172–73)

Masters and Servants (6:5–9)

ESV	KJV
[5]Slaves, obey your earthly masters with fear and trembling, with a sincere heart, as you would Christ, [6]not by the way of eye-service, as people-pleasers, but as servants of Christ, doing the will of God from the heart, [7]rendering service with a good will as to the Lord and not to man, [8]knowing that whatever good anyone does, this he will receive back from the Lord, whether he is a slave or free. [9]Masters, do the same to them, and stop your threatening, knowing that he who is both their Master and yours is in heaven, and that there is no partiality with him.	[5]Servants, be obedient to them that are your masters according to the flesh, with fear and trembling, in singleness of your heart, as unto Christ; [6]Not with eyeservice, as menpleasers; but as the servants of Christ, doing the will of God from the heart; [7]With good will doing service, as to the Lord, and not to men: [8]Knowing that whatsoever good thing any man doeth, the same shall he receive of the Lord, whether he be bond or free. [9]And, ye masters, do the same things unto them, forbearing threatening: knowing that your Master also is in heaven; neither is there respect of persons with him.

6:5 *Slaves.* Paul also addresses slaves directly as full members of the Church. Without questioning the institution of slavery—which was widespread in antiquity—he describes how slave owners and slaves alike are to serve their Lord within this social structure. *masters.* Paul uses the Gk word "lord" (*kyrios*) for the slave owner in this verse, and for the Lord Jesus in v. 9. The word play highlights the truth that the "lords" also have a "Lord" whom all Christians are to serve in whatever positions they find themselves.

6:6 *eye-service.* When slaves act this way, they serve only for the sake of appearances to make an impression on someone. Especially a slave accused of being lazy would be tempted to appear busy when the master was looking. Paul calls on the slaves to serve their masters with the pure motives, "doing the will of God from the heart" (Gk *psyche*, the inner being; v. 7). *servants of Christ.* The term translated "servants" in this verse is identical to the word for "slaves" in v. 5. This implies that the slaves in the Ephesian congregation are to consider themselves "owned" by Jesus Christ who bought them with a price (1Co 7:22–23). Paul, "a slave of Jesus Christ" (Rm 1:1), preached that we Christians have exchanged owners: "But now . . . you have been set free from sin and have become slaves of God" (Rm 6:22; cf. Gal 5:1). We are free from sin (Rm 6), from the condemnation of the Law (Rm 7), and from death (Rm 8).

6:8 *receive back.* Christians should not be discouraged when their good deeds go unnoticed by others. Their heavenly Master sees their faithful service as a result of their faith in Christ. He will reward them in heaven, not by merit, but by grace (Col 3:23–24; 1Co 3:8; Lk 14:14). Indeed, "God is not so unjust as to overlook your work and the love that you showed for His sake in serving the saints" (Heb 6:10). Imagine the positive effect Paul's encouragement could have on how employers and employees regard one another and their roles! *whether . . . slave or free.* Social status has no bearing on one's relationship to God in Christ (Col 3:11; 1Co 12:13; Gal 2:28).

6:9 *do the same to them.* Paul does not advocate here that slaves and masters should exchange roles. Rather, within their station in life they both serve the same Lord (v. 6), and thus must show mutual respect in words and actions. *threatening.* Threats of punishment may alter external behavior but they do not change the heart (vv. 6–7). Holding threats over someone's head must therefore be avoided. *no partiality.* The Gk term pictures lifting up the face of a person who has prostrated himself in greeting—body language showing a sign of special favor. In the NT the term has the negative connotation "partiality" (Rm 2:11; Col. 3:25; Jas 2:1; cf. Ac 10:34). The point is this: God shows no "social bias" or favoritism (1Pt 1:17).

Devotion and Prayer in 6:1–9 Paul concludes his "table of duties" by outlining responsibilities within the family and the slave/master relationships. Significantly, he begins by focusing on the subordinate member: children and slaves. The apostle does not reject all moral principles of his day, but shows how life "in the Lord" transforms inner attitudes and external behavior. Children must obey their parents, but do so because of God's command and His promises to bless them. Slaves must be obedient to their masters, but do so with pure motives and proper respect. Paul goes to an even higher level. Christian children and parents, slaves, and masters all have one Lord whom they serve. Before God they are equals and with this awareness they serve Christ as His redeemed servants in their callings. Remembering their allegiance and devotion to Christ, parents and slave owners (masters) must avoid doing what discourages or dispirits those under them. Paul's principles apply with special force today as Christians live in family and social environments in which cruelty, bigotry, and abuse are present. Such situations very often lead to despair and even rebellion. Paul urges that we "walk as children of light" (5:8) also—and especially—within our vocation or place in life.
• O Lord, mercifully forgive my failures to do Your will gladly from my heart and to find joy in being Your servant and a servant to my neighbor. Amen.

PART 6

BAPTISM EQUIPS WITH ARMOR (6:10–17)

ESV	KJV
¹⁰Finally, be strong in the Lord and in the strength of his might. ¹¹Put on the whole armor of God, that you may be able to stand against the schemes of the devil. ¹²For we do not wrestle against flesh and blood, but against the rulers, against the authorities, against the cosmic powers over this present darkness, against the spiritual forces of evil in the heavenly places. ¹³Therefore take up the whole armor of God, that you may be able to withstand in the evil day, and having done all, to stand firm. ¹⁴Stand therefore, having fastened on the belt of truth, and having put on the breastplate of righteousness, ¹⁵and, as shoes for your feet, having put on the readiness given by the gospel of peace. ¹⁶In all circumstances take up the shield of faith, with which you can extinguish all the flaming darts of the evil one; ¹⁷and take the helmet of salvation, and the sword of the Spirit, which is the word of God,	¹⁰Finally, my brethren, be strong in the Lord, and in the power of his might. ¹¹Put on the whole armour of God, that ye may be able to stand against the wiles of the devil. ¹²For we wrestle not against flesh and blood, but against principalities, against powers, against the rulers of the darkness of this world, against spiritual wickedness in high places. ¹³Wherefore take unto you the whole armour of God, that ye may be able to withstand in the evil day, and having done all, to stand. ¹⁴Stand therefore, having your loins girt about with truth, and having on the breastplate of righteousness; ¹⁵And your feet shod with the preparation of the gospel of peace; ¹⁶Above all, taking the shield of faith, wherewith ye shall be able to quench all the fiery darts of the wicked. ¹⁷And take the helmet of salvation, and the sword of the Spirit, which is the word of God:

Introduction to 6:10–17 "Onward, Christian soldiers, Marching as to war, With the cross of Jesus Going on before" (*LSB* 662; *H82* 562; *TUMH* 575). God's call (1:18; 4:1, 4) places the Church in hostile territory, a world in which spiritual forces ferociously oppose the advance of God's kingdom. Each Christian's life becomes an arena for conflict with the power of Satan. But God gives His saints strength for the daily battle, equipping each one with divine weapons. Paul draws from imagery in Isaiah and from the Roman soldier's military equipment as he issues a "call to arms" (cf. also Wis 5:16–20). God's armor equips Christians with defensive and offensive weapons. Like a general encouraging his troops, the apostle assures us that the victory is certain because Christ has already won the war. He has made us well-prepared to stand with Him against the remaining assaults of the devil. In ancient legends, the weapons and armor of a hero could give certain victory to anyone who wore them (cf. 1Sm 17:38). The armor Paul describes does not belong to us; it is in fact God's own armor. Since through Baptism we have "put on Christ" (Gal 3:27; cf. Eph 4:24; Rm 13:12–14), God gives us the mighty power that He exerted in Christ when He raised Him from the dead and seated Him triumphantly at His right hand in the heavenly places (1:19–20).

6:10 *be strong in the Lord.* See the notes on 1:19–20. Paul now forcefully issues a call to battle (6:10–20), summoning Christians to join the continuing fight against God's opponents with the proper weapons. Though He has won the war (Col 2:15), the mop-up operation continues until the final rout (1Co 15:24–25; cf. Ps 28:7; Col 1:11).

6:11 *Put on.* In 4:24 the Ephesians are told to "put on the new self" (same verb in Gk). *whole armor of God.* A single word in Gk, the expression would have conjured up images of the heavily armed and fully equipped Roman foot soldier. However, the apostle leaves out two essential items in a Roman soldier's equipment (spear and shin guards). It is probable that he primarily has in mind OT passages describing the armor with which God and His Messiah fight against His enemies (Is 59:14–17; cf. 11:4–5). *of God* stresses God's provision. *stand against.* The "armed" believer not only engages in defensive action (shielding against flaming darts, v. 16) but also offensive action (wielding the sword of the Spirit, v. 17). Paradoxically, the Christian stands his or her ground by taking an aggressive posture against evil. *schemes.* The Gk term connotes craftiness, with the intention to deceive (*methodeia,* "scheming"; see 2Co 2:11). It also occurs in 4:14 with reference to false teaching that through human cunning camouflages itself as truth. This should not surprise us, for the devil is "a liar and the father of lies" (Jn 8:44), ever disguising himself as an angel of light (2Co 11:14). He always has method in his madness.

6:12 *rulers . . . heavenly places.* See the notes on 1:3, 21. The struggle against the evil forces that oppose the Gospel and its power in our life rages as an intensely personal battle. Using whatever means available, the devil and his underlings seek to invade even our inner being (our thinking, motives, willing) where Christ now dwells through faith and the Spirit is at work in power (2:16–17). Personal demonic powers seek to bring evil where there is good and darkness where there is light (cf. 4:18–19; 5:8–9). Superhuman enemies require overwhelming power coming only from our victorious God. As Luther succinctly put it, "All our shelter and protection rest in prayer alone" (LC III 30).

6:13 *the evil day.* Paul says earlier that the "days are evil" (5:16). The singular "the evil day" narrows the focus to the time near the end when evil will intensify (Mt 24:3–14). The evil powers act more vigorously and attack more ferociously as time goes on and the moment of their final defeat approaches. *stand firm.* Fully equipped and defended by God, Christians trust that they are able to resist and to hold their ground against sin and every evil (cf. Ex 14:13–14; 2Th 2:15).

6:14 *belt of truth.* The "belt" or "girdle" (sash) may refer to the leather apron beneath the armor, or the metal studded belt protecting the lower abdomen. Either way, girding oneself designated preparation for activity and for ease of movement (Lk 12:35, 37; Rv 1:13; cf. Ex 12:11; Heb 12:1). See Is 11:4–5. God's truth alone can counter the devil's lies (1:14; 4:14–15), and truthful conduct characterizes our new life in Christ (4:25; 5:9). *breastplate of righteousness.* See Is 59:17. The Roman soldier's breastplate was generally made of leather overlaid with metal. It served as protection for the chest's vital organs in battle. In Paul's Letters "righteousness" refers primarily to God's justification of the sinner by grace through faith for the sake of Christ (Rm 1:16–17; 3:21–26; 5:1–3; Gal 2:15–16; Ti 3:4–7). Such faith produces righteousness or holiness in the believer's life (Eph 4:24; 5:9; Rm 6:16, 18–19).

6:15 *shoes . . . gospel of peace.* See Is 52:7. A Roman soldier wore leather half boots tied to ankles and shins with straps, with the soles studded with nails and the toes left free. They equipped him for long marches and gave him firm footing when using his weapons. The Gospel of peace is a powerful and sturdy offensive weapon against the devil. It rescues people from his tyranny and his efforts to block free access to God's forgiving grace (1:17; 2:18) and the inner peace it brings (Rm 5:1–2).

6:16 *shield of faith.* Arrows were dipped in pitch and set on fire. Soldiers were equipped with rectangular shields made of wood covered with a thick coat of leather, which before battle was soaked to quench any fiery darts launched against the soldier. In the OT, especially in the Psalms, the shield symbolized God's protection (e.g., 18:2, 30, 35). Because faith—mentioned often in Ephesians (1:13, 15; 2:8; 3:12, 7; 4:5, 13; 6:23)—lays hold of the risen and reigning Christ, it receives His mighty strength in order to resist "the evil one's" onslaughts (cf. 1Pt 5:9). Luther wrote that the devil

> is a liar, to lead the heart astray from God's Word and to blind it, so that you cannot feel your distress or come to Christ. . . . If you could see how many knives, darts, and arrows are every moment aimed at you [Ephesians 6:16], you would be glad to come to the Sacrament as often as possible. (LC V 81–82)

Calvin wrote,

> The most necessary instruments of warfare—a sword and a shield—are compared to faith, and to the word of God. In the spiritual combat, these two hold the highest rank. By faith we repel all the attacks of the devil, and by the word of God the enemy himself is slain. If we find the word of God through faith to be 'quick and powerful,' we shall be more than sufficiently armed both for opposing the enemy and for putting him to flight. (Calvin, *Ephesians* 323)

6:17 *helmet of salvation.* See Is 59:17 and 11:5. The helmet was made of bronze and equipped with cheek pieces for protection of the head. The helmet corresponds to our salvation, which is both a present reality (2:5, 8) and a future hope (1:14; 1Th 5:8). God has rescued us from bondage to the world, the devil, and our flesh by making us alive together with Christ (2:1–5). We now have ironclad protection against our archenemy. *sword of the Spirit . . . word of God.* The Gk term suggests the 20–24 inch sword used in close combat. The "word of truth, the gospel of [our] salvation" (1:13) is a sharp offensive weapon given to us "in power and in the Holy Spirit" (1Th 1:5; cf. Heb 4:12). Through the Word the Spirit gives and strengthens faith (Gal 3:2; Rm 10:16–17). "One little Word can fell" the devil, sang Luther. Wesley wrote,

> Till now our armour has been only defensive. But we are to attack Satan, as well as secure ourselves; the shield in one hand, and the sword in the other. Whoever fights with the powers of hell will need both. He that is covered with armour from head to foot, and neglects this [shield and sword], will be foiled after all. This whole description shows us how great a thing it is to be a Christian. The want of any one thing makes him incomplete. Though he has his loins girt with truth, righteousness for a breastplate, his feet shod with the preparation of the gospel, the shield of faith, the helmet of salvation, and the sword of the Spirit; yet one thing he wants after all[: prayer]. (Wesley 503)

PART 7

CONCLUSION (6:18–24)

Exhortation (6:18–20)

ESV	KJV
[18]praying at all times in the Spirit, with all prayer and supplication. To that end keep alert with all perseverance, making supplication for all the saints, [19]and also for me, that words may be given to me in opening my mouth boldly to proclaim the mystery of the gospel, [20]for which I am an ambassador in chains, that I may declare it boldly, as I ought to speak.	[18]Praying always with all prayer and supplication in the Spirit, and watching thereunto with all perseverance and supplication for all saints; [19]And for me, that utterance may be given unto me, that I may open my mouth boldly, to make known the mystery of the gospel, [20]For which I am an ambassador in bonds: that therein I may speak boldly, as I ought to speak.

6:18 Military conflict requires that when a combatant takes his stand (vv. 13–14) he must be continually vigilant and prepared for any unexpected attack. For Christians waging the battle against "the spiritual forces of evil," vigilant and persistent prayer is more than advisable; it is necessary. The fourfold use of "all," as well as the terms for prayer, reveal Paul's intensity. He had begun his Letter with prayer for all the saints (1:15–23), and now closes it by urging prayer for all the saints (cf. 1:6). *at all times.* See the note on 1:16. *in the Spirit.* The Spirit enables us to call upon God as our Father (Rm 8:15–16) and helps us in our weakness. He intercedes for us when we do not know how to pray as we ought (Rm 8:26–27). *supplication.* This Gk term *deesis* in the NT most often refers to an urgent request to meet a specific need, addressed exclusively to God.

6:19 *words may be given.* Paul asks his readers to pray that he may receive the words necessary to make the Gospel known clearly and boldly. Jesus promised that the Spirit would give His disciples the words to speak (cf. Mt 10:19–20). God answered the Church's prayers for Paul. He filled Paul's two years under house arrest in Rome with opportunities to proclaim God's kingdom and teach "the Lord Jesus Christ with all boldness and without hindrance" (Ac 28:31). *mystery of the gospel.* See the note on 1:9.

6:20 *ambassador.* See the note on 1:1 *chains.* See the note 3:1. Paul views his imprisonment as a validation of the mission God gave to him.

Devotion and Prayer in 6:10–20 Paul sees many threats to an unhindered proclamation of the Gospel. Christians may be tempted to regard the spiritual forces opposed to the Gospel as fairly harmless—even though Paul says they have superhuman power and can be lethal. These forces are pervasive, sinister, and intensely aggressive in their efforts to destroy saving faith in Christians. Many think that they can solve this problem themselves, looking to resources within themselves to overcome threats to faith. Spiritual complacency may also cause them to let down their guard. Paul, the "ambassador in chains," issues a triumphant "call to arms." Stand, fight, and pray constantly, Paul urges. God is our ever-present help and supplies us with His weapons and the power of His Spirit to use them: truth, righteousness, the Gospel of peace, faith, salvation, the Word of God. This is the equipment in God's spiritual armor as we fight our daily battles against the devil, the world, and our sinful flesh. • Lord, teach us to pray without giving up. May Your Word not be bound but have free course and be preached to the joy and edifying of Your holy people. Amen.

Commendation to Letter-Bearer (6:21–22)

ESV	KJV
[21]So that you also may know how I am and what I am doing, Tychicus the beloved brother and faithful minister in the Lord will tell you everything. [22]I have sent him to you for this very purpose, that you may know how we are, and that he may encourage your hearts.	[21]But that ye also may know my affairs, and how I do, Tychicus, a beloved brother and faithful minister in the Lord, shall make known to you all things: [22]Whom I have sent unto you for the same purpose, that ye might know our affairs, and that he might comfort your hearts.

6:21 *Tychicus.* A native of Asia, he was a close friend and associate of Paul. Here and in Col 4:7 Paul calls him "the beloved brother and faithful minister"—and in Colossians he adds "fellow servant" (literally, "fellow slave") in the Lord. Luke reports in Acts that at the end of the third missionary journey Tychicus accompanied Paul and traveled with him to Troas (Ac 20:4). He was part of the delegation that carried the collection that had been gathered from the Gentile churches to the poor Christians in Jerusalem. Evidently Tychicus was known in Ephesus (2Tm 4:12). Paul mentions him at Ti 3:12 as his possible emissary to Crete. He sent Tychicus to deliver the Letter to the Ephesians and inform the congregation fully about Paul and his situation in Rome.

6:22 *we.* Even while in prison Paul received guests and coworkers who supported him. Timothy, for example, served his needs (see 2Tm 4:9; cf. v. 12) and joined Paul in greeting the churches that received his Letters from prison (Col 1:1; cf. 4:9–14). One NT scholar notes that Paul attracted friends around him like a magnet attracts iron filings. See also the note on 1:15.

Final Greeting and Blessing (6:23–24)

ESV	KJV
²³Peace be to the brothers, and love with faith, from God the Father and the Lord Jesus Christ. ²⁴Grace be with all who love our Lord Jesus Christ with love incorruptible.	²³Peace be to the brethren, and love with faith, from God the Father and the Lord Jesus Christ. ²⁴Grace be with all them that love our Lord Jesus Christ in sincerity. Amen.

6:23 *brothers.* Ancient letters closed with a farewell wish like "Be strong" or "Prosper!" Paul's final greetings were totally Christian in content, reflecting the unity in Christ that he shared with fellow members of the household of God (2:19). The familial "brothers" occurs only here in Ephesians.

6:24 *all who love our Lord.* In the OT God's covenant love is promised to all those who love God (Ex 20:6; Dt 5:10; Ne 1:5). Here Paul applies the promise to all who love the Lord Jesus Christ. (Cf. 1Pt 1:8; 1Co 8:3). *love incorruptible.* The Gk term refers to a state of not being subject to decay, that is, that which is imperishable. Just as

Christ's love for us is undying (Rm 8:39), so also our love for Christ extends into eternity, the realm where our life in the resurrection will remain forever untouched by the forces of decay (1Co 15:42–53; 1Pt 1:4).

Devotion and Prayer in 6:21–24 The Letter to the Ephesians is bracketed with an opening grace/peace greeting and a closing blessing of peace/grace—both extended in the name of God the Father and our Lord Jesus Christ. In between these "bookends" Paul has made known "the mystery of the gospel" (v. 19), summarized best by these two colossal blessings intended to bring forth our praise to the triune God.

> Maker of all things, all Thy creatures praise Thee; All for Thy worship were and are created; Now, as we also worship Thee devoutly, Hear Thou our voices. Lord God Almighty, unto Thee be glory, One in three persons, over all exalted! Glory we offer, praise Thee and adore Thee, Now and forever. (*LSB* 504:3–4)
>
> Amen.

PHILIPPIANS

Introduction to Philippians

Overview

Author
Paul the apostle

Date
c. AD 60

Places
Philippi (Macedonia); Thessalonica

People
Paul; Timothy; Epaphroditus; Euodia; Syntyche; the imperial guard; "those of Caesar's household"

Purpose
Paul describes a life worthy of the Gospel (1:27)

Law Themes
Suffering, uncertainty, and personal sacrifice; rivalry over the Gospel; growth in humility and right-mindedness

Gospel Themes
Joy in Christ; Jesus' exaltation after the cross; righteousness through faith in Christ; heavenly citizenship

Memory Verses
To live is Christ (1:21–26); Christ's humility and exaltation (2:4–11); righteous through faith (3:7–11); press on (3:12–14); citizenship in heaven (3:20–21)

Reading Philippians

A foreign-born man received his citizenship document from the hands of an imperial clerk as others might receive and cradle a child. To be born a citizen of Tarsus or some other city might stir a person's pride. But to receive Roman citizenship—that came with privileges, which a father passed to his sons. Roman citizenship elevated a family above the tortured rabble who could only hope to prove themselves worthy and free.

Paul appealed to his Roman citizenship when he first visited Philippi (Ac 16:35–39). As residents of a Roman colony populated by former Roman soldiers, the Philippians well understood and appreciated citizenship. Paul reminded the Philippian congregation that, through Christ, they had received citizenship in heaven. Christ's heroic efforts on their behalf allowed them to enjoy a manner of life worthy of His Gospel.

Setting

After a decisive battle in 42 BC, Emperor Octavian established Philippi as a Roman colony and gave the city a special status, equal to that of cities in Italy and free from direct taxation. Though there are many inscriptions and relief carvings for various deities on the acropolis at Philippi, the favored god was Silvanus, the Roman god of the countryside and agriculture. Paul would have entered Philippi on the Via Egnatia, the great road through Macedonia. He likely met with Lydia (Ac 16:11–15) beside the stream that flowed near the east gate. Churches dedicated to Paul were built on this location. Archaeologists have located the Roman forum at the city center, lined with shops and fountains, where Paul likely stood before the city magistrates after his arrest and public beating (Ac 16:19–23). They have also identified a possible site nearby for the prison (Ac 16:24).

Central Issue

Philippians is a missionary thank-you letter. Scholars have carefully studied Paul's style in the Letter because of its relationship to Greek rhetoric. Paul's opening prayer (1:3–11) anticipates all the major themes of the Book (see Luther's summary below). Paul stated the key theme in 1:27—living in accord with the Gospel of Christ. He illustrated the paradox of human responsibility in view of God's work in us and the paradox of joy during suffering. Paul presented Jesus and himself as examples of living worthy of the Gospel.

Paul also warned the Philippians about (1) people who spread the Gospel from bad motives (1:15–17), (2) the circumcision group (3:2–7; see note, Gal 2:4), and (3) "enemies of the cross" (3:18). These groups were not necessarily part of the congregation at Philippi, but were affecting other congregations and spreading problems.

Luther on Philippians

In this epistle St. Paul praises and admonishes the Philippians that they abide and carry on in the true faith and increase in love. But since injury is always done to faith by false apostles and teachers of works, he warns them against these men and points out to them many different preachers—some good, some bad—including even himself and his disciples, Timothy and Epaphroditus. This he does in chapters 1 and 2.

In chapter 3 he rejects that human righteousness not based on faith, which is taught and held by the false apostles. He offers himself as an example: he had lived gloriously in this kind of righteousness, and yet now holds it to be nothing, for the sake of the righteousness of Christ. For human righteousness makes the belly its god, and makes men enemies of the cross of Christ.

In chapter 4 he exhorts them to peace and good outward conduct toward each other, and thanks them for the gift they sent him. (LW 35:385)

Calvin on Philippians

It is generally known that Philippi was a city of Macedonia, situated on the confines of Thrace, on the plains of which Pompey was conquered by Caesar; and Brutus and Cassius were afterwards conquered by Antony and Octavius. Thus Roman insurrections rendered this place illustrious by two memorable engagements. When Paul was called into Macedonia by an express revelation, he first founded a Church in that city, (as is related by Luke in Acts xvi. 12,) which did not merely persevere steadfastly in the faith, but was also, in process of time, as this Epistle bears evidence, enlarged both in the number of individuals, and in their proficiency in respect of attainments.

The occasion of Paul's writing to the Philippians was this,—As they had sent to him by Epaphroditus, their pastor, such things as were needed by him when in prison, for sustaining life, and for other more than ordinary expenses, there can be no doubt that Epaphroditus explained to him at the same time the entire condition of the Church, and acted the part of an adviser in suggesting those things, respecting which they required to be admonished. It appears, however, that attempts had been made upon them by false apostles, who wandered hither and thither, with the view of spreading corruptions of sound doctrine; but as they had remained steadfast in the truth, the Apostle commends their steadfastness. Keeping, however, in mind human frailty, and having, perhaps, been instructed by Epaphroditus that they required to be seasonably confirmed, lest they should in process of time fall away, he subjoins such admonitions as he knew to be suitable to them. (Calvin, *Philippians* 20–21)

Wesley on Philippians

PHILIPPI was so called from Philip, king of Macedonia, who much enlarged and beautified it. Afterwards it became a Roman colony, and the chief city of that part of Macedonia. Hither St. Paul was sent by a vision to preach and here, not long after his coming, he was shamefully entreated. Nevertheless many were converted by him, during the short time of his abode there; by whose liberality he was more assisted than by any other Church of his planting. And they had now sent large assistance to him by Epaphroditus; by whom he returns them this epistle. (Wesley 505)

Challenges for Readers

Place and Date. The Letter does not make absolutely clear when or where Paul wrote it. Traditionally, it is regarded as one of Paul's Prison Epistles written from Rome.

Composition. Paul made a concluding statement at 3:1 and changed his tone thereafter. Also, 4:10–20 could stand as a separate Letter. In view of these points, some critics have described Philippians as a collection of separate letters combined by a later editor. However, these points could simply indicate how Paul worked on this Epistle. Notably, the themes for the entire Letter are introduced in ch. 1.

The Humility of Christ. The Christ-hymn in 2:4–11 has challenged interpreters. The early Church Fathers struggled with the statement that Christ "made Himself nothing" or "emptied Himself" (see note, 2:7). Critics have struggled to reconcile the hymn's advanced Christology with their theories that distinguishing Jesus' divine and human natures was a late development in Christian teachings. Though early Christians did not settle on specific wording right away, these doctrines of the creeds were certainly taught.

Suffering. Paul's intensely personal reflections on suffering and God's will (1:19–26; 3:10–11) illustrate his maturity in the faith as well as his human weaknesses. It is not always clear how his reflections apply to us personally.

Blessings for Readers

Philippians reveals Paul's intense love for and joy in this congregation. The warmth he shows toward them is unique among his Letters, since the congregation seems to need less discipline than others. He describes the Christian life in all its blessings and goodness, which come from the Lord's work in us.

As you study Philippians, the Lord will work in your life, transforming your mind to be like Christ's. Pray that you may receive the fullness of His joy in all circumstances and live worthy of His Gospel. For your righteousness is through faith in Christ alone. Knowing Him has "surpassing worth" (3:8).

Outline

I. Salutation (1:1–2)
II. Thanksgiving and Prayer (1:3–11)
III. News about Paul's Preaching (1:12–26)
    A. Paul's Imprisonment (1:12–18)
    B. Life in Christ (1:19–26)
IV. Exhortations (1:27–2:18)
    A. Behave as Citizens Worthy of the Gospel (1:27–30)
    B. Christ's Example of Humility (2:1–11)
    C. Lights in the World (2:12–18)
V. Travel Plans for Timothy and Epaphroditus (2:19–30)
VI. Further Exhortations (3:1–4:9)
    A. Warning against Mutilators (3:1–11)
    B. Straining toward the Goal by Imitating Paul (3:12–4:1)
    C. Exhortation, Encouragement, and Prayer (4:2–9)
VII. Thanks for God's Provision and the Gifts Received (4:10–20)
VIII. Final Greetings (4:21–23)

PART 1

SALUTATION (1:1–2)

ESV	KJV
1 ¹Paul and Timothy, servants of Christ Jesus, To all the saints in Christ Jesus who are at Philippi, with the overseers and deacons: ²Grace to you and peace from God our Father and the Lord Jesus Christ.	1 ¹Paul and Timotheus, the servants of Jesus Christ, to all the saints in Christ Jesus which are at Philippi, with the bishops and deacons: ²Grace be unto you, and peace, from God our Father, and from the Lord Jesus Christ.

1:1 *Timothy.* In six of his Letters, Paul associates Timothy with himself (2Co 1:1; Col 1:1; Phm 1; 1Th 1:1; 2Th 1:1). Timothy was part of Paul's inner circle of close friends and coworkers (Rm 16:21). A native of Lystra in Lycaonia and the son of a Jewish mother and Greek father, he became a Christian when Paul and Barnabas came to his hometown during Paul's first missionary journey (Ac 14:8–20). He joined Paul in his missionary work (Ac 16–18). Timothy supported Paul in his imprisonment and had a special relationship with the Philippians (2:19–24). *servants.* Paul and Timothy bore the title ("slaves" in Gk; cf. Rm 1:1; Ti 1:1) with honor, identifying themselves with Christ who took upon Himself the form of a slave (2:7). They were utterly dependent on Christ, freed from bondage (of sin, death, and the Law) and now as Christians were owned by Him (1Co 3:23; 7:22). They also stood in a long line of God's servants in the OT chosen to bear His name and speak His Word: Moses (Ne 10:29), Joshua (Jsh 24:29), David (Ps 89:20), and Jonah (2Ki 4:25). Paul does not emphasize his apostolic authority in greeting the Philippians, but indicates that he is bound to Christ (cf. Eph 6:20; cf. Eph 3:1). *saints.* See the comments on Eph 1:1. *Philippi.* See "Introduction to Philippians," "Setting" on p. 178. *overseers and deacons.* This general description of church leaders in local congregations points to the responsibilities of persons chosen to guard the apostolic doctrine ("overseers," equated with "elders" in Ti 1:5, 7; cf. Ac 20:17, 28) and to serve the daily needs of a congregation (1Tm 3:8–13).

1:2 Paul gives Christian content to a customary ancient greeting form. See commentary on Eph 1:2.

Devotion and Prayer in 1:1–2 In his first Letter to Timothy Paul calls him "my true child in the faith" (1Tm 1:2) and in the second Letter, "my child" (2Tm 2:1). Awaiting execution in a Roman jail, he writes to his young co-worker and friend Timothy, "I long to see you, that I may be filled with joy" (2Tm 1:4). Paul's deep affection for Timothy and gratitude for his support leads Paul to include him in his apostolic greetings as a "fellow slave" of Christ Jesus. Through His Son Jesus Christ, God the Father revealed His grace and brought peace to humankind. Bound to Christ and at His complete disposal, Paul and Timothy bore the title "slave" as did their master Himself. The opening words of this Letter already breathe a spirit of pastoral, evangelical concern for God's dear saints at Philippi. The congregation there suffered its share of problems despite the joy in Christ present there. We all can learn from Paul and Timothy that service in the Church for the sake of Christ is a privilege and an honor, not a drudgery to be avoided and left to others. Paul's greeting in this Letter is intended for all saints of all times and places. We pray that we may receive it not as some pious wish, but as words through which God's blessings come upon us. • Thank You, dear heavenly Father, for making us Your saints through Jesus, Your Son, and for providing Your Word of grace and peace to sustain us. Amen.

PART 2

THANKSGIVING AND PRAYER (1:3–11)

ESV	KJV
³I thank my God in all my remembrance of you, ⁴always in every prayer of mine for you all making my prayer with joy, ⁵because of your partnership in the gospel from the first day until now. ⁶And I am sure of this, that he who began a good work in you will bring it to completion at the day of Jesus Christ. ⁷It is right for me to feel this way about you all, because I hold you in my heart, for you are all partakers with me of grace, both in my imprisonment and in the defense and confirmation of the gospel. ⁸For God is my witness, how I yearn for you all with the affection of Christ Jesus. ⁹And it is my prayer that your love may abound more and more, with knowledge and all discernment, ¹⁰so that you may approve what is excellent, and so be pure and blameless for the day of Christ, ¹¹filled with the fruit of righteousness that comes through Jesus Christ, to the glory and praise of God.	³I thank my God upon every remembrance of you, ⁴Always in every prayer of mine for you all making request with joy, ⁵For your fellowship in the gospel from the first day until now; ⁶Being confident of this very thing, that he which hath begun a good work in you will perform it until the day of Jesus Christ: ⁷Even as it is meet for me to think this of you all, because I have you in my heart; inasmuch as both in my bonds, and in the defence and confirmation of the gospel, ye all are partakers of my grace. ⁸For God is my record, how greatly I long after you all in the bowels of Jesus Christ. ⁹And this I pray, that your love may abound yet more and more in knowledge and in all judgment; ¹⁰That ye may approve things that are excellent; that ye may be sincere and without offence till the day of Christ. ¹¹Being filled with the fruits of righteousness, which are by Jesus Christ, unto the glory and praise of God.

1:3 Every time Paul thinks of the Philippians he is moved to thank God for their faith and the encouraging support that they provided him.

1:4 *joy.* The apostle Paul knew joy even in the midst of suffering and conflict. Beaten and imprisoned at Philippi during his second missionary journey, he and Silas "were praying and singing hymns" at midnight. Paul's prayer here reflects the "jubilant note" that reverberates throughout this entire Letter (1:18, 25; 2:2, 17, 18, 28, 29; 3:1; 4:1, 4, 10).

1:5 From the very first day (Ac 20:18) that Paul shared the Gospel with the Philippians, they joined together with him by believing the Gospel and seeking to extend that Gospel to others. Some "labored" with him in the Gospel (4:3). They prayed for Paul (1:19). They received Paul's messenger Epaphroditus (2:25–30) and entered into partnership with Paul in "giving and receiving" (4:15). They participated generously in the offering gathered for the saints in Jerusalem (2Co 8:1–5). *partnership.* The Gk word here is *koinonia.* This beautiful concept for sharing in something features prominently in Philippians (see 1:7 [compound noun "partakers with"]; 2:1, 3:10 [noun]; 4:14 [compound verb, "share in"]; 4:15 [verb]).

1:6 *bring it to completion.* The Gk word in this expression carries the idea of finishing or bringing something to an end. God will carry out to its conclusion the work He has begun among the Philippians when they came to faith in Christ (cf. Ac 16:14). The word occurs again at 2Co 8:6, 11, where Paul describes bringing the offering for saints to completion. God will bring to consummation Christ's redemption, working in Christians "both to will and to work for his good pleasure" (2:13). Calvin wrote,

> Paul, assuredly, did not derive this confidence from the steadfastness or excellence of men, but simply from the fact, that God had manifested his love to the Philippians. And undoubtedly this is the true manner of acknowledging God's benefits—when we derive from them occasion of hoping well as to the future. For as they are tokens at once of his goodness, and of his fatherly benevolence towards us, what ingratitude were it to derive from this no confirmation of hope and good courage! (Calvin, *Philippians* 25–26)

day of Jesus Christ. In the OT the "day of the Lord" is the day when God reveals/executes His judgment. In the NT "the day of Christ" (see also 1:10; 2:16) is the day when He will return to judge the living and the dead (Mt 26:64).

1:7 *heart.* See the commentary on Eph 1:18. "Heart" stands for a person's inner life, not only as the center and source of thinking and volition, but also of feeling. This is evident from the way the ESV translates the Gk word for "think" in this context with "feel." Paul's thanksgiving to God for the Philippian Christians and their relationship to him flows out of his deep affection for them. *partakers.* See the note on v. 5. The Gk word *sygkoinonos* conveys the idea of joint participation, and thus is usually translated "share in" (cf. Rm 11:17; 1Co 9:23; Rv 1:9 [ESV, "partner"]). The same is true of the corresponding verb (4:14), which means "be associated in a joint activity." Paul's love for the Philippians grew out of their common participation in God's grace (note Paul's closing words in 4:23). In Paul's personal life God's grace was especially manifested in his call to be an apostle (Rm 1:5; 1Co 15:9–10; Eph 3:7–8; 1Tm 1:14). The Philippians' "partnership in the gospel" (see the note on v. 5) included their generous and heartfelt support of Paul and his apostolic witness from the beginning (4:10–20; Ac 16:14–15). *imprisonment.* Paul specifically mentions his imprisonment four times in ch. 1 (here, and vv.12–14, 17). He speaks of it with a note of joy, absent of any self-pity and accepted as an opportunity for the Gospel's advance. *defense and confirmation of the gospel.* This is language common in legal proceedings of Paul's day. He may be alluding to a coming appearance in court before Roman authorities. His more basic interest, however, is making a strong case for the Gospel itself and confirming its truth so that people may accept it as trustworthy. Paul's speeches in Acts showcase his method of provided proof that the Gospel is not his concoction but is a fulfillment of what "Moses and the prophets" had foretold concerning the Christ (see Ac 17:2–3 and 24:10–21; 26:2–23).

1:8 *witness.* Only God knows the genuineness of Paul's convictions and the depth of his emotional ties to the Philippians (cf. Jn 2:25). He therefore calls upon God as his witness to verify the truth of what he is saying (cf. Rm 1:9; 2Co 11:11, 31; 1Th 2:5). Paul appeals to God as a witness of how strong his affections are toward the Philippians. *yearn . . . affection.* Nowhere else in his Letters does Paul express with such intensity an affectionate yearning to see his friends (cf. Rm 1:11; 1Th 3:6; 2Tm 1:4). The term "affection" translates the Gk *splanchna* which refers literally to the viscera or entrails of a person, which were thought to be the seat and source of human emotions.

187

In Phm twelve English translations render the term with "heart" (KJV, "bowels"), and in the present verse, "affection" (KJV, "bowels"). One might say today that Paul's love for the Philippians was "visceral." But more, his love for them was an outpouring of the compassionate heart of Christ Himself (Mt 9:36). Christ was expressing His love through the apostle himself. Every faithful pastor has some experience of this feeling that overcame Paul as he wrote to this beloved congregation.

1:9–11 Paul's introductory prayer of thanksgiving flows naturally into an intercessory prayer for them. The prayer itself actually touches on the Letter's main themes. Like David in Psalm 119, Paul prays that Christians may receive the understanding they need to grasp and learn divine teaching properly. The Lutheran reformers wrote,

> These prayers and passages about our ignorance and inability have been written for us. They are not written to make us idle and remiss in reading, hearing, and meditating on God's Word, but that we should first thank God from the heart that by His Son He has delivered us from the darkness of ignorance and the captivity of sin and death [Ephesians 4:8]. (FC SD II 15)

Paul prays that the Philippians will grow in the love they have come to know in Christ Jesus, with all knowledge and discernment. A discerning love has an eye for the things that really matter now in the life of a Christian awaiting Christ's coming. Paul knows God's desired end for His own, and thus prays that the Philippians (and hence all Christians) be filled with the fruit of righteousness to "the glory and praise of God" (v. 11).

1:9–10 Elsewhere in Paul's Letters, love consistently heads the list of the Spirit's fruits (e.g., Gal 5:22; 1Co 13:13). But the love for which Paul prays in the Philippians' lives is not to be understood merely as an emotion. Nor is it ever blind. On the contrary, he prays that it will be informed and morally discriminating—a love that is able to know what is right on the basis of God's will and to make wise, tactful decisions in practical situations (cf. Heb 5:14). The Gk word for "discernment" means "the capacity to understand" something (the noun occurs only here in the NT). Paul begins his Letter to Philemon with a similar prayer. Grateful to God for Philemon's love and faith, he prays that his "faith may become effective for the full knowledge of every good thing that is in us for the sake of Christ" (Phm 6). *approve what is excellent.* The purpose of informed and intelligent love is to choose those options that stand out as the best. This presumes that some moral choices are more advisable than others (see 4:8). In contrast to the "debased mind" of those who "do not see fit to acknowledge God" (Rm 1:28), believers are to have a mind that by testing "may discern what is the will of God, what is good and acceptable and perfect" (Rm 12:2; cf. Col 1:9–10; Eph 1:17; 5:9–10). *pure and blameless.* As he prays, Paul wants the Philippians to approach Christ's coming with transparently pure motives. He deeply desires that they not slip and fall away from their faith in Christ. Only by God's grace can we Christians act "with simplicity and godly sincerity" toward our fellow Christians (2Co 1:12). *day of Christ.* God is faithful and will surely keep our "whole spirit and soul and body . . . blameless at the coming of our Lord Jesus Christ" (1Th 5:23). See the note on v. 6.

1:11 *fruit of righteousness.* In Philippians Paul uses the term "righteousness" to refer to righteousness that comes from the Law, and the righteousness that "comes through faith in Christ, the righteousness from God that depends on faith" (3:9)—the central theme of the Gospel Paul proclaimed (Rm 1:17; 3:21–31; 1Co 3:9; 5:21). The righteousness of God, His justification of the sinner, produces fruit in the lives of those who believe in Christ by the Spirit's power (Gal 5:22). Through Baptism God unites us with Jesus Christ and gives us new life, so that we actually think, speak, and do what is "good, right, and true" (Rm 6:1–14; Eph 5:9). James calls such fruit "the harvest of righteousness" (Jas 3:17–18). *through Jesus Christ.* Just as God's justifying grace comes to us through faith in Jesus Christ, so also the "fruits" come to us as a result of the new life that flows from Him (Jn 15:5–8). "It is God who works in you, both to will and to work for His good pleasure," Paul writes after singing of the death and glorious exaltation of Jesus at whose name every knee should bow and confess to be Lord (Php 2:13).

Devotion and Prayer in 1:3–11 Opening thanksgivings customarily introduce the main themes present in Paul's Letters, setting the tone for what follows. His opening prayers also reveal his pastoral concern for his readers. This is especially true of his Letter to the Philippians. These verses breathe a profound pastoral love in the heart of Paul for this congregation. He regards them as his beloved "joy and crown" (4:1). With joyful confidence in God's grace he gives thanks to God every time they cross his mind. He is grateful especially for their partnership in the Gospel and the good work that God has begun and will complete in them. He cannot forget that they have stood by him and supported him in his imprisonment. They stood by him in his defense and confirmation of the Gospel. With the affection of Christ Jesus, Paul yearns for them and prays for the increase of a discerning love within their own lives as they await the coming of their Savior. We can learn much from the example the apostle sets for us. His intercessory prayer (vv. 9–11) reminds us that genuine Christ-like love requires thoughtful and wise judgment aimed at choosing what is first-rate for the Church (4:8; cf. Rm 12:2). Few things undermine believers' partnership in Christ and His Gospel like uninformed, shortsighted and tactless disregard for the spiritual welfare of others. Despite his imprisonment and sufferings, Paul looked not to his own interests but to their interests (2:4). He found great joy in their progress in the Christian faith. • Dear Lord Jesus, fill our lives with the fruit of Your righteousness that we might abound in love, approve what is excellent, and be pure and blameless on the day of Your return. Amen.

PART 3

NEWS ABOUT PAUL'S PREACHING (1:12–26)

Paul's Imprisonment (1:12–18)

ESV	KJV
¹²I want you to know, brothers, that what has happened to me has really served to advance the gospel, ¹³so that it has become known throughout the whole imperial guard and to all the rest that my imprisonment is for Christ. ¹⁴And most of the brothers, having become confident in the Lord by my imprisonment, are much more bold to speak the word without fear. ¹⁵Some indeed preach Christ from envy and rivalry, but others from good will. ¹⁶The latter do it out of love, knowing that I am put here for the defense of the gospel. ¹⁷The former proclaim Christ out of rivalry, not sincerely but thinking to afflict me in my imprisonment. ¹⁸What then? Only that in every way, whether in pretense or in truth, Christ is proclaimed, and in that I rejoice. Yes, and I will rejoice,	¹²But I would ye should understand, brethren, that the things which happened unto me have fallen out rather unto the furtherance of the gospel; ¹³So that my bonds in Christ are manifest in all the palace, and in all other places; ¹⁴And many of the brethren in the Lord, waxing confident by my bonds, are much more bold to speak the word without fear. ¹⁵Some indeed preach Christ even of envy and strife; and some also of good will: ¹⁶The one preach Christ of contention, not sincerely, supposing to add affliction to my bonds: ¹⁷But the other of love, knowing that I am set for the defence of the gospel. ¹⁸What then? notwithstanding, every way, whether in pretence, or in truth, Christ is preached; and I therein do rejoice, yea, and will rejoice.

1:12 *brothers.* This address occurs nine times in Philippians (v. 14; 2:25; 3:1, 13, 17; 4:1, 8, 21). Jesus calls everyone devoted to Him by this name (Mt 12:50; Mk 3:35). While the term sometimes designates a male follower of Jesus (2:25; Mt 28:10; Jn 20:17; Col 1:1), it also is used often for Christian men and women in their relationship to each other and to their membership in the Christian community in general (Rm 8:29; 16:23; Eph 6:23; 1Co 5:11, etc.). *what has happened.* The phrase means, literally, "the things pertaining to me." It is likely that the Philippians had inquired about how Paul was doing in his imprisonment. No doubt they expressed concern about his impending trial and related matters. Perhaps they received a report about this from Epaphroditus (2:25). *advance the gospel.* The phrase "I want you to know" probably confirms that Paul is responding to a specific concern the Philippians had raised: that his imprisonment could deal a severe blow to the Gospel's proclamation. Quite the contrary, says God's ambassador in chains. To Timothy (perhaps from the same prison) he declares: "The word of God is not bound!" (2Tm 2:9). With his usual positive outlook on things, Paul sees an unprecedented opportunity ahead for declaring the Gospel at the heart of the Roman empire. This verse leaves the unmistakable impression that he is someone more interested in the spread of the Gospel than in his own well-being.

1:13 *imperial guard.* If Paul's imprisonment here was in Rome, this was likely the emperor's elite body guard which consisted of about thirteen to fourteen thousand Italian soldiers. They were among the highest paid soldiers in the Roman military. One of these soldiers (no doubt in a rotating shift) was assigned to guard Paul while he was under house arrest in Rome (Ac 28:16). *all the rest.* Paul's imprisonment became known to a wider circle of people (Christians and non-Christians alike), but he does not specify exactly who they were. *my imprisonment is for Christ.* Word had spread that the apostle was in custody because he was a Christian. The civil authorities would likely not have understood how the charges against him squared with the message he proclaimed and the manner in which he conducted himself. Jewish authorities in Rome had received no adverse information about Paul, though they were aware that Christianity had been spoken against (Ac 28:21–22). Paul reported to them that he had been compelled to appeal to Caesar because Jews in Caesarea objected to the Roman authorities' desire to free him (28:18–19).

1:14 *brothers.* See the note on v. 12. Some commentators believe that this term refers to public ministers or Paul's coworkers. Others conclude that it is a general reference to Paul's fellow Christians in the church at Rome. The responsibility to proclaim the Gospel belongs to the whole Church. Accordingly, ministers were appointed and chosen to proclaim "the word of grace" publicly in behalf of the congregations they served (Ac 20:32). See the note on 1:1. *confident . . . by my imprisonment.* Paul's Christian friends would have had reason to be intimidated by his imprisonment and the uncertain outcome of the charges leveled against him. The words "without fear" seem to imply that this was the case. But Paul saw God's hand at work in what was happening to him, with many new opportunities to proclaim Christ opening up before him. His cheerful confidence in the Lord rubbed off on the majority of them (see the similar situation following the release of John and Peter from custody in Ac 4:23–31). Especially those who visited Paul in his imprisonment would have seen and heard for themselves how providential for him this development had become under the Lord's direction (cf. Ac 28:31). *bold to speak the word.* In Acts this specific expression occurs for apostolic proclamation (4:29, 31; 13:46; 14:25). The "word of God" or "word of the Lord" (which "continued to increase and prevail mightily," Ac 19:20) is an equivalent for the Gospel (6:2, 7; 8:4; 11:19; 13:5, 5, 44, 46; etc.).

1:15 For most Christians in Rome Paul's example triggered a renewed zeal for evangelism. But the motives of some were less than laudable. Personal envy—though apparently not theological disagreement—prompted them to use their proclamation as a way of getting the better of him or sidelining him. They may even have secretly welcomed his "misfortune" for such reasons. Others were very kindly disposed toward Paul. Their proclamation of Christ reflected a wholehearted support for the apostle personally. Paul labels envy, and the ensuing partisanship it most often breeds, as a "work of the flesh" (Gal 5:20–21). God, who has demonstrated kindliness and goodness toward humankind, is pleased when people share His Good News enthusiastically and with pure motives (Php 2:13).

1:16 *defense of the gospel.* See the note on v. 7. Note the subtle contrast between those who "know" and those who were "thinking" (i.e., "supposing" or "imagining").

1:17 *rivalry.* See the note on v. 15. The Gk term (*eritheia*) means "selfish ambition" (see Jas 3:14, 16; Php 2:3). An English dictionary definition of "ambition" captures its force: "an ardent desire for rank, fame, or power." *thinking to afflict me.* The Gk expression is, literally, "raise trouble." The apostle remains unperturbed by the insincerity of those who wish to make his life more difficult or exacerbate his situation.

1:18 *What then?* That is, "what should we make of this?" Amazingly, Paul does not become defensive or resentful, or resort to giving a "positive spin" to gain political points. And he does not accuse others of pretending to be Christians. Rather, he expresses genuine happiness that Christ is proclaimed, whether under pretense (Gk, *prophasis*, falsely alleged motive) or with absolute integrity. Ironically, the selfishly ambitious end up advancing Paul's principal interests in spite of themselves. Cyprian wrote,

> Paul . . . was not speaking of heretics. . . . He was speaking of brethren, whether as walking disorderly and against the discipline of the Church, or as keeping the truth of the Gospel with the fear of God. (*ANF* 5:382)

Devotion and Prayer in 1:12–18 Whatever the frustrations Paul experienced while in prison, they could easily have dampened his enthusiasm for proclaiming Christ and quenched his joy in the Gospel. We become especially "stressed out" when someone out of self-interest makes an outward show of friendship while inwardly filled with envy and resentment. We feel a sense of betrayal. Paul knew many good-hearted Christian supporters while in prison. But he also knew those who preached Christ out of pretense, with personal animosity toward him. As was typical of this great apostle, he maintained his focus and rose above it all. What really mattered was that Christ was proclaimed. He makes the special point that his imprisonment did not spell a defeat for the Gospel, as some had feared. On the contrary, he saw God at work to accomplish His gracious purposes in Christ through the seemingly adverse circumstances in Rome. Paul's faithful testimony and his unremitting joy in all circumstances encourage all Christians undergoing stresses and strains in their personal lives—including pressures from those who oppose the Christian message. • Almighty and merciful God, forgive our failure to trust in Your promise to work all things for our good, and give us grace in every situation to share the Gospel with others. Amen.

Life in Christ (1:19–26)

ESV	KJV
¹⁹for I know that through your prayers and the help of the Spirit of Jesus Christ this will turn out for my deliverance, ²⁰as it is my eager expectation and hope that I will not be at all ashamed, but that with full courage now as always Christ will be honored in my body, whether by life or by death. ²¹For to me to live is Christ, and to die is gain. ²²If I am to live in the flesh, that means fruitful labor for me. Yet which I shall choose I cannot tell. ²³I am hard pressed between the two. My desire is to depart and be with Christ, for that is far better. ²⁴But to remain in the flesh is more necessary on your account. ²⁵Convinced of this, I know that I will remain and continue with you all, for your progress and joy in the faith, ²⁶so that in me you may have ample cause to glory in Christ Jesus, because of my coming to you again.	¹⁹For I know that this shall turn to my salvation through your prayer, and the supply of the Spirit of Jesus Christ, ²⁰According to my earnest expectation and my hope, that in nothing I shall be ashamed, but that with all boldness, as always, so now also Christ shall be magnified in my body, whether it be by life, or by death. ²¹For to me to live is Christ, and to die is gain. ²²But if I live in the flesh, this is the fruit of my labour: yet what I shall choose I wot not. ²³For I am in a strait betwixt two, having a desire to depart, and to be with Christ; which is far better: ²⁴Nevertheless to abide in the flesh is more needful for you. ²⁵And having this confidence, I know that I shall abide and continue with you all for your furtherance and joy of faith; ²⁶That your rejoicing may be more abundant in Jesus Christ for me by my coming to you again.

1:19 *Spirit of Jesus Christ.* The Holy Spirit is called "the Spirit *of* Jesus Christ." The Spirit descended upon Jesus at His Baptism (Mk 1:10; Jn 1:32). Jesus is the Son of God and Second Person of the Trinity and now sends the Spirit to His disciples (3:34; 16:7). He prays to His Father who promises to send the Spirit to those who believe in Him (Jn 14:16). The Father sends the Spirit in Jesus' name (Jn 14:26). Our Heavenly Father gives the Holy Spirit to all those who ask Him in Jesus' name (Lk 11:13). Jesus has promised the Spirit's help to Christians especially when they are called to bear witness before governing authorities (Mk 13:11; Mt 10:20; Lk 12:12). Paul finds comfort and strength in the knowledge that the Philippians are praying for him and that the Spirit will support (ESV, "help" [Gk, *epichoregia*]) him in what he must face. *my deliverance.* The Gk term here is translated, generally, with "salvation." Various explanations of its precise meaning have been offered (future salvation at the end of time, rescue from the situation in Rome, general sense of everything turning out for good in the end). Noteworthy is Paul's allusion here to Jb 13:16 (the words correspond directly to Job's words) and Job's final vindication before God in view of accusations leveled against him. Likewise also Paul confidently believes that in the end everything will turn out for his salvation or vindication, whether in life or in death in Rome (v. 20). In the final analysis, in all things "we are more than conquerors" in Christ who has loved us (Rm 8:31, 37).

1:20 *honored in my body.* In some passages of Paul's Letters the term "body" is almost synonymous with the whole personality of an individual (e.g., Rm 12:1; Eph 5:28). Paul certainly has in mind the physical aspects of his earthly life—which was in jeopardy. But this does not mean that he sought to glorify Christ only in this dimension of his being. With his entire person, whether in death or in life, Paul sought to magnify Christ's name. If he lived, he would honor Jesus Christ by continuing his apostolic ministry. If he died, he would enlarge the name of Christ and advance His prestige by his faithful witness to the end. Paul's death would itself give testimony to a living hope, the consummation of which he awaited with eager expectation (3:20–21; Rm 8:19). The Lutheran reformers wrote,

> By God's help, we will retain this Confession to our last breath, when we shall go forth from this life to the heavenly fatherland, to appear with a joyful, undaunted mind and a pure conscience before the court of our Lord Jesus Christ [2 Corinthians 5:9–10]. (Preface to *The Book of Concord* 16)

1:21 Paul's thought parallels what he wrote to the Galatians: "It is no longer I who live, but Christ who lives in me. And the life I now live in the flesh I live by faith in the Son of God, who loved me and gave Himself for me" (Gal 2:20). For him to be found in Christ means that he can look forward to experiencing the power of Christ's resurrection and "by any means possible I may attain the resurrection from the dead" (3:10–11). For someone to lose his earthly life, therefore, would be an enormous gain! In both his life and death he believed that the cause of the Gospel would be advanced and promoted.

1:22 *live in the flesh*. The term "flesh" (*sarx*) can have a range of meanings in the NT. In this context it refers to a person's physical life on earth (cf. v. 24). *fruitful labor.* Paul wrote that his brother and "fellow soldier" Epaphroditus "nearly died for the work of Christ" (2:30; cf. 2:25). Paul often sums up his vocation and that of his co-workers as God's "work" (cf. 1Co 3:13–15; 16:10; 1:58). Through their labors God produces results in the lives of believers (1:6). In fact, Paul can even boldly declare that his converts are "my workman-ship" (literally, "my work") because of the power of God operative in the Word he proclaimed (1Co 9:1; 1:18; cf. 2:15–16; see the note on Eph 2:10). *choose.* God will have to decide which option He has in mind for Paul: continued labor for Christ on earth, or departure to be with Christ in heaven. In humble submission to the will of God, Paul knows that the number of his days belongs in God's providence alone (Ps 139:16). The Bible does not give us much information about our state between death and our resurrection. It is enough to know that we will be with Christ. To be with Him and look forward to our resurrection is to have everything that matters!

1:23 Paul admits that his mind is being pulled in two direc-tions, as if emotionally hemmed in on two sides. If he could chose, he would far and away prefer to depart this life and be with Christ. Calvin wrote,

> Death of itself will never be desired, because such a desire is at variance with natural feeling, but is desired for some particu-lar reason, or with a view to some other end. Persons in despair have recourse to it from having become weary of life; believers, on the other hand, willingly hasten forward to it, because it is a deliverance from the bondage of sin, and an introduction into the kingdom of heaven. . . . In the mean time, believers do not cease to regard death with horror, but when they turn their eyes to that life which follows death, they easily overcome all dread by means of that consolation. (Calvin, *Philippians* 43)

1:24 *remain in the flesh*. Paul's pastoral heart shines through once again as he weighs his desire to "depart" and be with Christ, or to "stay" and serve the Philippians' needs. In the end, the Church's needs vastly outweigh his own personal desires (2:4). Christians of-

197

ten say when they escape death, "Perhaps the Lord still has something left for me to do."

1:25 *remain and continue.* The terms share the same Gk root. The thought of his possible release from prison inspires in Paul a renewed confidence ("I know") that God will grant him the opportunity to resume his apostolic work on the Philippians' behalf. *progress and joy.* Earlier Paul used the term "progress" (Gk, *prokope*; elsewhere in NT only at 1Tm 4:15) to say that his imprisonment served the Gospel's progress (1:12). Now the apostle envisions that his future presence with the Philippians will help them to experience not only a stronger faith but also increased joy in believing the Gospel. Words that express the inner joy residing in a believer's heart occur sixteen times in Philippians alone (see note on 1:4). Paul's future sense of joy ("I will rejoice"; 1:18) indicates that a believer's joy is not a passing emotion. It is a deep, settled disposition that will outlast present troubles since it is rooted in the knowledge that "The Lord is at hand" (4:4–5). Moving forward in the Christian faith and life increases our joy as we experience God's will for us, even in times of anxiety (4:6; cf. Jn 16:24).

1:26 *glory in Christ Jesus.* Paul's release from prison and presence among the Philippians would be the occasion for them to be proud of Paul, but not the basic reason for that pride. Above all, Paul takes pride in Christ Jesus ("glory in Christ Jesus"; 3:3), his Savior (3:20). Everything else in life is secondary to "the surpassing worth of knowing Christ Jesus" the Lord (3:8). All human boasting therefore must be "in the Lord" (1Co 1:31), not in human wisdom or achievement. *my coming to you again.* "Coming" (Gk, *parousia*) often refers to Christ's Second Coming (e.g., Mt 24:3, 27, 37, 39). But here it is used in the non-technical sense of "return visit." Paul anticipated that Caesar would free him, after which he would revisit congregations.

PART 4

EXHORTATIONS (1:27–2:18)

Behave as Citizens Worthy of the Gospel (1:27–30)

ESV	KJV
²⁷Only let your manner of life be worthy of the gospel of Christ, so that whether I come and see you or am absent, I may hear of you that you are standing firm in one spirit, with one mind striving side by side for the faith of the gospel, ²⁸and not frightened in anything by your opponents. This is a clear sign to them of their destruction, but of your salvation, and that from God. ²⁹For it has been granted to you that for the sake of Christ you should not only believe in him but also suffer for his sake, ³⁰engaged in the same conflict that you saw I had and now hear that I still have.	²⁷Only let your conversation be as it becometh the gospel of Christ: that whether I come and see you, or else be absent, I may hear of your affairs, that ye stand fast in one spirit, with one mind striving together for the faith of the gospel; ²⁸And in nothing terrified by your adversaries: which is to them an evident token of perdition, but to you of salvation, and that of God. ²⁹For unto you it is given in the behalf of Christ, not only to believe on him, but also to suffer for his sake; ³⁰Having the same conflict which ye saw in me, and now hear to be in me.

1:27 *worthy of the gospel.* This comprises the underlying theme for the "exhortations" to follow (1:17–2:18; see Outline, p. 181; cf. Eph 4:1; Col 1:10). Through the Gospel, which Paul has defended and confirmed (1:7), God has begun His "good work" in the Philippians (1:6). God is now in the process of completing it. Paul wants to see progress in their faith (1:25). Thus he is ready to expand on what it means to live a life that corresponds to the powerful, saving message they have received. *in one spirit, with one mind.* The Philippians stand "arm in arm" with each other. They are kindred spirits united in a common fellowship and purpose (1:5). God's Spirit alone can give such inner unanimity (2:1–2, 5; see note on Eph 4:3).

striving . . . for the faith. The active imagery suggested by "striving" (Gk, *synathleo*) could be either athletic (contestants competing in an arena; 2Tm 2:5) or military (like a body of soldiers fighting in closed ranks). The word occurs again at 4:3 of two women who labored with him "side by side . . . in the gospel." *faith of the gospel.* The Gospel produces faith in Christ in our hearts, the faith on which our righteousness before God depends (3:9). But the Gospel not only produces saving faith (Rm 10:17); its content is also the object of our faith (cf. 1Tm 1:19; 4:1). Such faith brings us joy in our life with fellow Christians (1:25).

1:28 *opponents.* Paul does not specifically identify these opponents. In his missionary endeavors he met opposition both from Gentiles (Ac 17:32) and from Jews (Ac 13:45, 15:1). The Philippians, Paul notes in v. 30, "engaged in the same conflict" that Paul himself experienced in the past (in Philippi) and "now" as he writes in Rome. This may indicate that the opposition is primarily from non-Christians who sought also to intimidate them and make them skittish about living and sharing their faith (cf. 2:15). *their destruction.* The Philippians' steadfastness in the faith points not only to their salvation, but signals God's impending judgment on those who oppose the Gospel (see 2Th 1:5–10).

1:29 Believers do not find it shocking that they must suffer because of their faith in Christ (1Pt 4:12–13; 2Tm 3:12; Ac 14:22; cf. Ac 9:16). Participating in the sufferings Jesus endured (3:10) "is a gracious thing in the sight of God" (1Pt 2:20; cf. 2Th 1:5). Just as the apostles were happy that they "were counted worthy to suffer dishonor for the name [of Jesus]" (Ac 5:41), so we can count it a privilege granted to us by God when we experience criticism, social pressure, and even hostility because we confess Christ (Mt 5:10–12). Both faith in Christ and suffering for Him are God's gifts.

1:30 *same conflict.* See the note on v. 28. Paul recalls the intense struggle he experienced at Philippi when he was publicly mistreated (1Th 2:2) for casting a demon out of a young woman who told fortunes for her masters (Ac 16:16–24). He suffered severe physical abuse, was beaten with rods (cf. 2Co 11:25) and then jailed. He wants to comfort the Philippians in the knowledge that their "partnership in the gospel" with him "from the first day until now" (1:5, 27) included a partnership also in suffering. God gives us strength and courage to accept our own personal struggles with confidence and joy.

Devotion and Prayer in 1:19–30 No doubt word had reached Paul that the Philippians were deeply concerned about his imprisonment and its implications for the Gospel's advancement. He likely also learned that they were struggling because of mistreatment they were receiving from pagan neighbors because of their allegiance to Christ. Hostility against the Christian faith had lingered and perhaps even intensified since the days Paul was with them. Like Paul, they may have wished for some relief from the stresses they were experiencing. Paul lays bare his pastoral heart in this section. While he longs to depart this life and to be with Christ (truly a better place!), he remains hopeful that he will be released from prison and be able to fulfill their need. His interests are secondary to their progress and joy in the Christian faith. He and the Philippians are truly partners in the Gospel, wearing their sufferings for Christ as a badge of honor given to them by God. Sadly, the fear of embarrassment and sensitivity to public criticism often induces Christians to keep their faith in Christ under wraps. To be honest, they become ashamed of Christ and His Word. Extreme pressure may even drive them to avenues of escape or withdrawal from the battle into which their profession of faith thrusts them (see Eph 6:10–20 and commentary notes). By His grace, however, God promises to give us confidence and courage to say with Paul, "I am not ashamed of the gospel, for it is the power of God for salvation to everyone who believes" (Rm 1:16). Our Lord enables us to give glory to Him in everything. • O Lord Jesus, Author and Finisher of our faith, give us the strength to suffer, if need be, the abuse and hatred of this world and to regard such hardship as an honor and privilege to endure for Your name's sake. Amen.

Christ's Example of Humility (2:1–11)

ESV	KJV
2 ¹So if there is any encouragement in Christ, any comfort from love, any participation in the Spirit, any affection and sympathy, ²complete my joy by being of the same mind, having the same love, being in full accord and of one mind.	2 ¹If there be therefore any consolation in Christ, if any comfort of love, if any fellowship of the Spirit, if any bowels and mercies, ²Fulfil ye my joy, that ye be likeminded, having the same love, being of one accord, of one mind.

³Do nothing from rivalry or conceit, but in humility count others more significant than yourselves. ⁴Let each of you look not only to his own interests, but also to the interests of others. ⁵Have this mind among yourselves, which is yours in Christ Jesus, ⁶who, though he was in the form of God, did not count equality with God a thing to be grasped, ⁷but made himself nothing, taking the form of a servant, being born in the likeness of men. ⁸And being found in human form, he humbled himself by becoming obedient to the point of death, even death on a cross. ⁹Therefore God has highly exalted him and bestowed on him the name that is above every name, ¹⁰so that at the name of Jesus every knee should bow, in heaven and on earth and under the earth, ¹¹and every tongue confess that Jesus Christ is Lord, to the glory of God the Father.

³Let nothing be done through strife or vainglory; but in lowliness of mind let each esteem other better than themselves. ⁴Look not every man on his own things, but every man also on the things of others. ⁵Let this mind be in you, which was also in Christ Jesus: ⁶Who, being in the form of God, thought it not robbery to be equal with God: ⁷But made himself of no reputation, and took upon him the form of a servant, and was made in the likeness of men: ⁸And being found in fashion as a man, he humbled himself, and became obedient unto death, even the death of the cross. ⁹Wherefore God also hath highly exalted him, and given him a name which is above every name: ¹⁰That at the name of Jesus every knee should bow, of things in heaven, and things in earth, and things under the earth; ¹¹And that every tongue should confess that Jesus Christ is Lord, to the glory of God the Father.

2:1 *participation in the Spirit.* See the notes on 1:5 and Eph 4:3–4. Paul uses a similar phrase in his final blessing at 2Co 13:13. "Fellowship" here cannot simply be equated with a feeling of social togetherness. It is joint participation in the Holy Spirit and His gifts. The Spirit creates, preserves, and strengthens believers' oneness in Christ through Baptism and the Lord's Supper (1Co 12:13).

2:2 *one mind.* A surface congeniality that seeks to cover up dissension—as if to paste on a "smiley face"—will not go very far in solving a divisive situation. The Philippians can increase Paul's joy by possessing and fostering a unity of heart and purpose. Twice in this verse alone the Gk word commonly denoting an inner attitude or disposition occurs (*phroneo*; total of 10 times in Philippians—more than any other book in the NT!). A word meaning "harmonious" (ESV, "full accord" [Gk, *sympsychos*]) adds to what appears to be an expression of major concern about the Philippian congregation. Unanimity of heart and mind in a Christian congregation does not rule out vigorous debate and the frank interchange of opinions or views. Quite the contrary, healthy give-and-take can be expected among those who strive "side by side for the faith of the gospel" (1:27) and want to "approve what is excellent" (1:10) in their midst!

2:3 *count others more significant.* In the Greco-Roman world humility carried negative connotations. Self-disparagement signified that one was shamefully weak and poor. Jesus, who was "gentle and lowly in heart" (Mt 11:29), gave new meaning to this quality of the Christian life (cf. Mk 10:45). Paul here defines Christ-like humility: to consider others better then oneself. This presupposes a sober assessment of our sinfulness and the recognition that we creatures are utterly dependent on Him. Calvin wrote,

> Humility . . . is the mother of moderation, the effect of which is that, yielding up our own right, we give the preference to others, and are not easily thrown into agitation. He gives a definition of true humility—when every one esteems himself less than others. (Calvin, *Philippians* 52–53)

2:4 Paul elaborates on counting others more significant than ourselves (v. 3). Those who are prone always to be "looking out for number one" or demanding their "rights" (v. 21; cf. 3Jn 9) need to learn how to pay close attention to the best interests of others.

2:5 *Have this mind.* Verse 5 serves as a summary of vv. 1–4 and as a transitional verse introducing the supreme example of One who subordinated His interests below the interests of others. Since Christ has made Christians His own (3:12), their attitudes toward each other will be shaped by His humble and self-giving sacrifice. God wills that a humble mindset modeled after Christ's humility replace "rivalry" (i.e., selfish ambition) and "conceit" ("vainglory") (v. 3), which are destructive of harmony in the Christian congregation (cf. 3:15–16).

Introduction to 2:6–11 Paul encouraged the Colossian Christians to "teach and admonish one another in all wisdom, singing psalms and hymns and spiritual songs" (3:16). Early Christians likely developed their own hymns in poetic form. These spiritual songs contained a confession of their faith and expressed their praise to God. Such hymns, or fragments of them, have been identified and studied (e.g., Col 1:15–20; Eph 1:3–14; 1Tm 3:16). Some have called Php 2:6–11 a "Christ-hymn," for it serves not only to confess but also to teach the Gospel of Christ, who humbled Himself unto death for our salvation and was exalted to the throne of God to receive all honor and praise.

2:6 *form of God.* Even in His pre-existent state before His incarnation Jesus possessed the same nature as God (cf. Col 1:15). To say that He was in the form of God does not describe mere appearance, but rather means that He was of the same essence as God. Martin Chemnitz writes,

> Paul says [Php 2:6–9] that Christ was not only the actual form of God according to His deity, but he was also *in* the form of God, that is, in the highest glory, majesty, and power of God, indeed, true God equal with the Father . . . the whole fullness of God dwelt personally in the assumed [human] nature. (Chemnitz 6:326–27)

equality with God. A vast amount of literature has been written on the meaning of the phrase "form of God." Whatever its precise nuances, the ensuing phrase "equality with God" explains Paul's intended meaning. Full equality with God was something He possessed by nature since He was God, not something that was alien to Him. *grasped.* There was no need for God's Son to seize what He already possessed by nature. Therefore, Paul's meaning must be that Jesus did not regard equality with God as something to be exploited to His own advantage (Jn 13:3–4). Those who belong to Jesus find in their Savior encouragement to offer their lives in the service of others.

2:7 *made Himself nothing.* The Gk term meaning "emptied Himself" has also been interpreted in many ways over the years. For example, some have taken the expression to mean that Jesus actually exchanged His divine nature for human nature. Others have concluded that He was only a man who appeared to be divine. Still others have said that Jesus did not actually become human, but only appeared to be in human form. Taken within the context of the explanatory phrases to follow, "emptied Himself" means that Jesus gave up the appearance of His divinity (which He possessed) and took on the form of a slave (which He voluntarily assumed). The Lutheran reformers stated,

[The Son of Man] was received into God when He was conceived of the Holy Spirit in His mother's womb, and His human nature was personally united with the Son of the Highest. Christ always had this majesty according to the personal union. Yet He abstained from using it in the state of His humiliation, and because of this He truly increased in all wisdom and favor with God and men. Therefore, He did not always use this majesty, but only when it pleased Him. (FC Ep VIII 15–16)

form of a servant. Jesus took upon Himself the nature of a human being (note the "*of men*"). And He was, in every way, completely a servant to those around Him. See the note on v. 6. *likeness of men*. Paul uses a similar expression in Rm 8:3: "By sending His own Son in the *likeness* of sinful flesh and for sin, He condemned sin in the flesh." God's Son externally appeared similar to sinful human beings but He was not totally like them. That is, He wholly identified with sinful man and this was a full likeness. But it was only a "likeness" (Gk, *homoios*). He was fully human, yet a human without sin. As Paul writes, He "who knew no sin" was made "for our sake . . . to be sin" (2Co 5:21; cf. Rm 8:3; Heb 2:7, 14).

2:8 *human form*. See the note on v. 7. Jesus shared all the characteristics of a human being. He gave us glimpses of His "glory as of the only Son from the Father" (Jn 1:14). But He kept the full use of His glory veiled under His human form. *obedient*. Christ accepted death as obedience to His Father, praying in Gethsemane, "not My will, but Yours, be done" (Lk 22:42). Isaiah 53:7 prophesies how God's Suffering Servant would be mistreated but "opened not His mouth, "like a sheep that before its shearers is silent" (53:7). Isaiah 53:8, in the LXX, begins with the words "in lowliness" (ESV, "By oppression"). *death on a cross*. The Jewish historian Josephus described crucifixion as "the most wretched of deaths." Jesus' death on the cross meant that the rock bottom of humiliation was reached. In the Greco-Roman world, crucifixion was fairly widespread and was inflicted especially on the lower classes (e.g., slaves, violent criminals and rebels—people with no rights). An extreme form of human cruelty, it was regarded as offensive and obscene. The Romans crucified criminals publicly to humiliate them and to warn the people not to make the same mistake. Among Jews a crucified Messiah would have been inconceivable. In OT Law, being hung on a tree meant you were cursed before God (cf. Dt 21:22–23; Gal 3:13). To assert, as

Paul does, that God took the form of a slave and submitted to crucifixion to redeem the world would have seemed the height of folly
and madness to people of ancient times.

2:9 *above every name*. See the commentary notes on Eph 1:2. In
response to Jesus' voluntary act of humiliation, even to the point of
death on the despised cross, God exalted Jesus to the highest level of
dignity and honor. Paul uses a term (occurring only here in the NT)
to signify a person exceptionally honored by virtue of high status—a
status that belongs only to God Himself. Isaiah had prophesied of
God's Servant Messiah, "Behold, My servant shall act wisely; He shall
be high and lifted up, and shall be exalted" (Is 52:13). In fulfillment
of this prophecy, God conferred on Jesus, whose name means "save,"
the personal name by which the God of Israel revealed Himself in
the OT: "LORD" (v. 11; Yahweh, in Hbr; cf. Ex 3:13–14; Is 42:8). The
term "bestowed" (Gk *charizomai*) makes it clear that Jesus did not
seek after this title, but it was given to Him. In the state of exaltation
Jesus made full use of His divine powers: "[He entirely laid aside the
form of a servant, but not the human nature, and was established in
the full use, manifestation, and declaration of the divine majesty" (FC
Ep VIII 16).

2:10 *should bow*. See the commentary notes on Eph 3:13–14.
Paul's words correspond closely with the LXX text of Is 45:23: "To
Me [God] every knee shall bow, every tongue swear allegiance." Declaring that He alone is God and "there is no other," God summoned
"all the ends of the earth" to turn to Him "and be saved" (43:22).
Isaiah here points to the day when all people and powers will have
to acknowledge Jesus, God's Son, as the supreme Lord over every
corner of the universe. *under the earth*. Paul speaks figuratively of
a realm occupied perhaps by personal beings (including the dead),
or powers.

2:11 *Jesus Christ is Lord*. In the Pauline Letters the names "Christ,"
"Jesus Christ," or "Christ Jesus" occurs 271 times. "Jesus is Lord" is fit-
tingly called the first creed of the Christian Church (v. 11; 1Co 12:3;
cf. Mk 8:29; Ac 5:42). The name *Jesus* (Gk *iesous*) corresponds to the
Hbr name *Joshua*, which means "Yahweh is salvation," or "saves" or
"will save." God the Holy Spirit gave this name to the Virgin Mary's
child to signify who He is and what He would do: "He will save
His people from their sins" (Mt 1:21). The name *Christ* is the Gk
form (*christos*) of the Hbr for "Messiah" (*Meshiach*), which means

"Anointed One." God anointed Jesus of Nazareth to be the Christ in fulfillment of His OT promises, that He might save people from their sins through His suffering, death, and resurrection (Ac 4:24–31; 10:34–43). The Gospel proclaimed by the apostles and believed by those who receive Him is "the gospel of Jesus Christ" (Mk 1:1; Mt 1:1, 16, 18; Lk 2:26; Jn 4:25–26). In subsequent decades the Philippians and other Christians would know what a serious choice they would face when confessing "Jesus is Lord," especially in periods when the refusal to say "Caesar is lord" could place them in danger. Also today when hostility against the Christian faith seems on the increase, allegiance to Jesus Christ can entail great personal cost.

Devotion and Prayer in 2:1–11 The church at Philippi was not without its internal difficulties. There was a tendency among some "to seek their own interests, not those of Jesus Christ" (2:21). Paul's exhortation that the Philippians "do nothing from rivalry or conceit" mirrors some dissension there caused by self-assertive behavior. By and large, however, Paul is pleased that they are single-mindedly striving "side by side for the faith of the gospel" (1:27), which Paul is fond of calling a "partnership" (1:5; 4:15). This section of ch. 2 reads like a warm and loving word of pastoral encouragement. Paul wants the Philippians to continue placing the interests of others above their own interests. In a sense, he wants the congregation to have a distinct "personality," to have an attitude and character that is shaped by the Lord Jesus Himself. Christ Jesus has modeled the meaning of humble submission to the needs of others. He Himself, who possessed equality with God, lowered Himself to take on the form and life of a slave. He was obedient to His Father even to death on a cross. Therefore God exalted Him to the highest possible place of honor, bestowing on Him the name *Lord*, a title that is only God's prerogative to bear. At the name of Jesus, therefore, every knee must bow and every tongue confess in reverent and humble submission.

• Dear Lord Jesus, give us a spirit of humility, that we may set aside selfish pursuits and join with our fellow believers in the common task of proclaiming the glory of Your name. Amen.

Lights in the World (2:12–18)

ESV	KJV
¹²Therefore, my beloved, as you have always obeyed, so now, not only as in my presence but much more in my absence, work out your own salvation with fear and trembling, ¹³for it is God who works in you, both to will and to work for his good pleasure. ¹⁴Do all things without grumbling or questioning, ¹⁵that you may be blameless and innocent, children of God without blemish in the midst of a crooked and twisted generation, among whom you shine as lights in the world, ¹⁶holding fast to the word of life, so that in the day of Christ I may be proud that I did not run in vain or labor in vain. ¹⁷Even if I am to be poured out as a drink offering upon the sacrificial offering of your faith, I am glad and rejoice with you all. ¹⁸Likewise you also should be glad and rejoice with me.	¹²Wherefore, my beloved, as ye have always obeyed, not as in my presence only, but now much more in my absence, work out your own salvation with fear and trembling. ¹³For it is God which worketh in you both to will and to do of his good pleasure. ¹⁴Do all things without murmurings and disputings: ¹⁵That ye may be blameless and harmless, the sons of God, without rebuke, in the midst of a crooked and perverse nation, among whom ye shine as lights in the world; ¹⁶Holding forth the word of life; that I may rejoice in the day of Christ, that I have not run in vain, neither laboured in vain. ¹⁷Yea, and if I be offered upon the sacrifice and service of your faith, I joy, and rejoice with you all. ¹⁸For the same cause also do ye joy, and rejoice with me.

2:12–18 *Therefore.* Paul's teaching in vv. 12–18 flows from his teaching about Christ's humility in vv. 1–11.

2:12 *my beloved.* Paul often addresses those whom he dearly loved—but especially those whom God loved—by this affectionate term (4:1; Rm 12:19; 2Co 7:1; 12:19; 15:58; cf. 1:8). The Gk word *agapetos*, meaning "beloved," derives from the familiar word for love in the NT, *agape. always obeyed.* A prominent theme in vv. 6–11 is the obedience of Christ. From the very beginning, the Philippians responded positively to Paul's preaching and emulated Christ's obedience (Ac 16:15; cf. 1:3–6). *work out your own salvation.* The ESV and KJV's "work out" (Gk *katergazomai*, "produce") captures well what Paul is saying. Believers do not save themselves by their good works.

But through the Spirit's work in them they do produce the practical results of God's saving grace in their personal lives (Gal 5:22–23; cf. Eph 2:11 and commentary notes). *with fear and trembling.* The awesomeness of the divine presence in the person of Jesus Christ requires that service to God be performed with reverence and awe. Just as earthly slaves were to serve their masters with "fear and trembling" (Eph 6:5), so also we serve our Master with profound respect, not with slavish dread. Of the Early Church Luke writes, "And walking in the fear of the Lord and in the comfort of the Holy Spirit, it multiplied" (Ac 9:31). Luther wrote, "With our whole heart we trust in Him and fear and love Him throughout all our lives" (LC I 103).

2:13 *God who works in you.* God causes or puts into operation both the willing and the doing of His will in Christians. The "power at work within us" (Eph 3:20) is nothing less than God's mighty power that raised Jesus from the dead (Eph 1:19–20). Without the operation of God's Holy Spirit the human will cannot submit to God's will (Rm 8:7; cf. Jn 15:5).

> Even in this life the regenerate advance to the point that they want to do what is good and love it, and even do good and grow in it. Still, this (as stated above) is not of our will and ability, but of the Holy Spirit. Paul himself speaks about this, saying that the Spirit works such *willing and doing* (Philippians 2:13). . . . For the preaching and hearing of God's Word are the Holy Spirit's instruments. By, with, and through these instruments the Spirit desires to work effectively, to convert people to God, and to work in them both to will and to do [Philippians 2:13]. (FC SD II 39, 52)

His good pleasure. The pronoun "His" is not in the Gk text, but the context makes it clear that it is God who is at work to accomplish in believers what pleases Him in keeping with His divine purposes (cf. Eph 1:5). Note that the verse begins with "for God is at work . . . " which gives the reason or basis for Paul's prior encouragement that the Philippians put into practice God's saving action in Christ (v. 12).

2:14 *grumbling or questioning.* Grumbling (the Gk word connotes something said in a low tone of voice) and argumentative complaining are hazardous to the health of a Christian congregation, producing the "side effect" of ill-will among members leading to divisiveness. See Nu 11:1–6; 14:1–4; 20:3–5; 21:4–5.

2:15 *children of God*. In v. 15 Paul quotes from the end of Dt 32:5, which he largely reproduces. This OT passage (in the Song of Moses) speaks of the Israelites as a crooked people and therefore not God's children (5a). Paul uses the language of this OT text to say in contrast that the Philippians are God's children, while their pagan neighbors are not. God's children are those whom He has adopted in love (Eph 1:5). They are all "sons of God through faith." They have been redeemed by God's Son and made His children through Baptism. By His Spirit they are able and privileged to call God "Father" (Gal 3:26–27; 4:6; Rm 8:15; Jn 1:12–13). *without blemish*. In the LXX the Gk term for "unblemished" (*amomos*) refers to the absence of defects in sacrificial animals (e.g., Nu 6:14; 19:2). We have been redeemed, writes Peter, by the precious blood of Christ, "like that of a lamb without blemish or spot" (1Pt 1:19). Jesus offered Himself "without blemish to God" that so we might be forgiven of our sins (Heb 9:14). Because of Christ we have been presented to God "holy and blameless and above reproach before Him" (Col 1:22). *a crooked and twisted generation*. We have here a vivid description of unregenerate, rebellious humankind "without God in the world" (Eph 2:12). The expression, lifted directly out of Dt 32:5, not only designates immoral behavior, but also a distorted sense of values. Such a generation is inherently dishonest and unscrupulous. *you shine as lights*. Jesus calls His followers "the light of the world" who must let their light shine so people will see their good works and give glory to their Father in heaven (Mt 5:14). They are like the sun, moon and stars that God created to give light to the world (Gn 1:14–19). God's children are "children of light" (Eph 5:8–9). This imagery contains a lesson for all of God's children. They are to live pure and upright lives not to call attention to their own religiosity, but to be bear witness in word and deed to the new life that is theirs in Christ (cf. 2Pt 1:19).

2:16 *the word of life*. Christ Jesus has "abolished death and brought life and immortality to light through the Gospel" (2Tm 1:10; cf. Ac 5:20; 1Jn 1:1). Life comes from the Gospel revealed in the Holy Scriptures because it proclaims Jesus who is the resurrection and the life. It reveals that "The righteous shall live by faith" in Christ (Rm 1:16–17). *the day of Christ*. See the note on 1:6. Paul mentions Christ's Second Coming to judge the world because he expects that he will have to give an account of his apostolic labors. *proud*. The apostle also confidently expects that he will have reason to boast (Gk *kauchema*) in the Philippians' extraordinary response to the Gospel (cf. 4:15). He especially hopes to take pride in the fruit that the Gospel has produced among them and in their growth in the faith (1:6). *run in vain or labor in vain.* The term "run" can refer literally to footracing in a stadium (1Co 9:24, 26). Figuratively, the various aspects of Paul's whole missionary enterprise resemble a runner straining forward and making progress toward the finish line (Rm 9:16; Gal 2:2; 5:7; 2Th 3:1). Similarly, a word for manual labor aptly conveys the exertion and hard work that Paul and his coworkers undertook so that their missionary endeavors might not be in vain (1Th 2:9; 3:5; 2Th 3:8; 1Tm 5:17).

2:17 *drink offering.* Some think that Paul has in mind a pagan cultic practice involving the pouring out of blood. It is more likely, however, that he is alluding to the OT sacrificial system in which a drink-offering or libation of wine or oil was poured out at the completion of the burnt offering (with the cereal offering) in the sanctuary (Nu 15:3–10). *sacrificial offering of your faith.* Paul regarded the Christian's life and service as together a sacrifice offered to God (Rm 12:1–3; Php 4:18). In this verse the Philippians' faith itself, demonstrated in acts of service, rises as a sacrifice pleasing to God. If Paul should have to give up his life (perhaps he was envisioning his impending death), he can regard that as a way of completing and crowning the spiritual sacrifice that the Philippians offered to God.

2:18 *rejoice.* See the commentary note on 1:4. Philippians is often called "The Letter of Joy."

Devotion and Prayer in 2:12–18 Paul has encouraged the Philippians to be of one mind and to show concern for one another (1:27–2:4). He has appealed to the example of Jesus, who was equal with God but voluntarily took on a servant's form on their behalf. Now Paul urges his Christian friends to work out their salvation in practical ways that please God because God is powerfully at work in them. And they are to do so with a deep sense of reverence for Christ. In their everyday lives Christians face serious challenges, because they live in an unprincipled and perverse world. They need to be keenly aware that their life and conduct within the Church can tarnish their witness to those on the "outside," that is, their unbelieving neighbors. Therefore, Paul gives two pieces of advice: avoid bickering and complaining, for this weakens your partnership in the faith and sets a bad example to others; and, hold fast to the Word of life and shine like lights before the world, that people may see Christ through your words and actions. Paul rejoices with the Philippians and wants to be proud of them on the day of Christ. Following the example of Christ, Paul would be happy and willing to give up his life as a way of concluding their sacrificial service to God. By God's Spirit Paul has written his encouraging words to Christians of every age, that we too might be God's children of light (Eph 5:8). • Dear Lord Jesus, help us to remain faithful to Your Word of life and live blameless lives in this morally perverse world. Amen.

PART 5

Travel Plans for Timothy and Epaphroditus (2:19–30)

ESV	KJV
[19]I hope in the Lord Jesus to send Timothy to you soon, so that I too may be cheered by news of you. [20]For I have no one like him, who will be genuinely concerned for your welfare. [21]For they all seek their own interests, not those of Jesus Christ. [22]But you know Timothy's proven worth, how as a son with a father he has served with me in the gospel. [23]I hope therefore to send him just as soon as I see how it will go with me, [24]and I trust in the Lord that shortly I myself will come also.	[19]But I trust in the Lord Jesus to send Timotheus shortly unto you, that I also may be of good comfort, when I know your state. [20]For I have no man likeminded, who will naturally care for your state. [21]For all seek their own, not the things which are Jesus Christ's. [22]But ye know the proof of him, that, as a son with the father, he hath served with me in the gospel. [23]Him therefore I hope to send presently, so soon as I shall see how it will go with me. [24]But I trust in the Lord that I also myself shall come shortly.
[25]I have thought it necessary to send to you Epaphroditus my brother and fellow worker and fellow soldier, and your messenger and minister to my need, [26]for he has been longing for you all and has been distressed because you heard that he was ill. [27]Indeed he was ill, near to death. But God had mercy on him, and not only on him but on me also, lest I should have sorrow upon sorrow. [28]I am the more eager to send him, therefore, that you may rejoice at seeing him again, and that I may be less anxious.	[25]Yet I supposed it necessary to send to you Epaphroditus, my brother, and companion in labour, and fellowsoldier, but your messenger, and he that ministered to my wants. [26]For he longed after you all, and was full of heaviness, because that ye had heard that he had been sick. [27]For indeed he was sick nigh unto death: but God had mercy on him; and not on him only, but on me also, lest I should have sorrow upon sorrow. [28]I sent him therefore the more carefully, that, when ye see him again, ye may rejoice, and that I may be the less sorrowful.

²⁹So receive him in the Lord with all joy, and honor such men, ³⁰for he nearly died for the work of Christ, risking his life to complete what was lacking in your service to me.	²⁹Receive him therefore in the Lord with all gladness; and hold such in reputation: ³⁰Because for the work of Christ he was nigh unto death, not regarding his life, to supply your lack of service toward me.

2:19–20 *Timothy.* See note on 1:1. Paul and the Philippians will be heartened by Timothy's ministry of encouragement as Paul's co-worker in the churches (cf. 1Th 3:1–5; 1Co 4:17; 16:10–11). *genuinely concerned.* Paul and Timothy were kindred spirits, sharing a deep concern for the welfare of the churches (v. 28; cf. 2Co 11:28).

2:21 See the notes on 1:15–18 and 2:2–4. Paul elaborates on what he means by "genuinely concerned" in v. 20. Calvin wrote,

> He does not speak of those who had openly abandoned the pursuit of piety, but of those very persons whom he reckoned brethren, nay, even those whom he admitted to familiar intercourse with him. These persons, he nevertheless says, were so warm in the pursuit of their own interests, that they were unbecomingly cold in the work of the Lord. . . . When, however, we hear Paul complaining, that in that golden age, in which all excellences flourished, that there were so few that were rightly affected, let us not be disheartened, if such is our condition in the present day: only let every one take heed to himself, that he be not justly reckoned to belong to that catalogue. (Calvin, *Philippians* 76, 78)

2:22 *as a son with a father.* Paul was instrumental in Timothy's conversion and thought of him as a son (1Tm 1:18; 2Tm 2:1). Teachers and their followers in Paul's day often developed an intimate relationship described as "father" and "son." A mutual trust borne out of a mutual devotion to Christ bound Paul and Timothy together. Paul felt the affection a father could feel for a likeminded son. In return, Paul received from Timothy the service and devotion that a son could give to a father. See Phm 10. *served with me.* Timothy traveled and worked with Paul and was sent on Paul's behalf to teach. Paul does not say "served me" but "served *with me*," because both bore the title "slaves of Christ Jesus" (1:1; ESV, "servants"). See the note on 1:1.

2:23 *how it will go.* Paul delays sending Timothy to Philippi until he knows more about how his trial will turn out.

2:24 Paul expresses confidence that he will be released from prison and permitted to work again among the Philippians. Cf. 1:19–26.

2:25 *Epaphroditus.* He delivered gifts from the Philippians to Paul (4:18), and probably the Letter to them. Paul warmly commends him with five terms, one of which is "messenger" (Gk *apostolos*, in its general meaning; cf. 2Co 8:23).

2:26–27 *ill . . . near to death.* Travel conditions in Paul's day could be dangerous and harsh. The frequent severe conditions for travel perhaps decreased resistance to the many diseases of antiquity. Epaphroditus was suffering from some physical ailment (the nature of which we do not know) that posed a real threat to his life. *God had mercy.* Due to God's merciful help, Epaphroditus was restored to health. Scripture urges us to cast all our anxieties on God, "because he cares for [us]" (1Pt 5:7). Together with Epaphroditus, Paul was also the recipient of God's mercy (v. 27). God shows deep consideration for the struggles His servants endure and grants relief. *sorrow upon sorrow.* Paul was deeply sorrowful over Epaphroditus's condition. His death would have added greatly to Paul's burden of sorrow. But God, by His mercy, prevented Epaphroditus's death and brought Paul relief. The news of Epaphroditus's recovery also brought the Philippians relief from the mental and spiritual distress they experienced upon the shocking news of his illness (v. 28).

2:30 *he nearly died for the work of Christ.* Epaphroditus worked and traveled extensively for the sake of Gospel of Christ. He served in partnership with Paul and the Philippians (1:5). He not only delivered to Paul a gift from the Philippians, but at the same time ministered to Paul's needs in prison. He carried out the work that Christ had assigned to him at great risk (see note on vv. 26–27). *what was lacking in your service to me.* Epaphroditus acted like a conduit of the Philippians' love and devotion. The Philippians wanted to support Paul in spreading the Gospel, but Paul had been traveling and now was under arrest in Rome. Epaphroditus performed this service on their behalf. The term "service" in v. 30 (Gk *leitourgia*) appears also in 2:17 in the expression "sacrificial offering" of faith. Epaphroditus's unselfish devotion to Christ's mission—as in the case of Paul and Timothy—was another example of the self-giving attitude that Christ Jesus displayed (2:5, 6–11).

Devotion and Prayer in 2:19–30 Paul digresses to present two tireless and selfless servants of the Lord Jesus and His Gospel: Timothy and Epaphroditus. He informs the Philippians about the significance and well-being of these two close associates and their partnership in the Gospel. Paul intentionally holds them up as a kind of "Exhibit B." Their humble submission to the needs of others (vv. 1–5) duplicates the submission of Christ (vv. 6–11). Of Timothy, for example, Paul writes, "I have no one like him, who will be genuinely concerned for your welfare" (v. 20). Paul's counsel in v. 29, "honor such men," has special application in situations where Christian congregations neglect to esteem their pastors and other workers "very highly in love because of their work" (1Th 5:13). Paul's counsel to receive Epaphroditus "with all joy" can lift our vision to see what is all-important in the Church: "the work of Christ" (Php 2:30). • Dear Lord Jesus, by Your mercy, make us faithful servants, looking after the welfare of one another and of Your humble servants of the Word. Amen.

PART 6

FURTHER EXHORTATIONS (3:1–4:9)

Warning against Mutilators (3:1–11)

ESV	KJV
3 ¹Finally, my brothers, rejoice in the Lord. To write the same things to you is no trouble to me and is safe for you. ²Look out for the dogs, look out for the evildoers, look out for those who mutilate the flesh. ³For we are the circumcision, who worship by the Spirit of God and glory in Christ Jesus and put no confidence in the flesh—⁴though I myself have reason for confidence in the flesh also. If anyone else thinks he has reason for confidence in the flesh, I have more: ⁵circumcised on the eighth day, of the people of Israel, of the tribe of Benjamin, a Hebrew of Hebrews; as to the law, a Pharisee; ⁶as to zeal, a persecutor of the church; as to righteousness under the law, blameless. ⁷But whatever gain I had, I counted as loss for the sake of Christ. ⁸Indeed, I count everything as loss because of the surpassing worth of knowing Christ Jesus my Lord. For his sake I have suffered the loss of all things and count them as rubbish, in order that I may gain Christ	3 ¹Finally, my brethren, rejoice in the Lord. To write the same things to you, to me indeed is not grievous, but for you it is safe. ²Beware of dogs, beware of evil workers, beware of the concision. ³For we are the circumcision, which worship God in the spirit, and rejoice in Christ Jesus, and have no confidence in the flesh. ⁴Though I might also have confidence in the flesh. If any other man thinketh that he hath whereof he might trust in the flesh, I more: ⁵Circumcised the eighth day, of the stock of Israel, of the tribe of Benjamin, an Hebrew of the Hebrews; as touching the law, a Pharisee; ⁶Concerning zeal, persecuting the church; touching the righteousness which is in the law, blameless. ⁷But what things were gain to me, those I counted loss for Christ. ⁸Yea doubtless, and I count all things but loss for the excellency of the knowledge of Christ Jesus my Lord: for whom I have suffered the loss of all things, and do count them but dung, that I may win Christ,

⁹and be found in him, not having a righteousness of my own that comes from the law, but that which comes through faith in Christ, the righteousness from God that depends on faith—¹⁰that I may know him and the power of his resurrection, and may share his sufferings, becoming like him in his death, ¹¹that by any means possible I may attain the resurrection from the dead.

⁹And be found in him, not having mine own righteousness, which is of the law, but that which is through the faith of Christ, the righteousness which is of God by faith: ¹⁰That I may know him, and the power of his resurrection, and the fellowship of his sufferings, being made conformable unto his death; ¹¹If by any means I might attain unto the resurrection of the dead.

3:1 *Finally*. This word can sometimes indicate the end of a Letter. But Paul also uses it on occasion to mark a transition to a new topic (cf. 1Co 4:2 where this word is translated as "Moreover"). Although he has two chapters yet to write, Paul embarks on new topics and emphases, extending his conclusion. *my brothers*. See the note on 1:12. *write the same things*. Commentators have disagreed regarding the precise meaning of this phrase. Some think it may refer to earlier letters (now lost) that Paul wrote to the Philippians. Some speculate that it may refer to the topic of rejoicing, in particular, or to other topics treated previously in the Letter. The general thrust of the words, however, is not difficult to understand. Paul prepares to repeat topics that he had previously discussed during his association and contacts with the Philippians (including, of course, the possibility of other correspondence). *safe for you*. Paul does not hesitate to turn to the next topics because he is confident that what he has to say will be in the Philippians' best interest. His ensuing warning against false teachers flows from his deep affection for the Philippians, for he desires to safeguard them against the spiritual dangers of errant teachings. The tone of his Letter is absent the kind of deep anguish present in Paul's correspondence with the Corinthians (2Co 2:1–4).

3:2 *dogs*. The very mention of "dogs" connoted uncleanness in Jewish minds. Dogs were a despised and repulsive animal because they ate animal flesh that was unclean (Ex 22:31) and even human flesh (1Ki 14:11; 16:4; 21:19, 23–24). They preyed on the sick, dying, or dead (e.g., dogs devoured Jezebel after she was thrown from her window, 2Ki 9:36). Dogs scavenged around the streets and garbage dumps of the towns. Jews used the term as a derogatory title for Gentiles (*1En* 89:42) because Gentiles were regarded as ritually unclean and outside God's covenant (cf. Mt 7:6; 15:26–27). With an ironic twist, Paul applies the word here to traveling Jewish-Christian teachers like those in Galatia (Judaizers whom Paul called the "circumcision party" in Gal 2:12) who insisted that Gentiles had to be circumcised to be saved (Ac 15:1). For this they deserved the title "evildoers." The biting sarcasm of Paul's words would not have escaped such people unnoticed. *mutilate the flesh.* "Mutilation" (Gk *katatome*) is a wordplay on the word for "circumcision" (*peritome*), the sign of the covenant between God and Israel (Gn 17:10–14). With the term "mutilation" Paul may be alluding to pagan practices of cutting the body, which were forbidden in OT law (Lv 19:28; 21:5; Dt 14:1; but see the note on Gal 5:12). Again, the derogatory nature of Paul's language against the intruding errorists is evident.

3:3 *we are the circumcision.* "The circumcision" means figuratively believers in Jesus Christ. They are the truly circumcised people who by faith are heirs of the promise (Rm 4:16). Paul also writes about a "true circumcision" that takes place in the life of believers (Rm 2:29). This "circumcision" is not an external rite done by hands, but a "matter of the heart, by the Spirit, not by the letter [the Law]." Believers "put off" the sinful flesh through God's work in Baptism (Col 2:11–12). They put to death the deeds of the flesh (Rm 6:11). Similarly, the OT speaks of a spiritual "circumcision of the heart" through repentance (Dt 10:16; 30:6; Jer 4:4; Lv 26:41). *worship by the Spirit of God.* The Holy Spirit inspires true worship (Jn 4:24). He creates within us a new heart that praises and serves God. When believers offer themselves up as living sacrifices to God in worship and service, that is truly their "spiritual worship" (Rm 12:1). *glory in Christ Jesus.* The Gk word for "glory" commonly refers to boasting or taking pride in oneself. But it can also mean taking pride in someone else, and in this verse the distinguishing feature of Christian worship is taking pride in or glorying in Christ Jesus. *no confidence in the flesh.* Paul no doubt is alluding to physical circumcision. But he wants to make the more general point that God's new people in Christ do not place their confidence in earthly things or external physical advantages.

3:4–6 Paul presents his resumé, enumerating the privileges of his Jewish descent and his personal achievements according to the Law. But he places his confidence only in Christ, not in his religious accomplishments.

3:4 Paul speaks as one who has more than enough credentials to place *confidence in the flesh*. His opponents cannot easily dismiss him by saying he has no right to speak.

3:5 *circumcised on the eighth day*. Paul regards himself as a true member of God's covenant people Israel, circumcised in keeping with the requirements of the Law (Gn 17:12; Lv 12:3). *of . . . Benjamin*. The Jews held the tribe of Benjamin in very high regard (cf. Rm 11:1). Benjamin was the only son of Jacob born in the land of promise (Gn 35:16–18). From his tribe came Israel's first king, Saul (1Sm 9:1–2), after whom Paul was named (cf. Ac 7:58; 1:9). *Hebrew of Hebrews*. A "Hebrew" referred to an Israelite who spoke Aramaic (a West Semitic dialect). Paul is claiming again that he is a full-blooded Jew, faithful to the customs and traditions of his Hebrew ancestors. *Pharisee*. The Pharisees were a Jewish sect that advocated strict adherence to the written Law and its many binding interpretations.

3:6 *persecutor of the church*. Paul's extreme zeal for traditions of his Jewish ancestors moved him to aggressively pursue Christians for the purpose of annihilating the Church (Gal 1:13–14; Ac 9:1–2; cf. 1Co 15:9; 1Tm 1:13). He presents this personal history as iron-clad evidence of his total commitment to the Jewish faith. *blameless*. Later compilations of the many-layered Jewish traditions contained a large number of individual rules into which the Torah (the Law) was developed in rabbinical teaching (oral law; 248 commandments, 365 prohibitions, a total of 613 laws). Paul claims to have strictly observed such detailed codes of ethical and ritual behavior. He explicitly refers to these "traditions" in Gal 1:14, where he means the tradition of the rabbis (the "traditions" or "sayings of the fathers," known as the *Pirqe Aboth*) accepted by the Pharisees but rejected by the Saduccees. In Mt 15:1–9 Jesus accuses the Pharisees and scribes of breaking "the commandment of God" for the sake of "the commandments of men." (cf. Mt 15:1–9).

3:7 *loss*. Paul is saying more by this term (Gk *zemia*, "damage," "disadvantage") than that his advantages as a Jew (moral superiority and blamelessness) have no more value to him because of Christ. He insists that such "advantages" are actually disadvantageous—that is, harmful. Moral achievements are spiritually harmful if someone believes that by them a person can merit favor before God. Paul says this most sharply by his words to the Galatians: "You are severed from Christ, you who would be justified by the law; you have fallen away from grace" (Gal 5:4). Those who "accept circumcision" (as a necessary requirement for Christians to be saved), make Christ of "no advantage," says Paul (Gal 5:2; cf. Mt 16:26). The Lutheran reformers poignantly declared,

> If anyone wants to drag good works into the article of justification, rest his righteousness or trust for salvation on them, and merit God's grace and be saved by them, St. Paul himself answers, not us. He says and repeats it three times (Philippians 3:7–8)—such a person's works are not only useless and a hindrance, but are also harmful. This is not the fault of the good works themselves, but of the false confidence placed in the works, contrary to God's clear Word. (FC SD IV 37)

To use a monetary comparison, what Paul formerly regarded as a credit (a plus) to his account has now been made into a debit (a minus).

3:8 *surpassing worth.* The surpassing greatness of personally knowing Jesus Christ puts everything else into its proper perspective. *rubbish.* The Gk word (*skybalon*; only occurrence in the NT) refers to useless or undesirable material ("crud") that is subject to disposal. (In Gk literature outside the Bible it can mean excrement, manure, garbage, or kitchen scraps.) *gain Christ.* To have Christ makes us heirs of everything that belongs to Him (Col 2:3, 20). Calvin wrote,

> Those who cast their merchandise and other things into the sea, that they may escape in safety, do not, therefore, despise riches, but act as persons prepared rather to live in misery and want, than to be drowned along with their riches. They part with them, indeed, but it is with regret and with a sigh; and when they have escaped, they bewail the loss of them. Paul, however, declares, on the other hand, that he had not merely abandoned everything that he formerly reckoned precious, but that they were like *dung*, offensive to him, or were disesteemed like things that are thrown away in contempt. (Calvin, *Philippians* 95–96)

3:9 *comes through faith in Christ.* See the commentary note on Eph 2:8–9. The Bible speaks of saving faith as the instrument or means through which a sinner receives and possesses as his or her own the righteousness and benefits of Christ, forgiveness of sins, and salvation (Rm 3:25, 28; Gal 2:16). *righteousness from God.* The righteousness from God stands in sharp contrast to human righteousness based on obedience to the Law (Paul had believed that his previously mentioned Jewish status and moral achievements merited God's favor). "Justify" in Scripture denotes a verdict, i.e., a forensic (legal) act whereby a person is counted righteous, declared righteous, reckoned to be righteous and absolved (Rm 3:20–28; 4:1–13; 5:1; 8:33). God not only does not count our sins against us and forgive us; He actually credits to our account the righteousness of Christ.

> The word *justify* here means to declare righteous and free from sins and to absolve a person from eternal punishment for the sake of Christ's righteousness, which is credited by God to faith (Philippians 3:9). (FC SD III 17)

Cranmer wrote,

> This sentence, that we be justified by faith only, is not so meant of them, that the said justifying faith is alone in man, without true repentance, hope, charity, dread, and the fear of God, at any time or season. Nor when they say, that we be justified freely, they mean not that we should or might afterward be idle, and that nothing should be required on our parts afterward. Neither they mean not so to be justified without good works, that we should do no good works at all, like as shall be more expressed at large hereafter. But this proposition, that we be justified by faith only, freely, and without works, is spoken for to take away clearly all merit of our works, as being insufficient to deserve our justification at God's hands, and thereby most plainly to express the weakness of man, and the goodness of God; the great infirmity of ourselves, and the might and power of God; the imperfectness of our own works, and the most abundant grace of our saviour Christ; and therefore wholly for to ascribe the merit and deserving of our justification unto Christ only, and his most precious blood-shedding. (Cranmer 2:143–44)

3:10–11 After being stoned by his enemies and left for dead, Paul encouraged Christians at Lystra in Asia Minor to continue in the faith. But he reminded them, "through many tribulations we must enter the kingdom of God" (Ac 14:22). He considered it an honor to participate in sufferings similar to those that Christ endured, and wanted the Philippians also to be encouraged in this regard.

3:10 *power of His resurrection.* See the note on Eph 1:19–20. Paul desires to experience ever more deeply his knowledge of Christ

Jesus his Lord (v. 8), now during his lifetime and in the future (see v. 11). When we know Christ we experience the power of His resurrection in this life—the power at work now in those who believe (Eph 1:19). We are united with Christ through Baptism, as we daily put away our sins and rise in newness of life (Rm 6:1–14). *share His sufferings.* The Lord made it known at Paul's conversion that he would have to suffer for the sake of His name (Ac 9:16). When God gave Paul and the Philippians faith in Jesus Christ, He also granted that they "also suffer for His sake" (1:29). Paul believed that the sufferings he endured for Christ's sake as God's apostolic messenger were a participation in Christ's sufferings (cf. Rm 8:16–17; 2Co 1:5–7; 11:23–28; Col 1:24). *becoming like Him.* Paul means more than Christians suffering martyrdom because they are witnesses to Christ's name. Through Baptism God conforms believers "to the image of His Son" who conquered death and rescues us from our own death (see note above and Rm 8:29; Eph 4:22–24).

3:11 *attain the resurrection.* Christ's resurrection guarantees our own resurrection (1Co 15:20; 2Co 4:14; cf. 1Jn 3:1–3), the day when our lowly bodies will be transformed to be like Christ's resurrected body (3:20). Paul may be uncertain about his immediate future, but not about his resurrection when Christ comes.

Devotion and Prayer in 3:1–11. Like a loving father concerned about the safety of his children, Paul issues a surprisingly stern warning to the Philippians: "Look out for the dogs!" (v. 2). This sarcastic epithet refers to the Judaizers, who persistently strayed around the churches Paul founded, telling them that Gentiles by birth (whom they in general regarded as unclean like dogs) must be circumcised in order to be saved. And they may have said, "Who is this Paul to talk?" Paul presents his impeccable credentials as a Jew, from pedigree to high moral achievements. All of that, however, is fit for disposal as garbage in comparison with the surpassing worth of knowing Christ and the righteousness that God gives to believers in Christ. Confidence in Him, His forgiveness, and the power of His resurrection—not trust in human righteousness based on the Law—produces in us a living hope, even in the midst of suffering. If we have to endure suffering for the sake of Christ, so be it: we shall consider it an honor and God's way of shaping us into the image of His Son.

• Dear Lord Jesus, help me always to cling to You by faith, that I may know Your righteousness and the power of Your resurrection in my daily life as a Christian. Amen.

Straining toward the Goal by Imitating Paul (3:12–4:1)

ESV	KJV

ESV

¹²Not that I have already obtained this or am already perfect, but I press on to make it my own, because Christ Jesus has made me his own. ¹³Brothers, I do not consider that I have made it my own. But one thing I do: forgetting what lies behind and straining forward to what lies ahead, ¹⁴I press on toward the goal for the prize of the upward call of God in Christ Jesus. ¹⁵Let those of us who are mature think this way, and if in anything you think otherwise, God will reveal that also to you. ¹⁶Only let us hold true to what we have attained.

¹⁷Brothers, join in imitating me, and keep your eyes on those who walk according to the example you have in us. ¹⁸For many, of whom I have often told you and now tell you even with tears, walk as enemies of the cross of Christ. ¹⁹Their end is destruction, their god is their belly, and they glory in their shame, with minds set on earthly things. ²⁰But our citizenship is in heaven, and from it we await a Savior, the Lord Jesus Christ, ²¹who will transform our lowly body to be like his glorious body, by the power that enables him even to subject all things to himself.

4 ¹Therefore, my brothers, whom I love and long for, my joy and crown, stand firm thus in the Lord, my beloved.

KJV

¹²Not as though I had already attained, either were already perfect: but I follow after, if that I may apprehend that for which also I am apprehended of Christ Jesus.

¹³Brethren, I count not myself to have apprehended: but this one thing I do, forgetting those things which are behind, and reaching forth unto those things which are before,

¹⁴I press toward the mark for the prize of the high calling of God in Christ Jesus.

¹⁵Let us therefore, as many as be perfect, be thus minded: and if in any thing ye be otherwise minded, God shall reveal even this unto you.

¹⁶Nevertheless, whereto we have already attained, let us walk by the same rule, let us mind the same thing.

¹⁷Brethren, be followers together of me, and mark them which walk so as ye have us for an ensample.

¹⁸(For many walk, of whom I have told you often, and now tell you even weeping, that they are the enemies of the cross of Christ:

¹⁹Whose end is destruction, whose God is their belly, and whose glory is in their shame, who mind earthly things.)

²⁰For our conversation is in heaven; from whence also we look for the Saviour, the Lord Jesus Christ:

²¹Who shall change our vile body, that it may be fashioned like unto his glorious body, according to the working whereby he is able even to subdue all things unto himself.

4 ¹Therefore, my brethren dearly beloved and longed for, my joy and crown, so stand fast in the Lord, my dearly beloved.

3:12 *obtained . . . make it my own . . . made me His own.* On the road to Damascus the risen Christ literally seized Paul (Ac 9:1–6; 22:10; 26:16–18). Like an athlete's desire to win, he strains with every fiber in his body to fully know Christ, to "gain" Him because Christ has already grabbed hold of him (vv. 8–9; cf. 1Co 9:24). Stressing our need for the Lord's Supper, Luther wrote,

> For by Baptism we are first born anew [John 3:5]. But, as we said before, there still remains the old vicious nature of flesh and blood in mankind. . . . The new life must be guided so that it continually increases and progresses. (LC V 23, 25)

perfect. Christians are not in heaven yet. God is not finished with them. They have not "arrived"; they are in the process of becoming what they already are (see "progress" in 1:25). They are pursuing what God has prepared for them to do (see commentary note on Eph 2:10). *make it my own.* The Gk word in this phrase occurs also in "made me His own." Chemnitz wrote,

> Certain passages point out the goal toward which we are tending in our course. For we do not run properly if we do not know where we are to run. Yet the goal in this life is not reached before the course is completed. Finally, there are certain passages which speak of spiritual blessings which have been begun and certain which will be consummated in eternal life and have only begun here in this life. (Chemnitz 2:607)

3:13–14 Luther wrote,

> There are so many hindrances and temptations of the devil and of the world that we often become weary and faint, and sometimes we also stumble [Hebrews 12:3]. Therefore, the Sacrament is given as a daily pasture and sustenance, that faith may refresh and strengthen itself [Psalm 23:1–3] so that it will not fall back in such a battle, but become ever stronger and stronger. (LC V 23–24)

3:13 Like a runner exerting himself to the uttermost, Paul does not look over his shoulder as he strains forward. Calvin wrote,

> He alludes to runners, who do not turn their eyes aside in any direction, lest they should slacken the speed of their course, and, more especially, do not look behind to see how much ground they have gone over, but hasten forward unremittingly towards the goal. (Calvin, *Philippians* 102)

3:14 *goal for the prize of the upward call.* Perhaps Paul was thinking of the Olympic games. At the conclusion of each race official messengers would proclaim the winner and call the contestant up to receive the prize (a palm branch, or a wreath of wild olive, green parsley, or pine). The term "prize" (*brabeion*) appears in this connection at 1Co 9:24. He fully expected to receive from his Lord the crown of righteousness reserved for him in heaven when the Lord comes on the Last Day (2Tm 4:8; 1Co 9:25; cf. 1Pt 5:4; Heb 12:1–2). Confident that our citizenship is in heaven, like Paul we await our Savior, the Lord Jesus Christ, who will, on that Day, transform us to be like Him (3:20–21). In the meantime, we must continually set our minds "on things that are above, not on things that are on the earth" (Col 3:2).

3:15 *mature.* Paul uses the same Gk word in Eph 4:13 and 1Co 14:20. To become spiritually mature, Christians obviously must grow into Christ. Good pastor that he was, Paul humbly recognized that not everyone among the Philippians would be able to receive his encouraging testimony at the same level of understanding (note the phrase "Let those of us who are mature"). "We're in this together," he is saying. *God will reveal that.* He urges patient reliance on God's guidance if there is anything more to which they need to give careful thought. He wants them finally to adopt his mindset (see 2:2 and commentary note).

3:16 *what we have attained.* Christian friends will bring joy to Paul's heart if they follow the principles that he taught and lived by in faithfulness to the Lord Jesus (1Co 4:17). He fervently desires that they not take steps backward from where God has led them.

3:17 *Brothers.* See the note on 1:12. *imitating me . . . the example.* Paul often admonishes his congregations to be imitators of him in all respects, even as he himself is an imitator of Christ (1Co 4:16–17; 11:1; 1Th 1:6; 2Th 3:7). He tells the Philippians to do what they have learned, received, heard, and seen in him (4:9). Thus, not only individuals, but congregations are to imitate him. *walk.* See the note on Eph 2:2.

3:18 *enemies of the cross.* Paul may be referring to Jewish Christian teachers such as those in Galatia. They may not have completely ignored Christ's death on the cross, but their teaching that the obedience to the Law was also necessary for salvation in effect rendered Christ's death unnecessary and without purpose (Gal 2:21). This constituted a direct rejection of its redemptive significance. Their lifestyle ("walk") as well contradicted the new life of those redeemed by the cross of Christ—conduct that Paul modeled (v. 17).

3:19 *destruction.* In the NT the Gk word (*apoleia*) designates almost exclusively eternal destruction under God's judgment (e.g., Mt 7:13; Rm 9:22; Php 1:28; 1Tm 6:9; 2Pt 3:7). While the enemies of Christ's cross may not think destruction immediately looms on their personal horizons, that will be the eventual outcome ("end," Gk *telos*) unless they see their error and repent. *their god is their belly.* These people have minds set "on earthly things." They are bent on satisfying their fleshly appetites. To set your mind on the flesh is death, but to set one's mind on the Spirit "is life and peace" (Rm 8:6). It has also been suggested that "belly" (cf. Rm 16:18) may possibly be a caustic allusion to false teachers who insisted that Gentiles keep Jewish food laws. *glory in their shame.* Paul may have been fighting hatred toward the cross of Christ on two fronts, rigid legalists on the one extreme, and on the other, those who thought they were free to do as they pleased as if they were above the Law. Whatever form their self-indulgence took, they compounded their error by bragging about things of which they should have been ashamed. It is common for those who believe that they do not need a Savior to commit shameful and immoral acts and then to trivialize them by joking about them.

3:20 *our citizenship is in heaven.* Believers in Christ are to live a life that corresponds to their citizenship in heaven, where Christ reigns. Pilgrims and aliens in this world (Heb 11:13; 1Pt. 1:1; 2:11), their true home is in heaven. Paul's use of the term "citizenship" or "commonwealth" (Gk *politeuma*; cf. 1:27 "let your manner of life be," which uses the corresponding Gk verb) may be intended as an allusion to Roman citizenship. Citizens of Philippi, a Roman colony, were automatically Roman citizens, with all the rights and privileges that entailed. The Philippians could easily understand what it meant to live as citizens in God's heavenly colony even though they do not yet live there. Melanchthon stressed the importance of distinguishing between the earthly and heavenly realms, in both of which we are citizens but in distinctively different senses:

> Therefore, the Church's authority and the State's authority must not be confused. The Church's authority has its own commission to teach the Gospel and to administer the Sacraments [Matthew

28:19–20]. Let it not break into the office of another. Let it not transfer the kingdoms of this world to itself. Let it not abolish the laws of civil rulers. Let it not abolish lawful obedience. Let it not interfere with judgments about civil ordinances or contracts. . . . Paul also says, "Our citizenship is in heaven" (Philippians 3:20). (AC XXVIII 12–13, 16)

3:21 *transform . . . to be like.* In their present form, our lowly bodies, which have been subjected to sin and death, are unsuitable for entry into heaven. Since "flesh and blood cannot inherit the kingdom of God" (1Co 15:50), our resurrection bodies will have to be radically different (though in continuity with our lowly bodies; 51–52). Thus, our earthly bodies will undergo a change. At the resurrection our bodies will become like resurrected and glorified body of Jesus Christ (1Co 15:38–49). *subject all things.* See the note on Eph 1:22. The transformation of our bodies to be like Christ's resurrection body will take place because the entire universe ("all things," Gk *ta panta*) has been placed under, and is in, His control (1Co 15:27–28). Death will be forever destroyed (1Co 15:26).

4:1 *brothers.* See the note on 1:12. Paul continues to express warm affection for the Philippians (see note on 1:8). *crown.* Like a star athlete wearing a victory prize of the highest honor (e.g., a token of victory in the World Cup), Paul was bursting with pride over the Philippians. Parents glow with pride when their children receive honors at awards assemblies. Paul can hardly wait until the Lord comes, so he can boast about the Philippians (cf. 1Th 2:19). *my beloved.* Twice Paul calls them beloved (see note on 2:12; cf. 1Th 1:4).

Devotion and Prayer in 3:12–4:1 Paul does not doubt that God has clothed him with the righteousness of Christ (3:9). He knows that God has forgiven him and given him the hope of heaven. He also knows, however, that he is not perfect. Life on this side of heaven involves a strenuous, tedious effort to be faithful to our calling—like an athlete straining toward the goal. As Paul puts it, we rigorously strive "to gain Christ" (v. 8). People all around us are involved in a highly competitive and fierce rat-race in the pursuit of selfish interests. The pressures on Christians often become intense. But since we are citizens of heaven, we receive from God's Spirit the energy to keep our eyes on the goal that God has set before us as we press toward the "finish line." We see ahead of us the ultimate prize that is in fact already ours: our glorious resurrection and transformation to be like Christ. • Dear Lord Jesus, help us continually to keep our eyes on You and on our heavenly calling every day. Amen.

Exhortation, Encouragement, and Prayer (4:2–9)

ESV	KJV
²I entreat Euodia and I entreat Syntyche to agree in the Lord. ³Yes, I ask you also, true companion, help these women, who have labored side by side with me in the gospel together with Clement and the rest of my fellow workers, whose names are in the book of life. ⁴Rejoice in the Lord always; again I will say, Rejoice. ⁵Let your reasonableness be known to everyone. The Lord is at hand; ⁶ do not be anxious about anything, but in everything by prayer and supplication with thanksgiving let your requests be made known to God. ⁷And the peace of God, which surpasses all understanding, will guard your hearts and your minds in Christ Jesus. ⁸Finally, brothers, whatever is true, whatever is honorable, whatever is just, whatever is pure, whatever is lovely, whatever is commendable, if there is any excellence, if there is anything worthy of praise, think about these things. ⁹What you have learned and received and heard and seen in me—practice these things, and the God of peace will be with you.	²I beseech Euodias, and beseech Syntyche, that they be of the same mind in the Lord. ³And I intreat thee also, true yokefellow, help those women which laboured with me in the gospel, with Clement also, and with other my fellowlabourers, whose names are in the book of life. ⁴Rejoice in the Lord always: and again I say, Rejoice. ⁵Let your moderation be known unto all men. The Lord is at hand. ⁶Be careful for nothing; but in every thing by prayer and supplication with thanksgiving let your requests be made known unto God. ⁷And the peace of God, which passeth all understanding, shall keep your hearts and minds through Christ Jesus. ⁸Finally, brethren, whatsoever things are true, whatsoever things are honest, whatsoever things are just, whatsoever things are pure, whatsoever things are lovely, whatsoever things are of good report; if there be any virtue, and if there be any praise, think on these things. ⁹Those things, which ye have both learned, and received, and heard, and seen in me, do: and the God of peace shall be with you.

4:2 *Euodia . . . Syntyche.* The tone of Paul's public appeal to these two women (Gk *parakaleo*, repeated twice) is not harsh, but respectful. They should not only be remembered—as is often the case—because they did not agree with each other. They were, after all, coworkers of Paul who "labored side by side" with him "in the gospel" (v. 3; see the note on 1:27). It should be noted, however, that in some way their disagreement was a threat to unity in the congregation and affected the work there. Therefore the matter required special mention, and additional help (v. 3). *agree in the Lord.* See the commentary note on 2:2. The Gk for "agree" is virtually the same as the "being of the same mind" in 2:2.

4:3 *true companion.* Paul does not mention the name of this fellow laborer, no doubt because he was well known to the Philippians (perhaps someone like Luke, the author of Acts). Some have suggested that "companion" was actually the proper name "Syzygos" (Gk word meaning "yokefellow"). No known instance of this name exists, however. In any case, there certainly were many other coworkers dear to Paul whose names remain anonymous (note the phrase "the rest of my fellow workers"). These are "unsung" heroes of the faith. *fellow workers.* See the notes on 1:27 and 4:2. *book of life.* In His heavenly register God has written the names of those who belong to Him (Rv 3:5; 13:8; 17:8; 20:15; cf. Ex 32:32; Dn 12:1; Lk 10:20; Heb 12:23). No one can delete from this book the names that God has signed into this divine registry. Their names prove their citizenship in heaven (3:20) and certify that they are heirs of eternal life. Bengel wrote,

> The allusion is to the victorious competitors in the public games, whose *names* were openly read and became famous. . . . Being associated with those who have died with honour, is to younger survivors a great recommendation [from Paul] who thus, as it were, stands in the middle place between those who are dead and those who are alive. (Bengel 150–51)

4:4 See the notes on 1:4 and 1:25. Jesus cautioned His disciples against a misplaced joy in personal "success" and urged them instead to "rejoice that your names are written in heaven" (Lk 10:20). Paul echoes this by saying that a Christian's happiness is centered *in the Lord.* Because it is rooted in God's grace in Christ, such joy is deep and lasting, independent of the sufferings and stresses of our earthly life. It rests still, calm, and undisturbed, like the deepest regions of the sea. Calvin wrote,

> If they are appalled by persecutions, or imprisonments, or exile, or death, here is the Apostle setting himself forward, who, amidst

imprisonments, in the very heat of persecution, and in fine, amidst apprehensions of death, is not merely himself joyful, but even stirs up others to joy. The sum, then, is this—that come what may, believers, having the Lord standing on their side, have amply sufficient ground of joy. . . . *That* only is a settled joy in God which is such as is never taken away from us. (Calvin, *Philippians* 116–17)

4:5 *reasonableness.* This gracious quality of a gentle, yielding spirit does not insist at all costs on keeping every minute detail of the Law or custom. Like our Savior, we want to show a readiness to forgive in our dealings not only with our fellow Christians but with all people (2Co 10:1; cf. Ps 86:5). *The Lord is at hand.* The Lord is close to us. We not only expect Him to arrive soon (cf. Rv 22:20; 1Co 16:22); He is also very near to us now, ready to help us in our need (Ps 145:18).

4:6 *prayer.* When we bring our anxieties and concerns to God in prayer, He helps us to deal with undue concern about every little thing in life. As someone has wisely said, "The way to be anxious about nothing is to be prayerful about everything." See the notes on Eph 1:16, 5:20 and 6:18. See also Col 4:2. *supplication.* God does not want us to hesitate one moment to come to Him for help in need. *thanksgiving.* Thanksgiving expresses trust that God provides all that we need in this body and life (cf. Mt 6:26–32). *requests.* God loves to hear prayers filled with specific requests. Wesley wrote,

They who by a preposterous shame or distrustful modesty, cover, stifle, or keep in their desires, as if they were either too small or too great, must be racked with care; from which they are entirely delivered, who pour them out with a free and filial confidence. (Wesley 513)

4:7 Paul bases his preceding exhortations on God's firm and certain promises (note the future tense of the verb, "will guard"). *peace of God . . . will guard.* The term "guard" (Gk *phroupeo*) has military connotations. A unit of the Roman army (garrison) stood guard to secure and maintain order in Philippi. With this imagery in the background, Paul declares that the saving peace that God has brought to the world through Christ will stand guard like a Roman sentinel over our hearts and minds. God will keep us in Christ, who is our Peace (Eph 2:14; cf. Jn 14:27; 16:33; Ac 10:36; Rm 5:1). God's peace, not only over us but also within us, will dispel anxiety. Hence also, it will determine how we think and decide what to do as Christians. *surpasses.* The same Gk term occurs in 3:8 (ESV, "surpassing worth").

4:8 An ancient philosopher wisely observed, "Your mind will be like its habitual thoughts . . . dyed with the color of its thoughts." Paul recognizes in this verse that what occupies the mind of a Christian shapes his or her character and conduct. He urges us all therefore to get into the habit of concentrating on what is truthful and honest, honorable, right, pure, lovely, and praiseworthy. Conversely, we must close our minds to thoughts that are unkind, unlovely, impure, dishonest, and ugly. This involves much more than practicing the power of positive thinking. When we take upon ourselves the mind of Christ Himself (cf. 2:5), we learn to occupy our minds with and radiate the kind of virtues listed in God's Word (see "practice," v. 9). In his Large Catechism, Luther urges that we "constantly keep God's Word in [our] heart, on [our] lips and in [our] ears" for this reason: "[The Word] always awakens new understanding, pleasure, and devoutness and produces a pure heart and pure thoughts [Philippians 4:8]" (LC I 101). *brothers.* See the note on 1:12.

4:9 *learned . . . received . . . heard . . . seen in me—practice.* Family traditions are passed on from one generation to another. Parents do this when they teach their children, tell them stories, and set an example for them to follow. With Christ's authority, the apostle Paul deliberately passed on to his congregations teachings and practices that he had received. He requested them to accept and live according to these traditions (what is "passed on"; see e.g., 1Co 15:1–11). Earlier in this Letter he had urged that the Philippians follow the example that he himself and others had set: "join in imitating me and keep your eyes on those who walk according to the example you have in us" (3:17; see note). He emphasizes this point once again in this verse. His counsel applies also today to pastors. The apostle urges "elders" who serve as shepherds of God's flock to be "examples to the flock." They are to remember that Christ is their "Chief Shepherd" who modeled for them a life of humility (1Pt 5:1–5). *God of peace.* See the notes on v. 7 and Eph 2:14. Paul often calls God "the God of peace" because God produces peace in and among Christians (Rm 15:33; 16:20; 2Co 13:11; 1Th 5:23; cf. Heb 13:20). God grants us peace through the Gospel of peace (Eph 6:15). We can have the inner peace of "consciences that are peaceful and joyful before God" because we have been justified by faith in Jesus Christ (Ap IV 91).

Such faith truly free us from things that tear us up inside. God also has united us with our fellow-Christians in the body of Christ, desiring that we live "in the bond of peace" (Eph 4:3; Php 2:13–18). *be with.* We not only have the gift of peace, but we have the God of peace Himself with us.

Devotion and Prayer in 4:2–9 Paul's closing words of encouragement begin with a surprisingly personal note addressed directly to two women who were not "on the same page" with one another. He also asks an unnamed person to help them settle their dispute. No doubt Paul also sensed the congregation needed a lift in the midst of some anxieties that threatened to dilute their joy in Christ. He cheers them up in the light of Christ's glorious coming and urges them to bring all their needs and burdens to God in earnest prayer. They needed to refocus their thoughts, and so Paul lifts their minds to the things that characterize people of hope—things worthy of praise and commendation. If they are looking for an example to follow, they can find none better than in Paul himself. He was in prison, and yet his strong faith in Christ had a lively buoyancy that the Philippians would do well to emulate. Paul desires more than anything else that the God of peace Himself be with them and give them His peace, which can shield them from inner and external fears. How fitting it is that pastors today often close their sermons proclaiming the Gospel of peace with the prayer that God's profound peace will keep the hearers' hearts and minds in Christ Jesus (v. 7). • Blessed Lord, give us the inner peace and joy that comes in knowing that through Jesus Christ our sins have been forgiven. Amen.

PART 7

THANKS FOR GOD'S PROVISION AND THE GIFTS RECEIVED (4:10–20)

ESV	KJV
[10]I rejoiced in the Lord greatly that now at length you have revived your concern for me. You were indeed concerned for me, but you had no opportunity. [11]Not that I am speaking of being in need, for I have learned in whatever situation I am to be content. [12]I know how to be brought low, and I know how to abound. In any and every circumstance, I have learned the secret of facing plenty and hunger, abundance and need. [13]I can do all things through him who strengthens me.	[10]But I rejoiced in the Lord greatly, that now at the last your care of me hath flourished again; wherein ye were also careful, but ye lacked opportunity. [11]Not that I speak in respect of want: for I have learned, in whatsoever state I am, therewith to be content. [12]I know both how to be abased, and I know how to abound: every where and in all things I am instructed both to be full and to be hungry, both to abound and to suffer need. [13]I can do all things through Christ which strengtheneth me.
[14]Yet it was kind of you to share my trouble. [15]And you Philippians yourselves know that in the beginning of the gospel, when I left Macedonia, no church entered into partnership with me in giving and receiving, except you only. [16]Even in Thessalonica you sent me help for my needs once and again. [17]Not that I seek the gift, but I seek the fruit that increases to your credit.	[14]Notwithstanding ye have well done, that ye did communicate with my affliction. [15]Now ye Philippians know also, that in the beginning of the gospel, when I departed from Macedonia, no church communicated with me as concerning giving and receiving, but ye only. [16]For even in Thessalonica ye sent once and again unto my necessity. [17]Not because I desire a gift: but I desire fruit that may abound to your account.

18I have received full payment, and more. I am well supplied, having received from Epaphroditus the gifts you sent, a fragrant offering, a sacrifice acceptable and pleasing to God. **19**And my God will supply every need of yours according to his riches in glory in Christ Jesus. **20**To our God and Father be glory forever and ever. Amen.

18But I have all, and abound: I am full, having received of Epaphroditus the things which were sent from you, an odour of a sweet smell, a sacrifice acceptable, wellpleasing to God. **19**But my God shall supply all your need according to his riches in glory by Christ Jesus. **20**Now unto God and our Father be glory for ever and ever. Amen.

4:10 *revived your concern.* Epaphroditus' arrival with a monetary gift (cf. v. 18) showed the Philippians' renewed concern (the Gk word for "revived" [*anathallo*] means, literally, "bloom again"). *At length* suggests a delay, but Paul does not specify what it might have been.

4:11 *content.* The Gk word *autarkes* means "self-sufficient" or content (cf. 1Tm 6:6). Paul's thankfulness and joy did not come simply from having his needs satisfied.

4:12 *learned the secret.* This is the word's only occurrence in the NT. Paul borrows a technical term found in mystery religions of his day, meaning "I am an initiate" (i.e., "I have learned the secret"). He adapts it to say that he has become adept at living in both abundance and want. He worked part-time as a tentmaker (Ac 18:3; 20:34). Expenses he likely incurred through some of his travels may partly explain why he had to toil night and day (1Th 2:9; 2Th 3:8). Coping with tough economic times requires that we learn to trust in the Lord's provision in all circumstances.

4:13 Paul did not believe that hardship in life should cause us to despair or to doubt God's grace. Rather, he was content with weaknesses, insults, hardships, persecution, and calamities. "For when I am weak, then I am strong," he wrote to the Corinthians (2Co 12:10). Through His mighty strength the Lord enabled Paul to overcome obstacles and difficulties and to accomplish His perfect purposes in his life (2Co 12:9). Even imprisonment could not dampen Paul's confidence in God's grace and power to sustain him. Come what may, we too can do all things through Christ who strengthens us.

4:14 *share my trouble.* See the note on 1:7 for what Paul means by the term "share," a key concept in the Letter. Paul regarded the

Philippians' gift to him as a sign of their partnership in the Gospel (cf. vv. 16–17). He was grateful to them because they prayerfully supported his apostolic ministry and showed a sympathetic interest in him while he was in prison.

4:15 See the note on 1:5. *beginning of the gospel.* Paul's warm interchanges with the Philippians for the sake of the Gospel stretched all the way back to the first time they heard and received the Gospel Paul proclaimed to them (cf. Ac 16).

4:18 *full payment.* Paul uses a technical term from the field of commerce ("provide a receipt for a sum paid in full"). He has received more than enough. *Epaphroditus.* See the note on 2:25. *fragrant offering, a sacrifice.* See the note on 2:17. In OT worship a "fragrant offering" qualified as a sacrifice acceptable and pleasing to God (Gn 8:21; Ex 29:18, 25, 41; Lv 1:9, 13, 17, etc.). The Philippians' offering belongs high on the list of spiritual sacrifices acceptable and pleasing to God. Calvin wrote,

> While God invites us with so much kindness to the honour of priesthood, and even puts sacrifices in our hands, we nevertheless do not sacrifice to him, and those things which were set apart for sacred oblations we not only lay out for profane uses, but squander them wickedly upon the most polluted contaminations. For the altars, on which sacrifices from our resources ought to be presented, are the poor, and the servants of Christ. To the neglect of these some squander their resources on every kind of luxury, others upon the palate, others upon immodest attire, others upon magnificent dwellings. (Calvin, *Philippians* 128)

4:19 *supply every need.* The churches in the Roman province of Macedonia (including Philippi) lived in extreme poverty at the time of Paul's missionary journeys. Yet they demonstrated a wealth of generosity when they participated with gladness and beyond their means in an offering for fellow Christians in Judea (2Co 8:1–5). God's promise to fulfill *every need* they had embraces not only physical, but also spiritual needs (Paul's primary concern in the Letter). *His riches in glory.* Even though the Philippians may have been very poor, they were actually extraordinarily wealthy. They may have known of Paul's teaching to the Corinthians: "For you know the grace of our Lord Jesus Christ, that though He was rich, yet for your sake He became poor, so that you by His poverty might become rich" (2Co 8:9; see note on Eph 1:18). God's inexhaustible treasury is thrown open

237

to us, with wealth flowing from the boundless love of His heart. The conduit through which this supply comes to us is Christ Jesus (cf. Jn 16:14). In times of need God calms our restless hearts. See the notes on 3:8, 12, 13–14.

4:20 *God and Father.* Paul always departed from the customary conclusion of a Hellenistic letter, which typically included a health wish or a simple farewell. Instead, he closes with a benediction (1Co 16:23; Gal 6:16, 18; Eph 6:23–24; 2Th 3:16, 18) or a doxology as in this verse (Rm 16:25–27). God the Father is *our* Father through Jesus Christ, as Christians have prayed together through the centuries ("Our Father. . . . ").

Devotion and Prayer in 4:10–20 With extraordinary graciousness and tact Paul thanks the Philippians for the gift they sent to him with Epaphroditus. Ever since they first received the Gospel Paul proclaimed to them, the Philippians happily locked arms with Paul in God's saving enterprise. Their love and generosity blossomed anew during his imprisonment by making a personal gift to him. But their greatest gift was the sacrificial offering of themselves in worship to God—to whom highest praise is to be given for His boundless grace (2Co 8:1). As God has looked after Paul's needs, so He will look after all of theirs. Luther reminds us that "the desire for wealth clings and sticks to our nature all the way to the grave." Those who have it want more, those who don't fret and complain. God's invitation is this:

> Whatever you lack of good things, expect it from Me. Look to Me for it. And whenever you suffer misfortune and distress, crawl and cling to Me. I, yes, I, will give you enough and help you out of every need. Only do not let your heart cleave to or rest on any other. (LC I 4)

• Heavenly Father, help me, Your child, to put away all anxiety and worry. Let me remember that You are rich in mercy and are willing and able to supply my every need through Christ Jesus. Amen.

PART 8

FINAL GREETINGS (4:21–23)

ESV	KJV
²¹Greet every saint in Christ Jesus. The brothers who are with me greet you. ²²All the saints greet you, especially those of Caesar's household. ²³The grace of the Lord Jesus Christ be with your spirit.	²¹Salute every saint in Christ Jesus. The brethren which are with me greet you. ²²All the saints salute you, chiefly they that are of Caesar's household. ²³The grace of our Lord Jesus Christ be with you all. Amen.

4:21 *saint.* See the note on Eph 1:1. In his final greetings Paul wants no one in the congregation to be excluded. *brothers.* These are probably his companions and coworkers. See the note on 1:12.

4:22 *saints.* The circle of believers is wider than his coworkers attending to his needs under house arrest. *Caesar's household.* Paul is probably not singling out (note "especially") members of Caesar's family. He could have been referring to anyone in Roman civil service dependent on Caesar (slaves and freedmen). Or perhaps they were members of the Praetorian Guard who became Christians (see note on 1:13).

4:23 Mindful that both he and the Philippians are partakers of God's grace (1:7), Paul ends the Letter where he began it—with a prayer that God's grace be with them. *be with.* Through the Word which Paul has written and proclaimed, God actually imparts His grace to Christians. *with your spirit.* An expression equivalent to "you" (cf. Gal 6:16; Phm 25).

Devotion and Prayer in 4:21–23 The way Paul closes his Letter to his Christian friends in Philippi reveals his deep affection for every one of them. He writes to "every saint" there without singling anyone out by name—a custom he often follows in other Letters.

He wants them to realize that they are all dear to him because of the grace of God that has been manifested in and through them. No doubt he made his love for them known also to his friends in Rome, including new converts in the Roman military ranks. So everyone in the circle of friends and coworkers in Rome greets everyone in the circle of coworkers and friends in Philippi. What a testimony to the unity of all believers who together are partakers in the grace of our Lord Jesus Christ, wherever they may be in the world (cf. 1Co 1:2)! Paul's magnificent Letter to the Philippians was written to give encouragement, strength, and joy to the Church of all ages. Written in prison by a man facing possible death, the Letter exposes the heart of a leader who lived in the hope and joy of Christ. All Christians can find in Paul an example to follow. However difficult life may become for us, God cares for our needs and by His strength leads us through all trouble in keeping with His gracious purposes. • O give thanks to the Lord for His abundant grace! May His grace come continually to us and through us to others. Amen.

BIOGRAPHICAL SKETCHES ◆

The following brief sketches introduce preachers and commentators cited or referenced in this volume. They appear in chronological order by the date of their death or era of influence. Although some of them are ancient and medieval Church Fathers respected by the reformers, they are primarily writers of the Reformation era and heirs of the Reformation approach to writing biblical commentary. This approach includes:

(1) Interpreting Scripture in view of Scripture and by faith, so that passages are understood in their literary and in their canonical contexts;

(2) Emphasis on the historic and ordinary meaning of the words and literary expressions;

(3) Careful review of manuscripts and texts in search of greater accuracy;

(4) Faith in the canonical Scripture as divinely inspired, truthful, and authoritative;

(5) Respect for the ancient, ecumenical creeds (Apostles', Nicene, and Athanasian) as touchstones of faithful interpretation and application of Scripture; and most importantly

(6) Focus on Christ and justification through Him as the chief message of Holy Scripture (e.g., the distinction of Law and Gospel or sin and grace in interpretation and application).

For more information about these figures, see Edward A. Engelbrecht, gen. ed., *The Church from Age to Age: A History from Galilee to Global Christianity* (St. Louis: Concordia, 2011).

Ancient and Medieval Fathers

Justin Martyr. (c. 100–c. 165) An early Christian apologist who taught at various places in the Roman empire, including Ephesus.

Cyprian. (d. 258) Bishop of Carthage, North Africa. One of the earliest Latin Church Fathers, known for his dedication and pastoral care.

John Chrysostom. (c. 347–407) Bishop of Constantinople and a key figure in the early Christological controversies. He was called "golden-mouthed" because of his brilliant oratory style. His commentaries on Scripture are sermons, valued by the Church from ancient times.

Augustine. (354–430) Bishop of Hippo Regius, near Carthage, North Africa. His extensive and profound writings, including commentary on Genesis, the Psalms, and the Gospels, made him the most influential theologian in western Christendom. The reformers drew constantly upon his insights.

Hus, John. (c. 1372–1415) Priest and martyr. Lecturer and rector at the University of Prague, an enormously popular preacher and writer, greatly influenced by Augustine's theology and John Wycliffe's writings. Hus was falsely accused of heresy and condemned at the Council of Constance when the medieval church was sorely divided. His efforts heralded the Reformation.

Reformers

Luther, Martin. (1483–1546) Augustinian friar and preeminent reformer, lecturer on the Bible at the University of Wittenberg. Luther's preaching, teaching, and writing renewed biblically based piety in western Christendom. His translation of the Bible influenced the work of Bible publication throughout Europe, notably that of William Tyndale and the King James translators.

Cranmer, Thomas. (1489–1556) Archbishop of Canterbury and martyr. Cranmer served as a writer and editor for the Book of Common Prayer, one of the most influential works of the Reformation.

Melanchthon, Philip. (1497–1560) Lecturer on classical literature and languages at the University of Wittenberg. Melanchthon's *Commonplaces* and the Augsburg Confession laid the foundation for all subsequent works of Protestant dogmatic theology. He also wrote significant biblical commentaries.

Calvin, John. (1509–64) Preacher and lecturer on theology, founder of the Academy of Geneva. Calvin organized reformation efforts for Swiss, French, Dutch, and English Protestants. Calvin's *Institutes of the Christian Religion* and his extensive commentaries on Scripture are the most influential works of the second generation reformers.

Knox, John. (c. 1513–72) Scottish preacher and reformer. Knox edited the Book of Common Order used in Scottish churches and wrote a history of the Reformation in Scotland.

Chemnitz, Martin. (1522–86) Pastor and theologian at Brunswick, Germany. Chemnitz was largely responsible for the Formula of Concord that unified churches in Lutheran territories following the deaths of Luther and Melanchthon. His *Examination of the Council of Trent* equipped Protestant churches for responding to the Roman Catholic Counter-Reformation.

Heirs of the Reformation

Gerhard, Johann. (1582–1637) Professor of theology at Jena and devotional writer. Gerhard wrote the most extensive dogmatic of the Protestant age of orthodoxy, the *Theological Commonplaces*, and was widely regarded for his knowledge of biblical Hebrew.

Bengel, Johann Albrecht. (1687–1752) New Testament scholar and professor. Bengel wrote the first scientific study of Greek New Testament manuscripts. His *Gnomon* on the New Testament is an influential, succinct commentary of enduring value.

Wesley, John. (1703–91) Missionary preacher. Wesley preached throughout England, Scotland, Ireland, and the American colonies. His *Explanatory Notes upon the New Testament* is a classic evangelical commentary, which drew upon principles and emphases of the Reformers.